The Pragmatic Philosophy
of C. S. Peirce

BY MANLEY THOMPSON

The Pragmatic Philosophy
of C. S. Peirce

Phoenix Books

THE UNIVERSITY OF CHICAGO PRESS

To

PHYLLIS AND KATHERINE

The University of Chicago Press, Chicago 37
The University of Toronto Press, Toronto 5, Canada

Copyright 1953 by the University of Chicago. All rights reserved. Published 1953. First Phoenix edition 1963 Second impression 1963. Composed and printed by The University of Chicago Press, Chicago, Illinois, U.S.A.

Foreword

THE decade since this book was first published has been a period of significant advances in Peircian scholarship. A considerable amount of hitherto unpublished material by Peirce has appeared, notably the material in Volumes VII and VIII of the *Collected Papers of Charles Sanders Peirce*, edited by Arthur W. Burks. There have been a number of important articles (too numerous for individual mention here) commenting on and making use of various of Peirce's many contributions to philosophy. Murray G. Murphey's *The Development of Peirce's Philosophy* (1961), which makes use of still unpublished material as well as the new material in the volumes edited by Burks, is a landmark in scholarly efforts to relate Peirce's thought to the dominant ideas of his period and to trace in detail the chronological development of his philosophy. Other important work on Peirce is now in progress, including a scholarly biography by Max Fisch.

The Pragmatic Philosophy of C. S. Peirce was originally offered "as an essential propaedeutic to the determination of Peirce's place in the history of ideas and to any evaluation of his contributions to specific issues." If I were writing the last sentence of the Introduction today, I would say "as part of an essential propaedeutic"; I never meant to imply that I was presenting all that is needed for this task. My aim, as stated earlier in the Introduction, was a commentary that approached the ideal Peirce expressed in the statement: "I have read and deeply pondered upon all the main systems, never being satisfied until I was able to think about them as their own advocates thought." Such a commentary has obvious limitations. It is of course necessary in the end to evaluate a philosopher's work by thinking about philosophical problems in the right way and not merely in the way he thought about them. Yet the wisdom of a philosopher is in danger of being obscured by whatever shortcomings lie in the commentator's view of the right way, and the danger may be minimized when commentary begins with a conscious effort to work through the material first from the philosopher's own point of view, or, at least, from as close an approximation to that point of view as the commentator is able to achieve.

The difficulties in Peirce's philosophy remarked in the present study, including the general points put briefly at the close of the final chapter, are all based on comments made by Peirce himself about his own philosophy or about philosophy generally. If I were to discuss the main philosophical issues raised by these difficulties, I would do so from a standpoint very different from that taken in the following pages, but then the discussion would be an expression of part of my own philosophy rather than part of anything that could be properly called a commentary on Peirce. With this qualification I still subscribe to the claims I made concerning difficulties in Peirce's philosophy.

The recent work on Peirce mentioned above in the opening paragraph has contributed substantially to the propaedeutic I wanted to present and has made some advances toward a final evaluation of Peirce. The material by Peirce that has become available since I wrote my book has made it possible to trace in more detail the chronological development of his thought and to state more fully his views on a number of topics. However, I have found nothing in the material that would lead me to alter rather than to claim that it further substantiates what I said about Peirce.

It should be emphasized, finally, that the present book, though a propaedeutic in the sense mentioned, is not something to be read before one reads some of Peirce. The reader will profit most who has read enough of Peirce to become aware of the difficulties in trying to fit together the many diverse strains of philosophical thought in the *Collected Papers*. This awareness in turn presupposes some familiarity with the major figures in the history of philosophy that Peirce refers to so often and uses as a background against which to present his own views. I have written for a reader who possesses this awareness and familiarity, and some readers may occasionally find it helpful to pause and review a point in, say, Kant or Aristotle, as well as to read a passage in Peirce.

Preface

THE present work is the outgrowth of an attempt to understand Peirce which started nearly thirteen years ago and was interrupted early in 1942 because of the war. The project was resumed when I returned to civilian life, and it has been going on intermittently since 1946.

I am profoundly indebted to Professor Richard McKeon, who first introduced me to Peirce as a philosopher unique in the pragmatic tradition. While in its later stages my work has been carried on without consultation with Professor McKeon, it has always been done in what has seemed to me the spirit of his initial suggestions. Professors Arthur W. Burks, Charles Hartshorne, C. W. Morris, and Paul Weiss read the manuscript and offered helpful criticisms.

A postwar fellowship grant from the Rockefeller Foundation and a leave of absence from teaching duties for the Easter Term of 1949 at the University of Toronto made possible an extended period of free time for final work on the project. The Division of the Humanities of the University of Chicago provided a generous grant in aid of publication. The Harvard University Press kindly gave me permission to publish the passages which I quote from the *Collected Papers of Charles Sanders Peirce*. To all these institutions I am sincerely grateful.

Without my wife's constant encouragement and her unfailing assistance in the preparation of the manuscript, reading the proof, and making the Index, this book would never have appeared.

M. H. T.

UNIVERSITY OF CHICAGO
March 1953

Table of Contents

ix

NOTES

SELECTED BIBLIOGRAPHY

INDEX

Introduction

THE problems confronting the commentator on the philosophy
of Charles Sanders Peirce are somewhat unique. On the one
hand, there seems to be almost universal agreement that Peirce
is of considerable importance for contemporary philosophy.
Since the publication of his *Collected Papers* by the Harvard
University Press, 1931–35, the interest in his philosophy has
been steadily mounting. The concern to elucidate his writings
has already yielded an impressive accumulation of commentary
and has resulted in the formation of a society devoted to "fur-
thering knowledge of, and interest in, the works of Peirce."[1] But,
on the other hand, despite this ever increasing interest in the
philosophy of Peirce, radical disagreement persists concerning
the fundamentals of interpretation.[2]

The causes of this disagreement are at least twofold. In the
first place, not only is Peirce a difficult and often obscure writer,
but the situation is complicated by the fact that the *Collected
Papers* contain no single work which professes to bring together
all the important parts of his philosophy. On the contrary, important statements for any aspect of his philosophy lie scattered
throughout the forty-odd years of his writing. The commentator, consequently, seems left with no other choice but to attempt evaluation of Peirce's writings through a selection which
he, the commentator, regards as containing all the philosophic
truths that are to be found in them. In the second place, contemporary philosophy no less than the philosophy of other pe-
riods is in disagreement over fundamental issues; and one can
only rely on his own philosophic convictions when he judges
the work of a past philosopher. It might well be expected, then,

that the disagreement concerning the importance and interpretation of various aspects of Peirce's philosophy would be about as great as the disagreement in contemporary philosophy itself. Thus, for those who see contemporary naturalism or logical empiricism as the culmination of all philosophic inquiry, Peirce presents a curious picture. He makes striking anticipations of current truth and even has suggestions still valuable for present inquiry. Yet he also says so much that seems imbued with the confusions of nineteenth-century transcendentalism that he appears to be a sort of split philosophic personality. For those, however, who are more influenced by other contemporary movements, such as the philosophy of A. N. Whitehead, Peirce is neither so split nor so confused, and where he does fall into error it seems more in the direction of old Newtonian naturalism than of nineteenth-century transcendentalism.

But to look at another aspect of the problem, if it is a primary function of the commentator before he attempts critical consideration and evaluation to explicate the philosophy upon which he is writing in terms which involve as little distortion and as much penetration as possible, Peirce's *Collected Papers* furnish peculiar advantages as well as disadvantages for this end. The failure to provide a single work which all commentators are forced to accept as definitive is offset, in part at least, by the fact that perhaps no other philosopher engaged more in self-commentary, more in the practice of appending explanatory and critical notes to his writings many years after they were written and in giving detailed intellectual autobiographies to explain the origin of his views, than did Peirce. By taking advantage of this circumstance, it seems possible to follow a method of exposition which to a large extent takes its crucial points of departure from statements that Peirce made about Peirce. Faithful adherence to such a method of exposition prior to any attempt at critical evaluation should provide some check against the danger of missing the importance of a philosophic statement by forcing it into a preconceived pattern of interpretation, consonant with the convictions of the commentator but utterly foreign to the original intention of the author. With such a method, in fact, the ideal which Peirce sought to attain in his own philosophic reading may not be so impossible. In a sketch of his intellectual autobiography ca. 1897 he remarked concerning his reading in metaphysics: "I have read and deeply pondered upon all the main systems, never being satisfied until I was able to think about them as their own advocates thought" (1.3).[3]

Even a cursory survey of Peirce's many later reflections on what he had intended by his pragmatism may suffice to show that this doctrine is connected with the very roots of his philosophy—so much so that a thorough exposition of his pragmatism would require consideration of it in the general context of all his writings. For his pragmatism, he declared, was "designed" and "constructed" "architectonically" (5.5). While pragmatism is itself a "maxim of logic" (5.18), to subject the doctrine to a "methodical, scientific, and thorough examination" requires the ordering of the sciences, as logic depends upon ethics, ethics upon phenomenology, and finally phenomenology upon pure mathematics (5.34-40). Pragmatism as a "doctrine concerning the logic of abduction" must be understood in a context relating it to induction and deduction (5.179), and a "proof" of pragmatism "would essentially involve the establishment of the truth of synechism" (5.415).

Since remarks of this sort, then, can be found in abundance throughout the Collected Papers, the problem of finding preliminary justification for treating Peirce's pragmatism in terms of the whole of his philosophy is in no way a serious one. A statement of the reasons for extending this procedure to the point of calling his whole philosophy "pragmatic" belongs properly in the conclusion rather than the introduction of such a study. Although pragmatism perhaps more than any other single doctrine in Peirce has been the beneficiary of self-commentary, the problem of determining the order to be followed in this study is not so easily settled. It might seem that the ordering of the sciences should itself furnish the order of commentary, so that the relevant aspects of pure mathematics, formal logic, and phenomenology would be considered first, and then, by proceeding to ethics and logic proper, pragmatism could be placed in its proper sphere and examined in the light of its presuppositions. Yet such a procedure would encounter almost insuperable difficulties. For the *Collected Papers* contain no complete work which itself follows this order, but, on the contrary, certain stages of the architectonic, such as ethics, have been given relatively slight treatment, while stages subsequent to these, such as logic proper, have received detailed treatment. It would therefore be necessary either to infer from an architectonically posterior stage much of what would have been the character of a prior stage had Peirce developed his consideration of it or else so to restrict the entire treatment that no subsequent stage will be given commentary which cannot be linked with Peirce's explicit statements about a higher stage. The first of these alternatives would result in an attempt to construct undeveloped parts of Peirce's philosophy rather than a commentary; the second would permit only a study which excluded about nine-tenths of the *Collected Papers*.

But then it must be remembered that Peirce never intended to complete even the main stages of his architectonic and that his intention here was rather "to outline a theory so comprehensive that, for a long time to come, the entire work of human reason, in philosophy of every school and kind, in mathematics, in psychology, in physical science, in history, in sociology, and in whatever other department there may be, shall appear as the filling up of its details" (1.1). The architectonic, consequently, is the result of a philosophic theory, and the ordering which it furnishes may itself be understood and examined prior to the detailed development of any of the stages ordered. The concern of Peirce's endeavors at architectonic, in other words, was "not so much to set each brick with nicest accuracy, as to lay the foundations deep and massive" (1.1). A commentary following the order of the architectonic is thus undesirable, not only since the character of Peirce's writings would render it practically impossible, but especially since by Peirce's own conception the architectonic is but a result of his philosophy rather than a presupposition giving an order for any consideration of his philosophy. While pragmatism must be treated in relation to the ordering of the sciences, there is no reason why this relation, rather than that to formal logic or to synechism, should give the order for the entire commentary.

Another possibility is to select from Peirce's writings those which definitely bear on the philosophic issues of pragmatism, either because they explicitly treat of these issues or because they are later mentioned by Peirce as relevant to them, and to consider these writings in chronological order. But this procedure must be subject to certain modifications. The explanatory and critical writings often involve comments made in the light of considerations developed many years after the original piece, so that it may frequently be desirable in commenting on an early position to explicate aspects of a later theory before touching on the intermediate stages. Again, since much of Peirce's writings consists in the continual development and restatement of the same theories, it may sometimes prove more profitable to begin consideration of a theory by turning first to a later statement before taking account of earlier versions.

The present study in Peirce's philosophy will proceed according to an order determined in this general fashion. When Peirce's writings are viewed in relation to the development of his pragmatism, it seems convenient first of all to classify them roughly into two groups—those written before 1890–93 and those written during and after this period. Justification for this division may be found in the fact that the period around 1893 marks the beginning of Peirce's persistent efforts to cull his writings, revise them, and put them in the form of completed volumes. During this brief period four separate works were projected: A Guess at the Riddle; the Short Logic; a collection of some twelve or fourteen essays entitled Search for a Method; and the Grand Logic. Only the last of these was ever brought to completion—the only one, in fact, in all of Peirce's writings—and even it failed to attain so much as the status of a galley proof.

The *Search for a Method* perhaps never received the careful consideration which Peirce gave to some of his other projects; at any event, either the numbering of the essays is incorrect or at least two of them are entirely missing and not even mentioned in any of his writings, and several of them appear also as chapters in the *Grand Logic*. Nevertheless, the *Search for a Method* has peculiar significance for a commentary on Peirce's pragmatism, since the extant collection of essays constitutes a chronological arrangement of virtually all the important papers bearing on pragmatism from Peirce's first published papers of 1867 to the Johns Hopkins *Studies in Logic* of 1883. If Peirce's later expositions of pragmatism, given from ten to fifteen years after the *Search for a Method* was projected, were taken as the basis for selecting those of his early papers which make essential contributions to pragmatism, the resulting list would be almost identical with that given by the *Search for a Method*. It would thus seem that Peirce must have regarded this collection of essays arranged in chronological order as exemplifying the search which finally led him to his conception of the scientific method and its dependence on the pragmatic maxim, and this fact alone affords a good reason for employing the collection as proper introductory subject matter for a commentary on his pragmatism. The numerous notes which Peirce appended in 1893 and later to several of the essays should also provide considerable aid for such a commentary.

Part I of the present study follows the order of these essays comprising the *Search for a Method*. The inauguration of a new approach to logic constitutes more than a chronological beginning of Peirce's endeavors to construct a pragmatic philosophy. In a fragment ca. 1905 he referred to "the traditional logic" as the "principal alternative" to pragmatism, "as presenting itself at the first and only great parting of the ways" (5.500). The fact that the first three essays of the *Search for a Method* are concerned with the fundamentals of a new logic is thus not merely an expression of Peirce's early interest. The considerations central to these three essays may properly stand first in a systematic presentation of Peirce's philosophy as well as in a chronological account of the development of his thought. The remaining essays in the series succeed in at least touching on the chief problems with which Peirce continued to occupy himself during his later writing. The faculties, objects, and methods of knowledge require new explanation when traditional distinctions like that between immediate and mediate inference are obliterated or radically modified. Part II of the study is concerned with Peirce's endeavors, after his search for a method, to develop such explanation, first, by the construction of a "scientific metaphysics"; second, by a philosophic ordering of the sciences, including metaphysics; and, finally, by a restatement of the principles underlying his pragmatism.

While Peirce read extensively in the history of philosophy, he seems to have been influenced by Kant far more than by anyone else; and, quite aside from the question of influence, Peirce's meaning at many points is most easily elucidated by comparison with Kant. Since the aim of the present undertaking is an exposition of Peirce's approach to philosophy and a consideration of the limitations that approach involves regardless of the place it may assume in the history of ideas, all contrasts with previous philosophers, including Kant, are made solely for the purpose of clarifying Peirce's position and are not intended to trace lines of influence. A similar remark obtains for all references to later philosophy, as no attempt is made to delineate those contemporary doctrines which may be rightly attributed to Peirce. Nor is any effort made to evaluate individually Peirce's contributions to particular philosophic problems, such as the nature of probability, the foundations of semiotic, or the source of mathematical certainty. His analyses of such problems will be considered only for the light they throw on the general pragmatic orientation of his philosophy and not for the individual merits they may possess. What is undertaken here is offered as an essential propaedeutic to the determination of Peirce's place in the history of ideas and to any evaluation of his contributions to specific issues.

PART I

I

New Logic and a New List of Categories

PEIRCE's first printed paper (privately printed, November, 1866) was entitled *Memoranda concerning the Aristotelian Syllogism* (2, App.);[1] it was subsequently revised and appeared as Part II of a paper, *On the Natural Classification of Arguments*, April, 1867 (2, Bk. III, chap. 2). This second paper, with notes and corrections added in 1893, was intended for Essay I of the *Search for a Method*; two papers closely following, *On a New List of Categories*, May, 1867 (1, Bk. III, chap. 6), and *Upon Logical Comprehension and Extension*, November, 1867 (2, Bk. II, chap. 5), were intended for Essays II and III, respectively. These three essays lay the foundations for the new approach to logic and indicate clearly Peirce's attitude toward the traditional logic of Kant and the errors it seemed to involve. But since the break with Kant is not complete until the development of the logic of relatives given in Peirce's paper of 1870 (3, Paper III), it will be necessary to refer to this paper and to the manner in which it modifies the conclusions of the three previous essays. Two short papers of 1867 on Boole's calculus and the logic of mathematics (3, Papers I and II) may be passed over as unimportant for the general concern here.[2] The importance attached here to the first three essays of the *Search for a Method* is substantiated by the references Peirce continued to make to them in his later writings. He wrote ca. 1895 concerning the *On a New List of Categories*: "The truth is that my paper of 1867 was perhaps the least unsatisfactory, from a logical point of view, that I ever succeeded in producing; and for a long time most of the modifications I attempted of it only led me further wrong" (2.340). References indicating similar approval continue to appear (cf. 4.2 ff. [1898]; 1.561 [1905]).

1. THE NATURAL CLASSIFICATION OF ARGUMENTS

A. Peirce continued throughout his writings to regard a classification of arguments as comprising the chief function of logic. He wrote in a paper published in 1878: "The chief business of the logician is to classify arguments; for all testing clearly depends on classification" (2.619); and again in a dictionary article (1901–2): "It will ... generally be conceded that its [logic's] central problem is the classification of arguments" (2.203). He found occasion in his lectures on pragmatism in 1903 to emphasize the importance of a classification of arguments and to reaffirm the general results of his paper of 1867 on this subject.

Peirce's paper on the Aristotelian syllogism and the subsequent development of the same analysis into the natural classification of arguments seem to have been directly occasioned by a reading of Kant's essay on the figures of the syllogism and to have been conceived with the conviction that there was a fundamental error in Kant's approach. According to the intellectual autobiography of 1898,

... I read every book I could lay my hands on upon logic, and of course Kant's essay on the *falsche Spitzfindigkeit der vier syllogistischen Figuren;*[3] and here I detected a fallacy similar to that of the phlogistic chemists. For Kant argues that the fact all syllogisms can be reduced to Barbara shows that they involve no logical principle that Barbara does not involve. A chemist might as well argue, that because water boiled with zinc dust evolves hydrogen, and the hydrogen does not come from the zinc, therefore water is a mere form of hydrogen. In short, Kant omits to inquire whether the very reasoning by which he reduces the indirect moods to Barbara may not itself introduce an additional logical principle. Pursuing this suggestion, I found that that was in truth the case, and I succeeded [in 1866] in demonstrating that the second and third figures each involved a special additional logical principle, both of which enter into the fourth figure [4.2].

4

An understanding of this "fallacy" in Kant's reasoning as well as an analysis of Peirce's classification of arguments may be best approached by reference to certain fundamental points made at the beginning of Peirce's paper on the classification of arguments.

(i) The paper *On the Natural Classification of Arguments* opens with a brief section on the "essential parts of an argument." An "argument" is to denote "a body of premisses considered as such"; the term "premiss"[4] is to "refer exclusively to something laid down (whether in any enduring and communicable form of expression, or only in some imagined sign), and not to anything only *virtually* contained in what is laid down which is (or is supposed to be) relevant to the conclusion" (2.461). Further, "every inference involves the judgment that, if such propositions as the premisses are true, then a proposition related to them, as the conclusion is, must be, or is likely to be, true. The principle implied in this judgment, respecting a genus of argument, is termed the *leading principle* of the argument" (2.462). Hence, "a valid argument is one whose leading principle is true" (2.463), and "in order that an argument should determine the necessary or probable truth of its conclusion, both the premisses and leading principle must be true" (2.464).

These considerations distinguish two fundamental concepts of logic: an argument, which is identical with a body of premisses in some way laid down; an inference, which is identical with (or at least involves) a judgment about the argument. Thus, a syllogism may be regarded either as merely certain things laid down or as a judgment respecting what is laid down in virtue of which something related to what is laid down is inferred. These two terms, "argument" and "inference," are mutually dependent on each other, and both are necessary if there is to be logic at all. If, on the one hand, an argument is considered simply as the premisses laid down without reference to anything else, the entire consideration becomes psychological rather than logical. What one person *lays down* as warrant for making a certain judgment about facts may be quite different from what another person would lay down for the same purpose, and a consideration

5

of arguments only in this sense would always involve "psychological perplexities" (cf. 2.466, n. 1) and render it impossible to distinguish anything called an "argument" which everyone would be forced to assume as basis for a given judgment. If, on the other hand, an inference is identified exclusively with the judgment that one proposition is true because others are so and no reference is made to what is *laid down* as basis for such judgment, logic becomes impossible; and there is not even a means of characterizing such an inference, "since all that we know of thought is but a reflection of what we know of its expression" (cf. 2.466, n. 1; cf. also 2.461, n. 1 [1893]). A science of logic, consequently, is possible only when a mean position is taken between the extremes of considering arguments exclusively in terms of what is actually laid down by a person as a basis for judgment and of considering inference in itself without reference to what is laid down. When this mean position is followed, argument and inference must be taken as mutually determining each other, and in virtue of this determination a "natural classification of arguments" is possible. An argument as "premisses laid down" becomes the subject matter of judgment for an inference, and as a subject matter its "natural" characteristics can be ascertained and its "genus" determined.

(ii) Those aspects of an argument which are natural can be distinguished from those which are not by determining the requirements imposed by the inference upon the argument as something laid down. That is, while at the extreme where an argument is considered only with respect to what is laid down, the extent of what is laid down is arbitrary; yet, when the argument in this sense is taken as relative to the inference involved and not to individual thinkers, it is possible to mark a point in the laying-down of premisses beyond which further addition would be irrelevant to the requirements of the given inference. This limitation is thus an aspect of the argument which is other than what is actually laid down in the premisses and which is nevertheless necessary for the constitution of an inference; such an aspect is called the "logical principle" of the argument and

6

is contained in what is called the "leading principle." This latter principle "contains, by definition, whatever is considered requisite besides the premises to determine the necessary or probable truth of the conclusion" (2.465); and, when it contains nothing more than this (i.e., when "no part" of it can be "eliminated" or "transferred to the premises"), it is identical with the logical principle (2.466). "An argument whose leading principle contains nothing which can be eliminated," that is, whose leading principle coincides with its logical principle, "is termed a *complete*, in opposition to an *incomplete, rhetorical, or enthymematic* argument" (2.466). The logical principle, consequently, is a requirement of inference which limits the laying-down of premises to the point where the argument becomes complete, and what is thus determinative of a complete argument will constitute the genus or natural class of the argument.

This procedure of determining a complete argument may be illustrated as follows.[5] The enthymematic argument,

> Enoch was a man,
> ∴ Enoch died,

can be expanded by laying down another premiss. Thus,

> All men die,
> Enoch was a man;
> ∴ Enoch was to die.

The next step in laying down premisses would give

> *Nota notae est nota rei ipsius*,
> Mortality is a mark of man, which is a
> mark of Enoch;
> ∴ Mortality is a mark of Enoch.

But then this third stage of the argument cannot be further expanded without again laying down something already laid down, since the principle of the *nota notae* is also operative here, and all that could be done would be to reassert its truth on the next level.

> *Nota notae* . . . is a true principle of inference.
> To say that mortality . . . , and that therefore Enoch
> . . . , is an inference drawn by this principle.
> ∴ This is a true inference.

7

Such a procedure leads to an infinite regress which can be avoided only by recognizing that an argument becomes complete as soon as its leading principle contains nothing which can be laid down as a premiss. If the leading principle of a given stage of the argument be understood as the first principle added in expanding that stage, then the second stage of the above argument, the first complete syllogism, is just as complete as any subsequent stage. For the leading principle of this second stage, the principle of the *nota notae*, is also the leading principle for any subsequent stage, so that nothing contributing to the completeness of the argument is given by proceeding to later stages. Thus, only in the case of the first stage, the enthymematic argument, does the leading principle add something factual to the premisses already laid down. "All men die" makes a factual assertion different from that made by "Enoch was a man" and can therefore be "eliminated" from the leading principle and "transferred to the premisses." But when the leading principle of this new stage of the argument—the principle of the *nota notae*—is added to the premisses to give the third stage, nothing factual is transferred to the premisses by such procedure. The leading principle, therefore, coincides with the logical principle, which is precisely that aspect of the argument which is other than what is laid down in the premisses and which is nevertheless necessary for the inference.

It results from this consideration that "every complete argument has at least two premisses" (2.469). For an inference always involves the condition that some fact have "such a relation to another that, if the former is true, the latter is necessarily or probably true" (2.469). But this relation itself also "constitutes a determinate fact," so that by the requirements of inference every complete argument must have one premiss expressing the fact in virtue of which the fact in the conclusion is said to be true and another premiss expressing the fact that these other two facts have such a relation. Since the "leading principle of a complete argument involves no matter of fact" (2.469), the premisses laid down need be no more than two. Moreover, since every con-

8

clusion may be regarded as a statement substituted for one of its premisses, the substitution being justified by the other premisses, no complete argument can have more than two premisses (cf. 2.470). Thus "all S is P" can be substituted for "all S is M" in virtue of the fact that "all M is P." Now, if there are also other premisses required to justify this substitution, there will be at least two more: one stating a new fact and one which allows a premiss of the original argument to be substituted for this new fact. Thus, "all M is N" may be taken as stating a new fact and "all N is P" as permitting it to be replaced by the original premiss "all M is P." But this is of course another complete argument with two premisses and a conclusion. By this procedure, "every argument of more than two premisses can be resolved into a series of arguments of two premisses each," and hence the distinction of "*simple* and *complex* arguments" (2.470). This "decomposition of arguments" is immediately consequent to the restrictions imposed by the requirements of inference upon the laying-down of premisses.

(iii) The process of decomposition may also be applied to a single argument. A "valid, complete, simple argument" or "syllogistic argument" can, by analysis of its premisses, be decomposed into terms. Every premiss or proposition "may, in at least one way, be put into the form, S is P; the import of which is, that the objects to which S, or the *total subject*, applics have the characteristics attributed to every object to which P, or the *total predicate*, applies" (2.472). Thus, in respect to the way in which terms function in an argument, "every term has two powers or significations, according as it is subject or predicate. The former, which will here be termed its *breadth*, comprises the objects to which it is applied; while the latter, which will here be termed its *depth*, comprises the characters which are attributed to every one of the objects to which it can be applied" (2.473). The substitution by which a conclusion is seen to follow from its premisses can be explained by these two powers. Since "every substitution of one proposition for another must consist in the substitution of term for term," and since "such substitution can

9

be justified only so far as the first term represents what is represented by the second," there are only two possible substitutions (2.474). "The substitution for a term fulfilling the function of a subject of another whose breadth is included in that of the former; and the substitution for a term fulfilling the function of a predicate of another whose depth is included in that of the former" (2.474).

Peirce extended this analysis to syllogisms with a particular premiss and conclusion. "Since some S means 'the part now meant of S,' a particular proposition is equivalent to a universal proposition with another subject" (2.478). Thus, "some men are animals" is equivalent to "all the men now meant are animals," and this may serve as a rule by which the conclusion "some men are mortals" is substituted for the premiss "all animals are mortals." For the breadth of "some men" as equivalent to "all the men now meant" is included in the breadth of "all animals."[6]

Since this analysis of substitution may be used to explain the fundamental operation in every simple, complete argument or syllogism, Peirce concludes that

the general formula of all argument must be:

M is P
S is M
.·. S is P;

which is to be understood in this sense—that the terms of every syllogistic argument fulfill functions of subject and predicate as here indicated, but not that the argument can be grammatically expressed in this way [2.474].

The way in which terms function as subject and predicate in a syllogism is thus determined entirely by the manner in which the requirements of inference govern the manipulation of terms and has nothing to do with a grammatical determination of subject and predicate. The logical function of subject and predicate is precisely what is in no way indicated by grammatical analysis; for the operation of substitution which expresses the inference is based solely on the breadth and depth of the terms involved

10

and proceeds indifferently with respect to whether the substitution is regarded as the replacement of the middle term in one premiss by the subject of the conclusion or of the middle term in the other premiss by the predicate of the conclusion. That is, the substitution is warranted by the breadth and depth of the terms, and either premiss may function indifferently as that in which the substitution is made or as that according to which it is made.

B. The "general formula of all argument" determined by this analysis corresponds of course to the first-figure syllogism in Barbara of traditional logic. However, a radically nontraditional treatment of the second and third figures follows from the analysis. These indirect figures can no longer be taken simply as imperfect syllogisms which must be completed by reduction to the first figure, for they now arise, like the first figure, out of the substitutions productive of inference. It is "always possible to substitute for any premiss the denial of the conclusion, provided the denial of that premiss be at the same time substituted for the conclusion." Hence, "corresponding to every syllogistic argument in the general form,

"S is M, M is P;
S is P.

"There are two others:

"It is false that S is P, M is P;
It is false that S is M.

"S is M, it is false that S is P;
It is false that M is P" [2.475].[7]

Peirce gives a rather lengthy examination of the various ways in which these two additional forms of reasoning (which he called "apagogical forms") can be reduced to the first figure and concludes: "It appears that no syllogism of an indirect figure can be reduced to the first figure without a substitution which has the form of the very figure from which the syllogism is reduced" (2.499). For example, Camestres and Baroco can be re-

11

duced "by introducing the term not-P, and defining it as that which S *is* when it is *not* P." Then, "the moods:

"Any   M is P,
Any or some S is not P;
∴ Any or some S is not M,

are reduced to:

"No   not-P is M,
Any or some S is not-P;
∴ Any or some S is not M" [2.487].

In this reduction the inference of "any S is not-P" from "any S is not P," while not "ordinary syllogism," can be said to be an inference "essentially of the second figure," with the "suppressed premiss" "any not-P is not P." Similarly, "no not-P is M" can be said to be inferred from "any M is P" in a second-figure syllogism with the same suppressed premiss (cf. note of 1893 to 2.487 and 2.496).

Peirce offers "ostensive reductions" of this type for all the moods of the indirect figures. When the premisses have been converted or contraposited in such a way that the converse or contrapositive of the original conclusion is obtained, the reduction is called "long" as opposed to the above example, which was a "short" reduction (cf. 2.486). All ostensive reductions can be said to involve an inference in the form of the very figure which is being reduced in so far as "the conversions and contrapositions can be expressed syllogistically . . . by taking as one of the premisses:

" 'All   N is   N,'
'Any   not-N is not N,'
or 'Some   N is some-N' " [2.496].

Nonetheless, conversion and contraposition are clearly not inferences in the strict sense defined at the beginning of Peirce's paper, for none of these premisses can be taken as properly a premiss of an argument, that is, as some matter of fact laid down. It would appear, indeed, that such premisses are "merely forms of words without meaning" (2.496). Yet the operations performed in conversion and contraposition are in fact operations of substitution: "no B is A" may be substituted for "no A is B" by virtue of the rule "all B is B."[8] Now,

> there is . . . an intention in which these substitutions are inferential. For, although the passage from holding for true a fact expressed in the form "No A is B," to holding its converse, is not an inference, because these facts being identical, the relation between them is not a fact; yet the passage from one of these forms taken merely as having some meaning, but not this or that meaning, to another, since these forms are not identical, and their logical relation is a fact, is an inference. This distinction may be expressed by saying that they are not inferences, but substitutions having the form of inferences [2.496].

The indirect figures, then, arise out of substitutions productive of inference and upon analysis are found to be irreducible to the first figure, inasmuch as any attempt at such reduction involves a substitution having the form of the indirect figure being reduced. The "so-called *reductio per impossibile*" is easily seen to provide no exception to these results derived from an examination of ostensive reductions, for this process of denying the conclusion is merely "the repetition or inversion of that contraposition of propositions by which the indirect figures have been obtained" (2.498). An examination of fourth-figure or Theophrastean syllogisms, both as arising out of substitutions productive of inference and as reducible to the first figure, reveals substitutions having the form of inferences in the second and third figures but none having an entirely unique form. The fourth figure "therefore belongs to a figure which unites the characters of the second and third, and which may be termed the second-third figure in Theophrastean syllogism" (2.505). Contrary to the classical analysis, Peirce's treatment of the syllogism as a substitution having the form of an inference thus exhibits a sense in which both the second and the third figures constitute forms of argument irreducible to the first figure. It is only with respect to the facts laid down by the premises that the indirect figures may be reduced to the first figure; with respect to the forms of substitution, three different classes of arguments must be recognized.

13

The "fallacy" in Kant's essay on "the mistaken subtlety of the four figures" can thus be explained as a result of the fact that he did not regard the process of inference constituting a syllogism as an operation of substitution performed upon the premisses laid down. Once this view has been taken, it becomes apparent that conversion and contraposition, inasmuch as they are operations of substitution, are forms of inference. Kant argues that what is laid down as warrant for drawing a conclusion has no essential bearing on the inference involved: "for the question is not what is said, but what it is indispensably necessary to think, in order that there may be a valid sequence." The essential point for logic, then, is that the conversion or contraposition necessary to validate an inference in an indirect figure is an "immediate consequence, which one must have at least in thought."[9] Kant found no problem in distinguishing immediate consequence and inference, since the latter is a process of thought which requires a middle term while the former does not. But if all processes of thought must be viewed as processes of substitution performed upon what is laid down, both immediate consequence and inference proper require a "middle" in the form of a rule which justifies the substitution. This non-Kantian view of inference as a form of substitution will be seen in the sequel to constitute a fundamental characteristic of Peirce's approach to logic.

Peirce concluded his paper *On the Natural Classification of Arguments* with a brief consideration of "probable inferences" in relation to the three genera of arguments. Presumably the first figure or "general formula of all arguments" embraces only necessary inferences, while, "among probable inferences, it is obvious that hypothesis corresponds to the second figure, induction to the third, and analogy to the second-third" (2.516). In his later writings Peirce came to regard abduction or hypothesis, deduction, and induction as constituting the three general classes of argument, and further development of his logic soon led him to perceive that they should not be based on the three figures of the syllogism.

14

A. Despite the fact that Peirce for the remainder of his life seems to have regarded this analysis of arguments as indicating at least certain of his fundamental conceptions of logic, there is an obvious sense in which the classification afforded by the analysis is inadequate. Peirce seems to have realized this inadequacy almost as soon as he wrote the paper, and, in fact, the inadequacy is clearly indicated in one passage appearing in the original version of the paper. In a sketch of his intellectual autobiography, 1898, Peirce wrote: "[With regard to] my logical studies in 1867, various facts proved to me beyond a doubt that my scheme of formal logic was still incomplete. For one thing, I found it quite impossible to represent in syllogisms any course of reasoning in geometry, or even any reasoning in algebra, except in Boole's logical algebra" (4.4). In the original On the Natural Classification of Arguments there is a section on "mathematical syllogisms." The section ends with the statement: "If logic is to take account of such syllogisms, it would be necessary to consider some propositions as having three terms, subject, predicate, and object; and such propositions would be divided into active and passive. The varieties in them would be endless" (2.507).

The difficulty here may be viewed as arising from the circumstance that the analysis in the classification of arguments was based on a single set of relations, viz., those arising from the substitution of terms in accordance with their logical breadth and depth. But mathematical reasoning by means of such relations as whole and part, and greater and less, cannot strictly be taken as inferences expressed by this one set of relations. When the proposition "A is greater than B" is analyzed as "A," the subject, "greater than," the predicate, and "B," the object to which the subject is referred by the predicate, the basis for relations of possible substitutions arising from the breadth and depth of terms is entirely destroyed.[10] Such relations of substitution, moreover, hold only between certain kinds of symbols, viz., terms, which are taken as constituting the fundamental units of a proposition. But the relations considered by mathematics are far more general and hold not only between other kinds of symbols besides terms but also between objects which are not symbols. The solution to the difficulty must thus come by making the narrower relations of substitution special cases of the wider relations occurring in mathematics rather than vice versa, which would be the course demanded by Peirce's original analysis. The development of this solution requires "the logic of relatives," which Peirce was on the verge of discovering by 1867 (cf. 4.4). According to the intellectual autobiography of 1898, "the great difference between the logic of relatives and ordinary logic is that the former regards the form of relations in all its generality and in its different possible species while the latter is tied down to the matter of the single special relation of similarity" (4.5).[11]

B. The passage from the analysis which afforded the natural classification of arguments to that which culminated in the logic of relatives does not necessarily imply a radical change in the fundamental conceptions of logic. There is good ground for regarding Peirce's continued esteem for his paper on the classification of arguments as indicative of a fundamental unity of approach underlying the two apparently opposed analyses. As was seen in the preceding section, despite Peirce's adherence to the Kantian position that all reasoning can be expressed syllogistically, his classification entailed radical departures from the Kantian interpretation of inference. Peirce remarked in his comments of 1898 concerning this classification:

I found that there was also a mode of probable reasoning in the second figure essentially different both from induction and from probable deduction. This was plainly what is called reasoning from consequent to antecedent, and in many books is called adopting a hypothesis for the sake of the explanation it affords of known facts. It would be tedious to show how this discovery led to the thorough refutation of the third and most important of Kant's triads, and the confirmation of the doctrine that for the purposes of ordinary syllogism categorical propositions and conditional propositions, which

16

Kant and his ignorant adherents call hypotheticals, are all one. This led me to see that the relation between subject and predicate, or antecedent and consequent, is essentially the same as that between premiss and conclusion [4.3].

However "tedious" may be the details of Peirce's intellectual autobiography, the essential connection between his analysis of the classification of arguments and the proposed identification of categorical and conditional propositions seems fairly obvious. If every syllogistic conclusion may be regarded as a statement substituted for either of its premisses, the substitution being justified by the other premiss, then every premiss, whether stated conditionally or categorically, is for syllogistic purposes a rule of substitution. The traditional "all M is P" means simply that the name "M" may always be replaced by the name "P," and this is the same relation as that expressed by "if M, then P" or "M implies P." The careful distinctions which Kant, following traditional logic, drew between terms, propositions, and arguments or inferences are as useless on this analysis as the distinction of categoricals from conditionals. As Peirce explained the point in 1880: "By thus identifying the relation expressed by the copula with that of illation, we identify the proposition with the inference, and the term with the proposition. This identification, by means of which all that is found true of term, proposition, or inference is at once known to be true of all three, is a most important engine of reasoning" (3.175).

As a result of this approach, all logical analysis is made ultimately a matter of relations; for any operation of substitution is based on a relation between the things substituted. The fact that the relations examined may be only those subsisting indifferently between terms, propositions, or arguments, but not between facts signified, does not alter the circumstance that such consideration falls under the general analysis of relations. The passage from the classification of arguments to the logic of relatives is, therefore, a passage from a less general analysis to a more general one actually necessitated by the former. The only modification of the original analysis needed is the stipulation that the

17

classification afforded thereby does not apply to all types of argument (cf. note of 1893, 2.469, n. 2).

The fundamental character of Peirce's approach to logic may now be indicated by a partial statement of his conception of the subject matter of logic and the type of analysis necessitated by that conception. Logic not only must be a study insusceptible of reduction to considerations either of ontological categories or of potentialities of the human mind; it also must have a subject matter determined without reference to such considerations. Terms, propositions, and arguments cannot, for example, as on many interpretations of traditional logic, be defined with reference either to kinds of being signified (as simple substances, immediate, and mediate connections) or to kinds of mental faculties involved (as conception, judgment, and reasoning). On the contrary, all classification in logic must be based solely on the forms of the operations employed in laying down premisses and in drawing conclusions, as these operations are limited by the requirements of inference. That is, the principles of classification must be found in the operations themselves rather than in the *things* which the operations seem to presuppose (as the things reasoned about or the things doing the reasoning). But, then, the only type of analysis possible is one which characterizes the operations by classifying the patterns of relations according to which the substitutions are performed. Different occurrences of these patterns within the process of logical operations will provide the proper means for distinguishing one form of substitution from another (as the substitution of predicate for subject from that of conclusion for premiss) and will also constitute the proper expression of the way in which the requirements of inference determine the process. Logic must thus be established in its full generality as the logic of relatives before an adequate classification of its basic concepts becomes possible.

The most general and fundamental principles of logic are thus to be found in the continual recurrence of relational patterns in the process of logical operations. Traditional logic, as Peirce interpreted it, tried to take first-figure syllogisms as yielding the

18

one recurring pattern in all reasoning but was then forced to establish the recurrence in many cases by contrived processes of reduction. If these reductions involve two new and irreducible patterns, as Peirce thought they did, there might still be a single triadic pattern which embraces in one of its occurrences the three forms of argument. In this way the artificial unity of forms of reasoning in the traditional analysis could be replaced by a more comprehensive and natural unity. The same triadic pattern in another of its occurrences might then embrace the three stages in the formation of an argument—the passage from term to proposition to syllogism.

3. THE FIRST STATEMENT OF THE CATEGORIES

A. Peirce was led by the analysis which culminated in his threefold classification of arguments to search at once for more fundamental patterns recurring in the process of logical operations. In the intellectual autobiography of 1898 he remarked:

Why should there be three principles of reasoning, and what have they to do with one another? This question, which was connected with other parts of my schedule of philosophical inquiry that need not be detailed, now came to the front. Even without Kant's categories, the recurrence of triads in logic was quite marked, and must be the croppings out of some fundamental conceptions. I now undertook to ascertain what the conceptions were. This search resulted in what I call my categories [4.3].

Just as in the essay on the classification of arguments Kant's treatment of the figures of the syllogism served as a point of departure for a radically different treatment of the same subject, so in the On a New List of Categories Kant's treatment of the categories serves a similar function. Peirce's analysis in the latter paper is sufficiently important for the subsequent development of his philosophy to justify a somewhat extensive paraphrase of his whole argument before turning to a consideration of the problems to which it led him.

The paper opens with an acceptance of a statement of the Kantian position on the nature of conception. "This paper is

19

based upon the theory already established, that the function of conceptions is to reduce the manifold of sensuous impressions to unity and that the validity of a conception consists in the impossibility of reducing the content of consciousness to unity without the introduction of it" (1.545). According to Peirce's interpretation: "This theory gives rise to a conception of gradation among those conceptions which are universal. For one such conception may unite the manifold of sense and yet another may be required to unite the conception and the manifold to which it is applied; and so on" (1.546). Such interpretation clearly implies a process in which several conceptions may have to be added to the original conception applying to the manifold before the latter can be completely reduced to a unity. The first requirement in determining the categories, then, must be the delimitation of this process by marking a beginning and an end, just as the determination of kinds of complete arguments could not be attempted until the process of constructing a complete argument was first delimited as beginning when something was laid down as premiss and as ending when the leading principle coincided with the logical principle.

The first step in this delimitation is the recognition that the "universal conception which is nearest to sense is that of *the present, in general*" (1.547). Since this is nothing but "the pure denotative power of the mind" and has "no connotation," it can have "no proper unity." It is the conception of "ɪᴛ in general" and "is rendered in philosophical language by the word 'substance' in one of its meanings." The next point for recognition is that "the unity to which the understanding reduces impressions is the unity of a proposition." "This unity consists in the connection of the predicate with the subject; and, therefore, that which is implied in the copula, or the conception of *being*, is that which completes the work of conceptions of reducing the manifold to unity" (1.548). This conception of *being*, while it "plainly has no content," differs from that of *substance* in that it does involve some connotation or determinability, even if only

20

in the sense of implying an "indefinite determinability of the predicate." Thus,

if one could know the copula and predicate of any proposition, as "... is a tailed-man," he would know the predicate to be applicable to something supposable, at least. Accordingly, we have propositions whose subjects are entirely indefinite, as "There is a beautiful ellipse," where the subject is merely *something actual or potential*; but we have no propositions whose predicate is entirely indeterminate, for it would be quite senseless to say, "A has the common characters of all things," inasmuch as there are no such characters.

The two conceptions, substance and being, thus provide the delimitation desired, for they denote, respectively, "the beginning and end of all conception." That which first claims the attention of the mind is the immediately present, completely indeterminate subject, which can only be reduced to unity by joining it to some kind of determinate predicate; and the first requirement for this reduction, before any reference is made to the subject (and hence in this sense at the opposite extreme from substance), is the mere indefinitely determinate predicate, as "... is a man," which is the only way the otherwise empty word "being" can be understood.

B. These two extremes, substance and being, are brought together into a determinate judgment by a process which Peirce terms *precision* or *abstraction*.[12] This process must be carefully distinguished from two others, *discrimination* and *dissociation*. The former "only draws a distinction in meaning," while the latter "is that separation which, in the absence of constant association, is permitted by the law of association of images" (1.549). Thus abstraction or precision "supposes a greater separation than discrimination, but a less separation than dissociation." For often discrimination in meaning can be made where no separation is possible in the natural process of abstraction—for example, color can be discriminated, but not abstracted, from space; yet separations can be made by abstraction where none is possible by dissociation—for example, space can be abstracted, but not dissociated, from color. Abstraction, moreover, is thus not a re-

21

ciprocal process. Space is an "elementary conception" which reduces "impressions" or "more immediate conceptions" to unity, and such impressions, like those of color, can therefore not be abstracted from space. But, once the conception of space has been obtained from those more immediate conceptions, "there is, in general, no reason why the premisses which have occasioned it should not be neglected, and therefore the explaining conception may frequently be prescinded from the more immediate ones and from the impressions."

The "facts" obtained from this consideration of mental processes afford "the basis for a systematic method of searching out whatever universal elementary conceptions there may be intermediate between the manifold of substance and the unity of being" (1.550). The immediately present, indeterminate subject, or substance, is reduced to unity by an elementary conception which can be prescinded or abstracted from it; this abstraction is possible only because another conception, which falls under the elementary conception and thus cannot be abstracted from it, "already lies in the data which is united to that of substance" by the elementary conception. Thus, the perception of a black stove can be reduced to a unity by means of such elementary conceptions as "color" and "space" and regarded as a "colored object," but this is possible only because a more immediate conception, "blackness," was already in the data from which the abstraction was made. "Empirical psychology" discovers the occasion for the introduction of such elementary conceptions, and the first stage in the passage from substance to being will be given by the character of the more immediate conception appearing in the data on any such occasion. This latter conception, however, is itself mediate in respect to that to which it is applied, as in the proposition, "this stove is black," *this stove* is more immediate than the *blackness* which is referred to it. Hence, the blackness can be abstracted from the immediate data and considered in itself; and, so considered, it affords the conception of a quality, or that which characterizes a substance.

Peirce remarked in respect to the above analysis that, "through-

22

out this process, *introspection* is not resorted to. Nothing is assumed respecting the subjective elements of consciousness which cannot be securely inferred from the objective elements" (1.550). If introspection is relied on, the conception of quality "seems at first sight to be given in the impression" (1.551). But this is clearly not the case, since "a proposition asserts the applicability of a mediate conception to a more immediate one," so that "the more mediate conception is clearly regarded independently of this circumstance." Otherwise, "the two conceptions would not be distinguished, but one would be thought through the other, without this latter being an object of thought, at all." The blackness, then, must be prescinded from the immediate data comprising the black stove, and only when this is done does the conception of a quality arise. Introspection is thus not resorted to in this process because, independently of any reference to individual thought-processes, the analysis of a proposition reveals the mediacy of the predicate and the necessity for the precision of the concept of quality from the immediate data. Empirical psychology (which Peirce regards here as involving introspection) serves only to show the occasion whereupon a certain process occurs, but this process itself is analyzable in terms of the proposition to which it gives rise independently of individual thought.

The conception of a pure abstraction is "indispensable, because we cannot comprehend an agreement of two things, except as an agreement in some respect, and this respect is such a pure abstraction as blackness" (1.551). Considered in this fashion, as the basis of all comparison, reference to a *quality* or general attribute may be termed "reference to a ground." "Reference to a ground cannot be prescinded from being, but being can be prescinded from it."

The next step in the passage from being to substance is shown by the very occasion which produced the first step. It has been established by empirical psychology that "we can know a quality only by means of its contrast with or similarity to another" (1.552). The blackness of the stove cannot be prescinded from

23

the manifold comprising the black stove and considered as something in itself without at the same time being recognized as other than anything else contained in the manifold. This recognition always involves a "reference to a correlate," that is, the blackness in being compared and contrasted with the rest of the manifold is referred to it as to a correlate. Thus, "the occasion of the introduction of the conception of reference to a ground is the reference to a correlate, and this is, therefore, the next conception in order." Hence, "reference to a correlate cannot be prescinded from reference to a ground; but reference to a ground may be prescinded from reference to a correlate."

Peirce begins his consideration of the next step in the process by remarking that the act of comparison "has not been sufficiently studied by psychologists, and it will, therefore, be necessary to adduce some examples to show in what it consists" (1.553). Any act of comparison, for example, that of comparing the letters *p* and *b*, involves a reference to some mode of representation whereby two objects can be compared. Thus, one of the letters may be imagined "to be turned over on the line of writing as an axis, then laid upon the other, and finally to become transparent so that the other can be seen through it. In this way we shall form a new image which mediates between the images of the two letters, inasmuch as it represents one of them to be (when turned over) the likeness of the other." Peirce considers other examples of acts of comparison and concludes that, "by a further accumulation of instances, it would be found that every comparison requires, besides the related thing, the ground, and the correlate, also a *mediating representation which represents the relate to be a representation of the same correlate which this mediating representation itself represents*" (italics in original). This mediating representation may be called an "*interpretant*, because it fulfills the office of an interpreter, who says that a foreigner says the same thing which he himself says." The very occasion which produced the second step in the process thus affords the third step. "Every reference to a correlate, then, conjoins to the substance the conception of a reference to an interpretant; and this is, therefore, the next conception in order in passing from being to substance. Reference to an interpretant cannot be prescinded from reference to a correlate; but the latter can be prescinded from the former."

Reference to an interpretant "is rendered possible and justified by that which renders possible and justifies comparison," viz., "the diversity of impressions" (1.554). There would be no problem of reducing a manifold to a unity, and no act of comparison, if there were but a single impression; and impressions "are not brought to a unity until we conceive them together as being ours, that is, until we refer them to a conception as their interpretant." Thus, blackness is first prescinded from the manifold of substance comprising the black stove, and, considered in itself, it joins to the substance the conception of a pure abstraction and affords a basis for comparison. In this sense it constitutes a reference to a ground, but the occasion of this reference involves the comparison of blackness with the manifold in terms of a relation, such as the "embodying" or "possessing" of a quality by a subject.[13] This latter consideration is itself a reference to a correlate and is possible only because blackness is conceived as a part of the manifold comprising the perception of a stove. The occasion of conceiving blackness in this way does not merely add a new conception but also affords a mediating representation in virtue of which black may be compared to the rest of the manifold in the relation expressed by the proposition, "the substance, stove, embodies black." "Thus, the reference to an interpretant arises upon the holding together of diverse impressions, and therefore it does not join a conception to the substance, as the two other references do, but unites directly the manifold of the substance itself. It is, therefore, the last conception in order in passing from being to substance."

C. The "five conceptions" obtained from this analysis "may be termed categories. That is,

> *Being*
> Quality (reference to a ground)
> Relation (reference to a correlate)
> Representation (reference to an interpretant)
> *Substance*" [1.555].

25

These five conceptions may be ordered in either of two ways. When they are considered according to degrees of precision or abstraction, being, the most abstract conception, stands first and can be prescinded from all the others; each of the remaining steps in the passage downward to the union of being with substance can be prescinded from the conceptions falling under it but not from those above it. When they are viewed in the reverse direction, as constituting a passage from the many (the manifold of substance) to the one (the unity of being), the order becomes "numerical."

The conception of a *third* is that of an object which is so related to two others, that one of these must be related to the other in the same way in which the third is related to that other. Now this coincides with the conception of an interpretant. An *other* is plainly equivalent to a correlate. The conception of second differs from that of other, in implying the possibility of a third. In the same way, the conception of *self* implies the possibility of an *other*. The *ground* is the self abstracted from the concreteness which implies the possibility of another [1.556].

If an abstraction always supposes a corresponding object, when the five conceptions are viewed in the order of abstraction, they afford a list of "supposable objects."

What is
Quale (that which refers to a ground)
Relate (that which refers to ground and correlate)
Representamen (that which refers to ground, correlate, and interpretant)
It [1.557].

Inasmuch as a relate and a representamen involve reference to more than one conception, it is possible to distinguish cases where a reference to one conception can be prescinded from other references and cases where this cannot be done. Thus, there are "relates whose reference to a ground is a prescindible or internal quality" and those "whose reference to a ground is an unprescindible or relative quality" (1.558). This distinction affords two fundamentally different kinds of relatives, those of similarity and those of any other form of dyadic relation (which, as a class, Peirce later called "dynamical relations").[14] In an instance of similarity, such as that of one blue patch to another, the ground of the comparison—the blueness—is prescindible from the manifold which contains it and, hence, from any reference to a correlate. But in an instance of an external relation—such as A is to the right of B—the ground of the comparison is the relative position of A and B, which is not prescindible from the manifold presenting the two objects in this position and, hence, not prescindible from reference to a correlate.[15]

In like manner, in the case of representations or "representamens," it is possible first to distinguish those whose reference to a ground is prescindible both from reference to a correlate and from reference to an interpretant. In this instance the relation of the representations to their objects "is a mere community in some quality" (1.558), so that such representations may be termed "likenesses" (later called "icons"). Second, there may be distinguished representations called "indices" (in 1867, also "signs"), "whose relation to their objects consists in a correspondence in fact." In this case the reference to a ground is prescindible from reference to an interpretant but not from reference to a correlate, as the ground of the relation between a pointer and the object pointed to is a certain external relation which cannot be prescinded from the manifold representing the relate and the correlate. Finally, representations may be distinguished which are properly "symbols" or "general signs," since their ground is prescindible neither from reference to a correlate nor from reference to an interpretant. For example, the ground of the relation between the word "man" and an actual man is unprescindible from a mediating conception such as that of the the imposition of words.

D. The consideration has now reached a point where it is possible to show that "the three conceptions of reference to a \ ground, reference to an object, and reference to an interpretant are the fundamental ones of at least one universal science, that of logic" (1.559). If logic be understood "to treat of second intentions as applied to first," the class of all symbols will constitute the "subject genus" of this science. The rules of logic will apply to external symbols, spoken or written, as well as to internal symbols or concepts, but they will "have no immediate application to likenesses or indices, because no arguments can be constructed of these alone." Since logic, then, will treat of "the reference of symbols in general to their objects," it becomes possible to distinguish three kinds of logic in accordance with the three references involved in any symbol. There is, first, the consideration of "the formal conditions of symbols having meaning, that is of the reference of symbols in general to their grounds or imputed characters, and this might be called formal grammar" (later, "speculative grammar"). Second, there is the consideration of "the formal conditions of the truth of symbols," which involves both reference to a ground and reference to the objects correlated with the symbols (later called "critical logic" or "critic"). Third, there is the consideration of "the formal conditions of the force of symbols, or their power of appealing to a mind, that is, of their reference in general to interpretants, and this might be called formal rhetoric" (later, "speculative rhetoric" or "methodeutic").

Application of the three references involved in any symbol also affords "a general division of symbols, common to all these sciences." Symbols "which directly determine only their *grounds* or imputed qualities" are terms; those which directly determine the second reference and thus become "capable of truth or falsehood" are propositions; and those which directly determine the third reference are arguments, since they determine "the minds to which they appeal, by premissing a proposition or propositions which such a mind is to admit" (1.559).

By a similar procedure, three kinds of arguments can be distinguished and identified with the three kinds afforded by the paper on the classification of arguments. For, "in an argument, the premisses form a representation of the conclusion, because they indicate the interpretant of the argument, or representation representing it to represent its object" (1.559). Hence, "the premisses may afford a likeness, index, or symbol of the con-

28

clusion." In the first case the argument is a hypothesis and the syllogism is in the second figure: M is P', P'', and P'''; S is P', P'', P'''; ∴ S is M. The characters P', P'', and P''' may be taken as showing what anything is like that is M, and thus "the premisses are or represent a likeness of the conclusion." In the second case the argument is an induction, and the syllogism is in the third figure: S', S'', S''' are samples of M; S', S'', S''' are P; ∴ all M is P. Here the S's form an index of the collection M, and thus the premisses form an index of the conclusion, which is about the character of all the M's. In the final case a deductive argument results, since "the conclusion is represented by the premisses as by a general sign under which it is contained."[16]

4. PROBLEMS IN THE THEORY OF THE CATEGORIES

A. By the continual application of the three intermediate categories, the conceptions of reference to a ground, to a correlate, and to an interpretant, in accordance with the possible abstractions arising from each application, Peirce has found what appear to be the fundamental patterns recurring in the process of logical operations. In his later writings his opinions varied as to the manner in which a threefold classification of arguments should constitute an expression of these three conceptions, and he found his characterization of the third conception especially needed refinement. But the most striking alteration is the complete disappearance of the first and last of the five conceptions in the original list of categories. Although it would be somewhat difficult to find a dozen or more consecutive pages anywhere in the *Collected Papers* which do not make some reference, direct or indirect, to the categories, in no such reference except in the original presentation are the conceptions of being and substance explicitly mentioned as categories. Yet, despite this apparently important omission, Peirce's frequent comments concerning his first paper on the problem leave no doubt as to his belief that in this work at least the proper outline of his categories had been indicated. An attempt to explain this circumstance may begin with the fact that the early paper on the categories, like the preceding one on the classification of arguments, professed to give revision and criticism of Kantian doctrines. In both cases an interpretation of Kantian statements affords the initial problem, while the solution obtained differs widely from that given by Kant. If the two papers, then, can be assumed to follow the same fundamental approach to different problems stated in Kantian terms, the manner in which the paper on the classification of arguments had to be altered by later treatments because of its Kantian point of departure should be similar to the manner in which the paper on the categories also required alteration.

The original treatment of the classification of arguments was modified by the logic of relatives in that the latter was a more general type of analysis ultimately necessitated by the former. The restrictions of the original analysis came from an initial acceptance of the Kantian position that the basis for any classification of arguments is the recognition that all reasoning can be put into syllogistic form. The collapse of this position, however, came as a result of the original analysis. For, since inference was regarded at the outset as a substitution performed upon the premises laid down, the principles of classification had to come ultimately from the relations according to which substitutions were made. The syllogism constituted only one such relation and therefore could not provide the general formula of all argument.

The original presentation of the categories was restricted by acceptance of the Kantian doctrine that the impressions of a manifold are reduced to unity by propositions and that consequently the search for the most universal conceptions must begin with an analysis of the proposition. The division of all propositions into subject and predicate afforded at once the conceptions of substance and being, and the problem of determining the categories became that of discovering the conceptions involved in passing from the manifold of substance to the unity of being. But if, as revealed by the classification of arguments, the relation between subject and predicate is the same as that between premiss and conclusion, then the essential aspect of the consideration lies in the analysis of the passage itself, irrespec-

30

tive of whether it is identified with that from substance to being /
or from premiss to conclusion. The concern is thus with the
fundamental forms of relation subsisting between any signs
whatsoever and not merely between those which constitute the
subject and predicate of a proposition. In a statement of intellectual autobiography ca. 1905, Peirce remarked concerning his
early investigations of the categories:

> After a series of inquiries, I came to see that Kant ought not
> to have confined himself to divisions of propositions, or "judg-
> ments," as the Germans confuse the subject by calling them, but
> ought to have taken account of all elementary and significant differ-
> ences of form among signs of all sorts, and that, above all, he ought
> not to have left out of account fundamental forms of reasonings.
> At last, after the hardest two years' mental work that I have ever
> done in my life, I found myself with but a single assured result of
> any positive importance. This was that there are but three elemen-
> tary forms of predication or signification . . . [1.561].

Once the treatment of the categories, then, is generalized so as
to accord with the logic of relatives rather than with a Kantian
interpretation of traditional logic, the conceptions of substance
and being disappear from the list of categories just as the syllogism as the fundamental form of all reasoning disappeared from
the analysis when the classification of arguments underwent such
generalization.

When the logic of relatives is properly recognized as the basis
for the treatment of the categories, the three fundamental conceptions may be generalized as nonrelative characters or pure
abstractions, dual relations, and plural relations.[17] According to
Peirce's comments ca. 1899, the restricted analysis of his early
paper prevented him from obtaining such a generalized conception of the third category.

> In 1867, although I had proof (duly published) that there was
> only a third category of characters besides non-relative characters and
> dual relations, yet I had not discovered that plural relations (which
> it had not occurred to me were sometimes not reducible to conjunc-
> tions of dual relations) constitute that third class. I saw that there
> must be a conception of which I could make out some features, but

31

being unfamiliar with it in its generality, I quite naturally mistook it for that conception of *representation* which I obtained by generalizing for this very purpose the idea of a sign. I did not generalize enough, a form of error into which greater minds than mine might fall [1.565].

B. Yet this determination of the categories at the highest level of generality is far from being the principal problem which Peirce encountered in revising his first presentation of them. The conceptions of substance and being did form a fundamental part of his early scheme, and they must be retained in some sense if the categories are not to become a mere curiosity of the logic of relatives. For it was precisely by means of these two conceptions that the process originally analyzed could be identified with that which renders experience intelligible. If these extreme conceptions are to be dispensed with as categories of experience, the intelligible *what is* of the predicate and the mere *it* of the subject must both be accounted for as ingredients of experience which fit into the triadic pattern given by the intermediate conceptions. The endeavor to accomplish this led Peirce to what he called in his later years phenomenology, a science which seeks to analyze whatever appears in consciousness without attaching any evaluation to the appearance, such as good or bad, true or false, real or illusory.

When such evaluation is made, however, the doctrine of the categories is faced with a new problem. The values assigned must themselves be brought into accord with the triadic scheme if the three intermediate conceptions are to have the complete universality demanded of categories. It is of course impossible to consider this problem without a careful examination of the different phases of Peirce's later philosophy, and this is the aim of the subsequent chapters of the present study. But it may be well to remark now, without examining them, the principal modifications which Peirce was led to make in his conception of logic in order to accommodate his theory of the categories. The purely formal study of the logic of relatives becomes part of the "simplest mathematics" or what is properly formal logic, while the three types of logic roughly distinguished in 1867 form the divisions of logic conceived as normative science. It is logic in this latter sense that examines the notions of reality and truth as values to be assigned by inquiry and considers the categories as determining modes of being. Phenomenology becomes necessary for the transition from formal to normative logic, and, when modes of being have been determined, Peirce thought it possible to speak of "objective logic," or "the logic of events," in connection with his theory of cosmic evolution. It becomes difficult to find adequate designations for the three categories as they are elucidated by phenomenology. After explaining in 1898 that quality, reaction, and mediation would do better than his original quality, relation, and representation, Peirce remarked, "but for scientific terms Firstness, Secondness, and Thirdness, are to be preferred as being entirely new words without any false associations whatever" (4.3). The incomplete state of his theory of the categories, however, did not prevent him from starting to use them at once as principles of order in all phases of his philosophy.

C. Further understanding of the importance of substance and being as well as definite indication that they do not occupy the same status as the three intermediate conceptions in Peirce's original scheme may be drawn from the Upon Logical Comprehension and Extension, the sequel to the first statement of the categories. The principal concern in this third essay is to examine the different senses of the breadth and depth of terms. The three intermediate conceptions as they are manifested in the "triple reference" of a symbol to its object give rise to what Peirce calls (1) "the informed breadth of the symbol," which corresponds to "its direct reference to its object, or the real things which it represents"; (2) "the informed depth of the symbol," which corresponds to "its reference to its ground through its object, or the common characters of those objects"; and (3) "the sum of synthetical propositions in which the symbol is subject or predicate, or the information concerning the symbol" (2.418). The last of these corresponds to the reference of the symbol

33

"to its interpretant through its object, or all the facts known about its object."

This threefold distinction provides the basic pattern for Peirce's doctrine of logical extension and comprehension. There is nothing in the definitions of the breadth, depth, and information of a symbol which corresponds to the notions of being and substance; and, in order to find a place for these notions in his analysis, Peirce turns to the kind of knowledge the information may convey. Being and substance may be taken as characterizing the knowledge given by two extreme states of information: "first, the state in which no fact would be known, but only the meaning of terms; and, second, the state in which the information would amount to an absolute intuition of all there is, so that the things we should know would be the very substances themselves, and the qualities we should know would be the very concrete forms themselves" (2.409). When breadth and depth are assumed with the knowledge determined by the first of these "imaginary extremes," they are called *essential*, and when assumed with that determined by the second, they are called *substantial*. Every symbol must have at least essential breadth and depth, though, if it possesses no more than this, the information corresponding to its third reference would be nil, since only analytic propositions would be known in which the symbol is subject or predicate. On the other hand, the information actually known concerning any symbol is never sufficient to fix its substantial breadth and depth unless there are a priori synthetic propositions.

Substance and being in the previous essay could be taken phenomenologically as factors actually present in experience—as the mere *it* of something which seems immediately present and the intelligible *what is* expressed in a perceptual judgment. But these conceptions are now taken so as to suggest epistemological and ontological problems. They raise questions as to the status of the real objects which are known through experience and the character of our knowledge of such objects. The effect of retaining substance and being as part of the categorial scheme is to make

34

a final determination of what is real lie beyond the process that gives rise to the three intermediate conceptions which properly constitute categories. In order to characterize this determination by means of firstness, secondness, and thirdness, Peirce was led to the problem of modes of being. He came to consider the extreme states of information in question here as forms of possibility. Thus, he explained in a paper of 1896,

possibility may be understood in many senses; but they may all be embraced under the definition that that is possible which, in a certain state of information, is not known to be false. By varying the supposed state of information all the varieties of possibility are obtained. Thus, *essential* possibility is that which supposes nothing to be known except logical rules. *Substantive* possibility, on the other hand, supposes a state of omniscience [3.442; cf. 4.67 (1893)].

Scarcely a year later (March, 1897) in a letter to William James, Peirce wrote that he had been struggling with the question, "Is possibility a mode of being?"[18]

It should also be remarked that Peirce's early essay on logical breadth and depth was arbitrarily limited to terms, as his first essay on the categories was limited to propositions. In 1893, when he selected the former as the third essay of the *Search for a Method*, he added in a footnote: "I restricted myself to *terms*, because at the time this chapter was first written (1867), I had not remarked that the whole doctrine of breadth and depth was equally applicable to *propositions* and to *arguments*" (2.407, n. 1). While Peirce left this wider use of "breadth" and "depth" a relatively undeveloped part of his logic, especially as it applies to arguments,[19] it is an extension clearly demanded by his new approach to logic. With an approach of the traditional sort, the substance-attribute character of reality affords the basis for an analysis of breadth and depth which is properly restricted to terms; but, with the peculiar character of classification in logic which results from the exclusive use of Peirce's three intermediate categories, the properties of breadth and depth should reappear on the level of propositions and again on that of arguments. Even if these properties are still taken as belonging primarily to terms, the nature of the classification entails, as Peirce remarked in his footnote, that "every proposition and every argument can be regarded as a term." This expansion of the analysis is of course possible only when the notions of substance and being in the traditional sense have been kept outside the proper scheme of logical classification.

The significance which these notions have for Peirce's ontology (as distinct from his phenomenology) is indicated by their positions in the original list. However Peirce may decide to define reality, in accordance with his categorial scheme the idea of a process must be taken as central to the definition. The movement from a manifold presented in experience through the three stages which properly constitute categories must somehow issue in a determination of reality. Whether this determination is to constitute a fourth step distinct from the three stages, or whether it can be achieved at the third stage, becomes a crucial problem for Peirce's philosophy. His original analysis would require a fourth step, since the formation of a proposition which marks the third stage accomplishes merely the unification of the manifold but does not guarantee that a true representation of reality is thereby attained. Yet this restriction to propositions is an arbitrary feature of the analysis, and the situation is changed when the third stage is generalized so as to accord with the logic of relatives.

II

The Faculties of Knowledge

THE next three essays of the *Search for a Method*, published serially in the *Journal of Speculative Philosophy* (1868–69), contain Peirce's first attempt to state the views on the nature of reality and the faculties of knowledge which seem to be demanded by his approach to logic and his theory of the categories. By way of contrast with the previous papers, the problem of this second group of essays may be regarded as that of determining the material conditions requisite for the existence of knowledge. The logical (and to some extent phenomenological) analysis given so far has determined at most only the formal conditions governing any rational process. The epistemological and ontological questions which were raised require consideration of the conditions which must be supposed for man and his environment if he is actually to obtain knowledge by participating in such a process. As with the logical analysis, the point of departure here is from an apparently Kantian statement of the problem, so that the faculties of knowledge as the necessary conditions of the knowing subject must be examined first rather than the objects of knowledge in themselves independent of such conditions.

1. THE METHOD OF DETERMINING THE FACULTIES OF MENTAL ACTION

A. The paper intended for Essay IV of the *Search for a Method* was entitled *Questions concerning Certain Faculties Claimed for Man* (5, Bk. II, Paper I) and examined seven questions pertaining to the existence of faculties seemingly demanded by a Kantian approach to the problem of knowledge. These seven questions in the order examined by Peirce are:

1. Whether by the simple contemplation of a cognition, independently of any previous knowledge and without reasoning from signs, we are enabled rightly to judge whether that cognition has been determined by a previous cognition or whether it refers immediately to its object.

2. Whether we have an intuitive self-consciousness.

3. Whether we have an intuitive power of distinguishing between the subjective elements of different kinds of cognitions.

4. Whether we have any power of introspection, or whether our whole knowledge of the internal world is derived from the observation of external facts.

5. Whether we can think without signs.

6. Whether a sign can have any meaning, if by its definition it is the sign of something absolutely incognizable.

7. Whether there is any cognition not determined by a previous cognition.

Peirce answers each of these questions negatively: none of the four faculties is required for the existence of knowledge, and the possibilities in the last three questions must be denied. The term "intuition" will be taken "as signifying a cognition not determined by a previous cognition of the same object, and therefore so determined by something out of the consciousness" (5.213). In this sense, "intuition" becomes "nearly the same as 'premiss not itself a conclusion'; the only difference being that premisses and conclusions are judgments, whereas an intuition may, as far as its definition states, be any kind of cognition whatever."

The examination of the three intuitive faculties seems clearly to follow the order of *precision* given in Peirce's essays of 1867. If it is assumed that the thought-process does require the three intuitive faculties in question, the ability to recognize intuitively the cognitions resulting from intuition may be prescinded from the other two faculties, and its existence may be questioned independently of them. After a negative answer to this first question, the faculty of an intuitive self-consciousness can be prescinded from the more special faculty pertaining only to the subjective elements of cognitions. When it is found that the self cannot be known intuitively, it is possible to prescind from any remaining faculties this faculty of discerning intuitively the subjective elements of cognitions; for example, whether a cognition has an element of "dreaming, imagining, conceiving, believing, etc." (cf. 5.238). The denial of this third faculty leaves only the faculty for distinguishing intuitively or otherwise between any cognitive aspects of the self not covered by the previous considerations and whatever is clearly derived from external facts.

The nature of Peirce's attack on the existence of intuitive faculties may be elucidated by a comparison with the analysis in his classification of arguments. Just as Kant's formal distinction between mediate and immediate inference failed when an argument was determined by forms of substitution in the process of laying down premisses and not by what could be taken for the indispensably necessary requirements of thought,[1] so Kant's material distinction between mediate and immediate cognition now fails when a cognition is determined by its character as an event in the thought-process and not by what can be taken for its object or content. In other words, what constituted a genus of arguments had to depend upon the formal relations proper to a sign-process and not upon the character of anything else the process purported to express. Similarly, what is a faculty necessary for the existence of thought must depend upon characteristics proper to the cognitive process itself and not upon objects of cognition—upon something "out of the consciousness."

Peirce offers rather detailed psychological arguments in support of his first negative conclusion. The manner in which each of these arguments rests finally upon the view that a cognition must be regarded as an event in the thought-process and not as an expression of its apparent content may be seen from the following examples. The cognition of the pitch of a tone seems immediate and simple in respect to its object or content, but in respect to events in the thought-process it is easily seen to be complex and to consist in a number of such events. For "the pitch of a tone depends upon the rapidity with which certain impressions are successively conveyed to the mind," and since "these impressions must exist previously to any tone, . . . the sensation of pitch is determined by previous cognitions" (5.222). Similarly, in respect to content the perception of two-dimensional space seems immediate, but in respect to events in the thought-process, since "the retina consists of innumerable needles pointing towards the light, and whose distances from one another are decidedly greater than the *minimum visible*," and since in a visual perception "each of those nerve-points conveys the sensation of a little colored surface, . . . what we immediately see must . . . be, not a continuous surface, but a collection of spots" (5.223). That event in the thought-process known as the cognition of two-dimensional space is thus determined by a series of previous cognitive events rather than immediately by something outside of consciousness.

An explanation for the circumstance that "the previous cognitions which determine" the conception of two-dimensional space "are not more clearly apprehended" can be seen from the analysis presented in the *On a New List of Categories* (5.223). For, when an elementary conception which reduces more immediate conceptions to unity has been obtained from these latter conceptions, it may be prescinded from them and considered in itself without reference to them (cf. 1.549 and above, p. 22). Thus, "in any case when the reasoning is easy and natural to us, however complex may be the premisses, they sink into insignificance and oblivion proportionately to the satisfactoriness of the theory based upon them" (5.223). In this way the conception of two-dimensional space tends to be regarded as immediate and independent of the previous cognitive events from which it has been derived. Peirce offers other examples of cognitions which are commonly supposed to be immediate but which are found not to be so when examined properly as events in the thought-process. He concludes: "We have, therefore, a variety of facts, all of which are most readily explained on the supposition that we have no intuitive faculty of distinguishing intuitive from mediate cognitions" (5.224).

If this general intuitive faculty cannot be admitted, an affirmative answer for any of the remaining questions about faculties would demand the existence of a special faculty, intuitive or otherwise, peculiarly adapted to its objects. But in all cases where the cognition in question can be explained by the existence of previous events in the thought-process, the assumption of a special faculty to account for the cognition only with respect to its object or content is unwarranted. Thus, self-consciousness can be explained as resulting from previous cognitions of ignorance and error. Such explanation is substantiated by observations of the behavior of children. "At the age at which we know children to be self-conscious, we know that they have been made aware of ignorance and error; and we know them to possess at that age powers of understanding sufficient to enable them to infer from ignorance and error their own existence" (5.236). There would appear to be no need to assume a special faculty for apprehending a cognition of the self.

Such analysis leads to the conclusion that every thought is a sign and that processes of thought are processes of signification. For knowledge of the subjective elements of cognition as well as any knowledge whatsoever about an internal as distinct from an external world can, as cognitive event, be explained as the result of previous events. Inasmuch as these events are always external facts (e.g., nerve impulses or sensations), it follows that thought itself can only be known as a process of external facts. Yet an external fact becomes a thought only in so far as it is related to something else as to an object, that is, in so far as it is a sign. "The only thought, then, which can possibly be cognized is thought in signs" (5.251). The distinction between a cognition as an event in the thought-process and the content

41

of the cognition is thus the distinction between a sign and its object.

The object of a cognition, moreover, can never be wholly outside of consciousness, wholly unrelated to cognition. The absolutely incognizable can never be signified. Since "the meaning of a term is the conception which it conveys" (5.255), the only kind of meaning a term supposed to signify the absolutely incognizable could have would be one which is "self-contradictory" (cf. 5.257). The assertion of such a term would be equivalent to the statement, "The not-cognizable is cognizable." Hence, ignorance and error can only be conceived as opposite to "an unknown but knowable reality," and, opposite to "all possible cognition, there is only the self-contradictory." The significance for metaphysics of this denial of meaning to the absolutely incognizable is that "*cognizability* (in its widest sense) and *being* are not merely metaphysically the same, but are synonymous terms." It is easily seen from these considerations that every cognition is determined by a previous cognition. The object, content, or meaning of a given cognition can only be referred to a previous cognition and never to something outside of consciousness.

B. The result of this critical examination is to leave the material or existential conditions of the thought-process with little positive determination. "Cognition" is a broad term referring to any event in the thought-process, and the only determination obtained thus far is that the thought-process is a continuous process of signification in which every event is preceded by another event. As with any other temporal process, this does not mean that a thought-process cannot have a beginning but only that any element in the series, in so far as it is a thought, can be analyzed into further thoughts. "To say . . . that thought cannot happen in an instant, but requires a time, is but another way of saying that every thought must be interpreted in another, or that all thought is in signs" (5.253). Apparent paradoxes which arise from the continuous nature of the thought-process are perfectly analogous to those about Achilles and the tortoise[2] and may be answered in the same way (cf. 5.263).

This general characterization of the existence of thought may be viewed as the initial specification of matter for the forms of logic treated in the first three essays of the *Search for a Method*. That is, to specify that the process of symbolic operations becomes a temporal process when it is regarded as productive of actual premisses and conclusions and not merely of the logical relations they express is to specify a matter for a form. The form is given by the types of relations which continually recur in the process; the matter is given by the specification that all such recurrences are temporal events called "cognitions."

Further specification of matter will involve a positive statement of the conditions necessary for the process to become an actual series of temporal events. For example, if various events or signs are related as premisses and conclusions, there must be the conditions requisite for drawing inferences. The method is thus always to begin with the actual events in the process and to infer the conditions probably necessary for the production of these events. The general statement of these conditions may be expressed by saying that there is a faculty of a certain type. The principle of economy in scientific procedure demands of course that no more faculties be assumed than are absolutely necessary for the production of the events in question. Peirce believed his critical examination of previous attempts to enumerate the faculties of mental action had disclosed in these attempts a marked tendency to assume the existence of faculties without adequate scrutiny of the evidence. This tendency could be explained as resulting from a failure to distinguish properly between a cognition as an event or sign in the thought-process and the object or content of the cognition, which latter always involves a reference to previous cognitions. The uncritical assumption that the object must be something outside of consciousness rather than a previous cognition thus led to unwarranted hypotheses about the existence of faculties. The

43

proper method for determining the faculties of mental action, on the contrary, must be one which begins with mental events as signs in the thought-process and recognizes the impossibility of referring to anything wholly outside the process.

2. THE FACULTIES OF MENTAL ACTION

A. Peirce sought further evidence for his seven negative conclusions by developing their consequences. Such development is tantamount to a positive statement of the material characteristics of the thought-process, in so far as these characteristics can be explained according to the method just indicated. Peirce begins this task in the fifth essay, *Some Consequences of Four Incapacities* (5, Bk. II, Paper II), with a brief explanation of the terms "doubt" and "belief."

It is impossible in the first place to begin a philosophic analysis with the "universal doubt" demanded by the Cartesian method, since doubt based solely on a maxim which enjoins one to doubt can only be a mere pretension which gives up beliefs "in form" but does not supply a "positive reason" for doing so (5.265). Moreover, the Cartesian criterion for resurrecting beliefs from the column of doubts also displays a similar "formalism" in that it consists only in the acceptance of what a person is "clearly convinced of." But to take this as a basis for truth is "to make single individuals absolute judges of truth" and to neglect the material factors which limit any individual's capacity for acquiring truth. An adequate criterion must take into account the fact that "we individually cannot reasonably hope to attain the ultimate philosophy which we pursue." Such a goal, therefore, can be sought only "for the *community* of philosophers," and a criterion of truth can be adequate only when it is modified so as to apply to social and not merely individual acceptance. Further, "philosophy ought to imitate the successful sciences in its methods, so far as to proceed only from tangible premises which can be subjected to careful scrutiny, and to trust rather to the multitude and variety of its arguments than to the conclusiveness of any one."

The formalism of the Cartesian approach, on the contrary, results in "a single thread of inference depending often upon inconspicuous premisses" (5.264). Finally, the supposition made by "every unidealistic philosophy" that there is "some absolutely inexplicable, unanalyzable ultimate" is "never allowable" (5.265), as was shown from the examination in the preceding paper. Such a supposition, consequently, can have no part in the consideration of doubt and belief, as it does in the Cartesian philosophy.

The seven negative conclusions whose consequences are to be explored may be reduced to four and ordered according to this fourfold criticism of the Cartesian philosophy (5.265).

1. With respect to what an individual privately may doubt or believe: "We have no power of Introspection, but all knowledge of the internal world is derived by hypothetical reasoning from our knowledge of external facts."

2. With respect to the criterion of truth: "We have no power of Intuition, but every cognition is determined logically by previous cognitions."

3. With respect to the treatment of premisses and inferences: "We have no power of thinking without signs."

4. With respect to the concept of an inexplicable ultimate: "We have no conception of the absolutely incognizable."

These four propositions "cannot be regarded as certain," and the procedure in "testing" them by "tracing them out to their consequences" will be to consider the "first alone," then to trace "the consequences of the first and second," next to see "what else will result from assuming the third also," and, finally, "add the fourth to these hypothetical premisses."

It seems possible to regard this reordering of the seven negative conclusions as an application of the categories and to justify such interpretation by textual evidence, although Peirce made no explicit statement of the principles he used in the reordering. According to the original presentation of the categories, reference to a ground can be viewed as reference to "the self abstracted from the concreteness which implies the possi-

45

bility of another" (cf. 1.556 and above, p. 26). A faculty of introspection yielding immediate knowledge of the internal world is thus equivalent to a faculty determining an immediate knowledge of the self as a firstness without any reference to secondness or something other than the self. Since the second of the four propositions in the reordering is concerned with the relational character of thought, with the fact that every cognition is determined by a previous cognition, it seems equivalent to saying that every thought involves secondness, or reference to a correlate. The third proposition expresses the fact that every thought is a sign, which clearly implies that it involves thirdness. The fourth proposition pertains to the significance of the previous propositions for ontological considerations. The manner of tracing the consequences of the first three propositions corresponds, of course, to the order of precision given for the categories.

The absence of any explicit mention in Peirce's paper of this interpretation of the four propositions may be explained as arising from the same circumstance as that which occasioned the restrictions on the mode of analysis used in the original classification of arguments and presentation of the categories. The essay in question was published (1868) two years before the first paper on the logic of relatives, and it is clear from the brief exposition of formal logic given in the investigation of the second proposition that Peirce at this time was still laboring under the attempt to reduce all reasoning to syllogistic form. But it is only when the categories are generalized so as to express, respectively, unrelated elements, dyadic relations, and polyadic relations that the interpretation in question becomes possible. This fact is particularly in evidence in the examination of the second proposition, where, in order to explain the relation between thought and its object, thought-processes are analyzed as always proceeding according to some one of the three general species of syllogistic argument. For, in this case, all three categories and not merely secondness are in a sense involved. However, this is true only in so far as the analysis is taken by itself without regard to the context which includes the first and third propositions. When it is taken as dealing with the relation between forms of reasoning and objective evidence, as such analysis is prescinded from the conception which mediates between the two, the relation is dyadic, and the analysis is therefore concerned with a secondness. Thus, the first proposition, in so far as it can, deals with the self as unrelated to anything else; the second, with the formal conditions of thought within the self as opposed to the conditions of evidence outside the self; and the third, with the conditions of thought as involving all three references of a sign and not merely the references to the self and something other than the self. A definition of the true and real as distinct from the untrue and unreal is then considered in the examination of the fourth proposition, where the consequences yielded by each of the three preceding propositions are to be applied conjointly to the general problem of ontology. Thus, according to the present interpretation of the propositions, Peirce believed at this time that only after the thought-process has been properly characterized by the aid of his categories can there be any final determination of the objects of thought. At the level of the second proposition such objects must be treated as relative to the conditions of evidence and not in their complete ontological determination.

B. If this interpretation of the four propositions is correct, the categories by repeated application thus supply the ordering principles for a positive statement of the material characteristics of the thought-process. A brief summary of the "consequences" by which Peirce "tests" each of his four propositions should provide further evidence for this conclusion as well as an exposition of Peirce's doctrine on the faculties of mental action.

The first proposition leads at once to the overthrow of that philosophy which "bases our knowledge of the external world on our self-consciousness" (5.266). Quite to the contrary, knowledge of ourselves can come only by inference from "what takes place in what we commonly call the external world." Inasmuch as this reduces kinds of knowing which are usually regarded as two separate actions, that is, knowing the self and knowing the external world, to a single mental action of drawing inferences, the principle of economy demands that no further kind of mental action be supposed unless it is impossible to explain the fact by this single kind of action already assumed. "In other words, we must, as far as we can do so without additional hypotheses, reduce all kinds of mental action to one general type."

When the second proposition is added to the first one, it is necessary to regard the cognitions from which we infer knowledge of the self and the external world as constituting a continuous process in which there is no absolutely first cognition. Since this process must be one "whose laws are best understood and most closely follow external fact," it can be "no other than the process of valid inference, which proceeds from its premiss, A, to its conclusion, B, only if, as a matter of fact, such a proposition as B is always or usually true when such a proposition as A is true" (5.267). While it is "certainly very doubtful" whether the mind does in fact go through the syllogistic process in the sense that "a conclusion—as something existing in the mind independently, like an image—suddenly displaces two premisses existing in the mind in a similar way," it is nevertheless "a matter of constant experience, that if a man is made to believe in the premisses, in the sense that he will act from them and will say that they are true, under favorable conditions he will also be ready to act from the conclusion and to say that that is true" (5.268). Hence there is something that "takes place within the organism which is equivalent to the syllogistic process." The formal analysis of the syllogism, then, will determine characteristics which are exhibited in the material or actual manifestations of the thought-process within the organism.

When the third proposition, viz., that "we have no power of thinking without signs," is added to the first two, it becomes possible to specify the nature of the events occurring in the thought-process as it exhibits the forms of valid inference. In the first place, since there is no immediate cognition of the self, that is, of the mind or the subject experiencing the process, but everything appears as a "phenomenal manifestation" of this subject, it follows that the self, as being thus in a sense identical with each event occurring in the process, is always a sign. In other words, "When we think, then, we ourselves, as we are at that moment, appear as a sign" (5.283). Moreover, since every event in the process appears as a "thought-sign," it may be characterized by the three references involved in any sign, namely, the reference "to some thought which interprets it"; the reference to some object for which it is a sign and "to which in that thought it is equivalent"; and, finally, the reference to the fact that it is a sign "in some respect or quality, which brings it into connection with its object."

It follows from the continuity of the thought-process that a thought-sign must always refer to a previous thought for its interpretant. There is thus a continuous "current of ideas" in which the introduction of new trains of thought and the acts of forgetting and remembering are explained as changes in degrees of prominence in consciousness (5.284). For since "the striking in of a new experience is never an instantaneous affair, but is an event occupying time, and coming to pass by a continuous process, . . . there is no sufficient cause for the thought which had been the leading one just before, to cease abruptly and instantaneously." The "prominence in consciousness" of any thought is therefore "probably . . . the consummation of a growing process." "There is no exception . . . to the law that every thought-sign is translated or interpreted in a subsequent one, unless it be that all thought comes to an abrupt and final end in death." The second reference of the thought-sign, that to its object or suppositum, is to an outward thing "when a real outward thing is thought of" (5.285). However, "as the thought is determined by a previous thought of the same object, it only refers to the thing through denoting this previous

49

thought." An examination of an actual instance in the thought-process seems to justify the generalization that "in every case the subsequent thought denotes what was thought in the previous thought." The third reference of the thought-sign, that in virtue of which it is a sign connected with its object, may be expressed simply by saying that the sign "stands for its object in the respect which is thought; that is to say, this respect is the immediate object of consciousness in the thought, or, in other words, it is the thought itself, or at least what the thought is thought to be in the subsequent thought to which it is a sign" (5.286).[3]

The consequences of this third proposition added to those of the other two afford a positive generalization concerning the faculties of mental action. "We have thus seen that every sort of modification of consciousness—Attention, Sensation, and Understanding—is an inference" (5.298).[4] Hence, as was implied in Peirce's examination of the first proposition, "all kinds of mental action" can be reduced "to one general type." There is no evidence for noninferential faculties when the impossibility of a cognition determined by something wholly outside of consciousness is recognized. All phenomena of consciousness seem explicable on the hypothesis that every event in the thought-process is a thought-sign referring to previous thought-signs for its objects. The triadic nature of this reference provides the ordering principles for further and more specific characterization of mental events. Attention can be distinguished from understanding and sensation, and "sensations proper," from "emotions" and "the feeling of a thought."[5] Events in the continuous process of mental action are thus to be ordered and characterized by repeated application of the categories, just as logical forms were ordered and characterized in the continuous process of symbolic operations.

When the fourth proposition, viz., that there is no absolutely incognizable, is added to the above three, the crucial problem becomes that of determining "the real" as something cognizable. In terms of the above characterization of the thought-process, it may be stated that the cognitions arising from the "infinite series of inductions and hypotheses (which though infinite *a parte ante logice*, is yet as one continuous process not without a beginning *in time*) are of two kinds, the true and the untrue, or cognitions whose objects are *real* and those whose objects are *unreal*" (5.311). Now the conception of something real and objective first arises when there is a recognition of error—when there is a distinction between "an *ens* relative to private inward determinations, to the negations belonging to idiosyncrasy, and an *ens* such as would stand in the long run." But since the real is thus something which transcends the "vagaries" of individual thinkers, it is a conception which "essentially involves the notion of a COMMUNITY, without definite limits, and capable of a definite increase of knowledge." Hence, "those two series of cognition—the real and the unreal—consist of those which, at a time sufficiently future, the community will always continue to re-affirm; and of those which, under the same conditions, will ever after be denied." It follows, then, that there is nothing "to prevent our knowing outward things as they really are, and it is most likely that we do thus know them in numberless cases, although we can never be absolutely certain of doing so in any special case."

A further consequence of this explanation of the real is that "generals must have a real existence" (5.312). This statement constitutes Peirce's first explicit declaration of his realism,[6] and it "follows" at once from the fact that "no cognition of ours is absolutely determinate." That is, since every cognition in the thought-process is unanalyzable in its immediacy, any determination of a cognition must be a generality which abstracts from its immediacy;[7] and, when such generality is true, it is also real. A "nominalist" in these terms is anyone who assumes that beneath the immediacy of a cognition is a "thing in itself, an incognizable reality"; while a "realist" is one who makes no such assumption but "is simply one who knows no more recondite reality than that which is represented in a true representation." In other words, nominalism assumes and realism denies that

51

"reality is something independent of representative relation."
The final question in developing the consequences of the fourth proposition is, "Such being the nature of reality in general, in what does the reality of the mind consist?" (5.313). Since from the consequences of the third proposition the self has been identified with an external sign, this question may be resolved into the question, "What distinguishes a man from a word?" There are certain obvious distinctions arising from the references involved in any sign. "The material qualities, the forces which constitute the pure denotative application, and the meaning of the human sign, are all exceedingly complicated in comparison with those of the word." But these differences are "only relative," and further examination reveals a real identification between man and an external sign. "The word or sign which the man uses is the man himself. For, as the fact that every thought is a sign, taken in conjunction with the fact that life is a train of thought, proves that man is a sign; so, that every thought is an *external* sign, proves that man is an external sign" (5.314).

Peirce's doctrine of the faculties of mental action has thus led him to a position on the reality of universals and the reality of mind. His philosophy is placed in sharp opposition to any form of dualism which holds that mind is a unique substance, capable of knowing itself and its objects immediately. The hypothesis of noninferential faculties, as viewed from the approach of Peirce, leads inevitably to the nominalistic and self-contradictory assumption of an incognizable particular, spiritual or material, underlying the immediacy of cognition. These ontological "consequences" of Peirce's negative conclusions are clarified and developed in the remaining essays of the *Search for a Method*.

3. THE FACULTIES OF INQUIRY

A. If every mental action is an inference, and there is never an immediate apprehension of absolute first principles, it follows that knowledge as a product of mental action is always probable and must be equated with belief rather than certainty. Hence, when the general characteristics of the faculties and products of mental action have been specified, the next step in the statement of the existential conditions of knowledge is an examination of the circumstances necessary for the production of belief. Just as any treatment of the material conditions of the thought-process was necessarily preceded by a specification of its formal conditions, so a consideration of the circumstances productive of belief must begin with an examination of the grounds for belief in the validity of these formal conditions presupposed by every inference before proceeding to the grounds for belief in the actual inferences constitutive of knowledge. In other words, if knowledge is always by inference and never by immediate apprehension, nothing can be absolutely inexplicable—not even the laws of logic presupposed by every inference. The next essay in the *Search for a Method* was entitled *Grounds of Validity of the Laws of Logic: Further Consequences of Four Incapacities* (5, Bk. II, Paper III) and began by accepting a challenge to show how, on the principles of the two preceding essays, "the validity of the laws of logic can be other than inexplicable" (5.318).

Peirce comments on his undertaking: "It will be said that my deduction of logical principles, being itself an argument, depends for its whole virtue upon the truth of the very principles in question; so that whatever my proof may be, it must take for granted the very things to be proved" (5.319). His reply to this is that he is "neither addressing absolute sceptics, nor men in any state of fictitious doubt whatever." The proposed explanation of logical principles can claim to be a deduction only in the sense that it aims to show how the validity of these principles is apparent in an adequate understanding of them. Since a man "may reason well without understanding the principles of reasoning," he may stand in need of such a deduction to enable him to overcome his doubts concerning the principles. The reader is warned that if he actually finds in the arguments "a convincing force," "it is a mere pretence to call them illogical." The use of "deduction" in this context clearly implies a Kantian point of departure, as in the preceding essays. Peirce undoubtedly had in mind Kant's "deduction" of the categories and, in analogy with it, wanted to show that the principles of logic are preconditions of all inquiry.

The first section of the essay attempts a "deduction of the general form of the syllogism" (5.320). This form is stated as a relation among three signs which yields the first figure Barbara, and the statement is "not doubted by anybody who distinctly apprehends the meaning of these words." The deduction of the form, then, will consist merely in an explication of its meaning. Peirce examines various objections that have been urged against the validity of the syllogism and attempts to show that in each case they are founded on a misconception of its meaning. But in some cases, and in one especially, the objection seems based on a misunderstanding of how a syllogism represents reality; so such an objection must be refuted by an explication of what is meant by "reality" as well as "syllogism." Peirce in these cases refers to his conclusions of the preceding essay that nothing is absolutely incognizable and that reality consists in the ultimate agreement of the community (cf. 5.330–31).

The close connection between reality and the validity of inference is clearly brought out by a comment Peirce makes immediately after giving his final attempt to reduce inferences involving relatives to syllogistic form.[8] The various formulae for valid syllogisms, including those involving relatives,

can all be deduced from the principle, that in a system of signs in which no sign is taken in two different senses, two signs which differ only in their manner of representing their object, but which are equivalent in meaning, can always be substituted for one another. Any case of the falsification of this principle would be a case of the dependence of the mode of existence of the thing represented upon the mode of this or that representation of it, which, as has been shown in the article in the last number, is contrary to the nature of reality [5.323].

The import of this last sentence may be illustrated by the following example. If "man is mortal" cannot be substituted for the true proposition "animal is mortal" by virtue of the true proposition "man is animal," then the reality represented by "man" would vary as it is represented by "animal" or "mortal," which is the same as to deny objective reality. While Peirce here gives no further explanation of his statement, it seems clear that he intends to imply the priority of logic for ontology and not vice versa. If we deny the principles of deductive reasoning, then we must deny reality. The order of priority is made clear by the argument in the preceding essay that reality cannot be defined except as the outcome or product of reasoning.

The second section of the essay is concerned with an examination of certain traditional sophisms "which really are extremely difficult to resolve by syllogistic rules" (5.333). The analysis comprises the most lengthy single treatment of the subject in the *Collected Papers*, and the solutions offered do not differ essentially from Peirce's later ones. His position here in summary form is that all the sophisms in question arise from one of three sources of confusion: (1) the nature of continuity; (2) the manner in which two true propositions may in form conflict with one another; (3) the manner in which a proposition may refer to itself. In the first case, the typical sophisms are Zeno's paradoxes, and the confusion lies in the assumption that "a *continuum* has ultimate parts" (5.335). But since "a continuum is precisely that, every part of which has parts, in the same sense," the assumption is seen to be self-contradictory, and the paradoxes are resolved. Sophisms from the second source of confusion are avoided by an understanding of the existential import of propositions. Two universal propositions may both be true and at the same time conflict in form, that is, be such that from one the contradictory of the other may be deduced, only when it is erroneously assumed that the particular propositions under both universals are true (cf. 5.337–39). A typical example of sophisms from the third source is the paradox of the liar. The confusion here arises from a failure to recognize that, since every proposition implies its own truth, no proposition can mean nothing but the assertion of its own falsity. The paradox in question thus depends on an erroneous assumption as

55

to the complete meaning of the proposition, "This proposition is not true" (cf. 5.340).[9]

／ Throughout this analysis of sophisms, Peirce's primary concern of course is simply to show that in no case does a formally ＼correct syllogism yield a false conclusion from true premises. The difficulty in resolving the sophisms by syllogistic rules would be in showing how in each instance a syllogistic rule has been violated. While Peirce certainly does not attempt to show this, he does state each sophism in syllogistic form, and his defense of the syllogism then consists in showing that the premises cannot be true, at least in the sense required for the paradoxical conclusion. There is thus no need to alter the principles of logic in order to cope with these sophisms, since the contradiction in each case arises from a misunderstanding of the premises rather than from the form of the argument. The syllogism in this context, then, is "deduced" not by explicating the meaning of the principle itself, as in the preceding section of the essay, but rather by making clear what is involved in particular cases where the principle is used. The fact that Peirce had not yet recognized a logic of relatives in addition to syllogistic logic when he wrote this exposé of sophisms does not affect his analysis. He continued throughout his logical writings to maintain essentially his present views on the subject.

The final section of the essay contains an examination of the validity of probable or inductive reasoning and constitutes what is certainly the most important consideration in the paper. The question of course is not the validity of probable as opposed to indubitable conclusions but rather of synthetic as opposed to analytic reasoning. In what follows, Peirce makes three points which remain fundamental in all his later treatments of the problem.

(i) The conception of a universe "in which probable arguments should fail as often as hold true, is absurd"; though "we can suppose it in general terms, . . . we cannot specify how it should be other than self-contradictory" (5.345). For any attempt to specify the character of a purely disordered universe leads to the description of a state of affairs in which "everything conceivable" would be found "with equal frequency." This "would not be disorder, but the simplest order." Hence, the validity of induction cannot be explained by an assumption about the peculiar constitution of the actual universe (as J. S. Mill's principle of the uniformity of nature) which distinguishes it from a purely disordered one. Such explanation would have force only if possible universes could be specified in which there would be no order or uniformity.

This logical impossibility of characterizing a universe that destroys the validity of probable inference is also of consequence for a theory of reality. The "nominalistic" hypothesis of a thing in itself, which Peirce rejected in the preceding essay because it presupposed noninferential faculties, can now be refuted in another way. Since this hypothesis supposes the objects of knowledge to possess characteristics as things in themselves independently of whether or not they are presented in experience, "inductions would not be true unless the world were so constituted that every object should be presented in experience as often as any other; and further, unless we were so constituted that we had no more tendency to make bad inductions than good ones" (5.353). While these assumptions about the constitution of the world and of ourselves "might be explained by the benevolence of the Creator," Peirce argues that the theory in question is nevertheless "absolutely refuted" because it fails to take account of "the fact that no state of things can be conceived in which probable arguments should not lead to the truth." In short, the notion of a reality as a thing in itself that might conceivably remain forever unintelligible involves a logical contradiction which is not avoided by special assumptions to explain why, in point of fact, reality is intelligible.

Peirce here refers to the theory of reality he refutes as the "idealistic theory" rather than the "nominalistic" one, as he termed it in the preceding essay (cf. 5.312 and above, p. 51). But it seems clear from the context that he means "idealistic" only in the sense of a theory which regards reality as composed

57

of absolutely determinate particulars which are given or presented in experience, as opposed to his own "realistic" theory
which holds that what is given is always a general susceptible
of further determination. It makes no difference for the refutation just considered whether a Kantian thing in itself, a Berkeleian mind of God, or something else is assumed to supply the
ultimate reality underlying the particulars given, or whether all
such assumptions are abandoned and the particulars themselves
are taken as ultimate. The important thing is simply that reality
cannot possibly be conceived in such a way as to make the intelligibility presupposed by induction depend upon the special
manner in which determinate particulars are presented in experience. Inasmuch as the crucial issue becomes the reality of
generals as opposed to that of absolutely determinate particulars, however the latter may be characterized, the adjective
"nominalistic" rather than "realistic" seems the appropriate one
for the opposing view. This of course is the terminology Peirce
adopted throughout his later writings, and his use of "idealistic"
here is undoubtedly due to the fact that at the time he had
Kant primarily in mind. In other meanings of the word, he frequently called his own philosophy idealistic.

(ii) Peirce argues next that his realistic theory provides the
basis for a satisfactory explanation of the validity of induction
and at the same time takes account of the fact that the conception of a universe in which there is no such validity is self-
contradictory. Since "all probable inference, whether induction
or hypothesis, is inference from the parts to the whole," it is
"essentially the same . . . as statistical inference" (5.349).
Hence, "the validity of induction depends simply upon the
fact that the parts make up and constitute the whole." But then
the question, "Why of all inductions premises for which occur,
the generality should hold good?" is easily answered if there is
"such a state of things that any general terms are possible."
By his theory of reality in the preceding essay which showed
that "being at all is being in general," Peirce concludes that
the answer to his question "depends merely on there being any

58

reality." In other words, the facts usually turn out to be as they
are represented by inductive conclusions from true premises because the reality signified by the premises usually constitutes a
part of the whole reality signified by the conclusion. This part-
whole relation is always at least possible, since all reality is general, that is, never absolutely determinate, whether it is that referred to by the most specific premiss or the broadest conclusion.
When every reality is thus conceived as a whole always susceptible of further analysis into parts, it of course cannot be conceived as a totally independent particular concerning which no
generalization would be possible.

The difficulty encountered by nominalism, however, seems
to break out in another direction. There remains the question,
"why men are not fated always to light upon those inductions
which are highly deceptive" (5.351). Even though part-whole
relations between premisses and conclusion are always possible,
there seems nothing impossible in the conception of a universe
in which men can learn nothing of reality because they are forever fated to be deceived in their attempts to discern genuine
part-whole relations. Peirce argues that, upon his theory of
reality, this conception is no more possible than that of a reality
which by its own nature would always remain unintelligible.
For his realism is not a simple equation of the real with the
general or universal; on the contrary, the crucial point is that
the real must be defined as "consisting in the ultimate agreement of all men." The fact that every reality is general and
therefore a whole with parts is a further consequence of the
approach. Now in a universe where men are always deceived
in their inductions, there must be as part of such a universe a
general law that all inductions will ultimately turn out to be
false. But this law itself eventually would be discovered by induction, and then by hypothesis it would turn out to be false.
Hence, there must be as another part of this universe a second
law which asserts that the first law will prove false once it has
been discovered. A similar argument will apply to the discovery
of this second law, and so on. Thus, the men in question con-

59

tinually would tend to reach agreement about the laws which make up the whole of their universe, and this agreement by definition would constitute reality. The original hypothesis that these men can learn nothing of reality is contradicted, and the difficulty of nominalism is avoided.

(iii) This explanation of the validity of induction entails a definite theory about the requirements of logic. Peirce remarks that upon his "theory of reality and of logic, it can be shown that no inference of any individual can be thoroughly logical without certain determinations of his mind which do not concern any one inference immediately" (5.354). For inasmuch as reality must be defined as consisting in the ultimate agreement of all men, as the long-run result of the continuous inquiry of the community, inferences determined only by individual interest have no assurance of being determined by reality. Thus, in the hypothetical universe just considered, an individual might be led by personal interest to accept an induction as true before there had been sufficient inquiry to prove it false. If everyone in the universe were fated to act in a similar manner, a state of affairs in which men could learn nothing of reality once again seems possible. This state of affairs becomes self-contradictory only if there are always at least some men in the universe who transcend their personal interest and pursue their inquiries sufficiently far. Only these men would necessarily tend to agreement in their inductions and, hence, to reality. Peirce is thus forced to conclude that "logic rigidly requires, before all else, that no determinate fact, nothing which can happen to a man's self, should be of more consequence to him than everything else. He who would not sacrifice his own soul to save the whole world, is illogical in all his inferences, collectively. So the social principle is rooted intrinsically in logic" (5.354).

This ultimate requirement of logic reduces to the assumption, or the "hope," as Peirce also calls it, that human inquiry will continue indefinitely. A man can transcend his personal interests only when he identifies his inductions with those of an unlimited community whose inquiry will never cease, for otherwise his interests would lie in a limited community with finite / objectives. Yet Peirce is well aware that this basic assumption of logic "is entirely unsupported by reasons" (5.357).

There cannot be a scintilla of evidence to show that at some time all living beings shall not be annihilated at once, and that forever after there shall be throughout the universe any intelligence whatever. Indeed, this very assumption involves itself a transcendent and supreme interest, and therefore from its very nature is unsusceptible of any support from reasons. . . . We do not want to know what are the weights of reasons *pro* and *con*—that is, how much odds we should wish to receive on such a venture in the long run—because there is no long run in the case; the question is single and supreme, and ALL is at stake upon it.

Peirce never departed from this view of the ultimate grounds for the explanation of true inductions. While his later writings give considerable elaboration and development in his analysis of the problem, the assumption stated above remains fundamental. The final remarks (1910) on probability in the *Collected Papers* refer with praise to these essays of 1868–69 for having made the point "still better" than the more extended treatment of the subject written ten years later (cf. 2.661).

B. Peirce began his essay on the grounds of validity of the laws of logic by accepting a challenge to show how these grounds could be "other than inexplicable," since the examination of the faculties of mental action had seemed to establish the principle that "nothing can be admitted to be absolutely inexplicable." The reader who was not an "absolute sceptic" or in a state of "fictitious doubt" was to find a "convincing force" in the arguments and warned that, if he actually did so, it would be a mere pretense on his part to call them illogical. Inasmuch as Peirce's attempts to answer the challenge in the case of synthetic reasoning ended with an assumption "entirely unsupported by reasons," and thus difficult to regard as having a convincing force, the result seems an intended paradox. The assumption here, unlike the principle of the syllogism, can hardly be pronounced indubitable once its meaning has been properly understood. However, Peirce gives no indication that he intended his answer to be paradoxical. On the contrary, his emphasis on the total lack of evidence for the assumption implies that he believed there was some obvious factor which saved him from self-contradiction. It is difficult to see what this factor might have been, except the utterly unique status that must be accorded the assumption. The question is, he states, "single and supreme, and ALL is at stake upon it." Since he defined reality as consisting in the ultimate agreement of all men, the assumption is crucial not merely for the attainment of true inductions but for the reality of anything at all. It is by means of this assumption, and only by means of it, that everything real becomes explicable. If convincing reasons for the assumption were sought, these reasons themselves would presuppose both true inductions and reality, and circular argument would be inevitable. Peirce appears to have believed, then, that only by insisting on the total lack of evidence for his assumption could he save himself from a paradoxical answer.

It seems possible to draw a parallel between the positions of Peirce and Kant which may throw some light on the problem. Since Peirce defined reality as the outcome or product of inquiry, he inevitably brought together questions which Kant distinguished under the headings of speculative and practical reason. For, by Peirce's approach, the attainment of anything true of reality just as much as of anything morally good depends upon the conduct of human action. Just as Kant argued that morality demands action totally unaffected by personal ends within the phenomenal world, so Peirce argues that reality demands inquiry totally unaffected by personal ends within finite experience. For Kant, a man would not be acting morally if he acted because of his own arguments rather than for the sake of the moral law, even though his particular action might conform to the categorical imperative; and, for Peirce, a man would not be conducting inquiry that would be certain in the long run to discover reality if his interests were limited by his own arguments rather than being identical with those of an unlimited community, even though his particular inquiry might

62

conform to the rules of induction. Thus, when Peirce speaks of the "logical necessity" for the identification of one's own interests with those of an unlimited community, he can hardly mean the kind of necessity which belongs to any logical principle, as the principle of the syllogism. He seems rather to mean something that might be called the necessary condition for the logical employment of logical principles—something which cannot itself have logical reasons to support it. Just as for Kant, morality demands the identification of one's own interests with those of a community of rational beings, so, for Peirce, inquiry demands the identification of one's own interests with those of a community of inquirers. Peirce's "logical necessity" here is perhaps, then, analogous to Kant's "moral necessity"; at any rate, they both, in their respective ways, express necessary preconditions for rational action.

C. Whether or not an appeal to the unique status of Peirce's fundamental assumption of logic can save him from self-contradiction, and regardless of analogies that may hold between his position and Kant's, there are some obvious problems which require further investigation before a complete statement of his position can be given. In the first place, the relation of the formal to the material or factual conditions of valid induction must be made out more clearly. The assumption in question may be necessary if valid inductions true of reality are sometime sure to exist in the minds of men, and there may still be a sense in which the principles of induction can be shown to be logically valid without this assumption. This formal view of the principles is certainly suggested by Peirce's contention that any notion of a universe in which inductions would not hold is self-contradictory. The complications which arise then involve the further point that reality is to be defined as the ultimate outcome of valid induction. Thus, in the second place, the implied dependence of ontology on logic must be clarified by working out the relation between mind and reality which follows when the latter is defined as the product of inquiry. This gives rise to metaphysical problems, such as that of explaining how both chance and necessity are possible when the universe cannot be conceived to have characteristics that might always remain undiscovered. Finally, what is perhaps most important, the nature of man as an inquiring organism must be taken into account more fully. While the discovery of truth has been made a social enterprise, little has been said, apart from the remarks about an ultimate hope, as to how an individual person can come to participate in the enterprise.

All these problems are given some treatment in Peirce's later writings, and most of them are taken up in the remaining essays of the *Search for a Method*. The essays immediately following the one just considered deal more specifically with the nature of man as an inquiring organism and the methods he should use in the practice of his inquiry. It may be well to close the present chapter with a brief statement of what can be concluded regarding Peirce's views on this subject as they now stand.

While his examination of the faculties of mental action led Peirce to the view that all cognition could be explained by a single faculty for drawing inferences, some of his comments in his essay on the validity of the laws of logic seem to imply that he regarded the process of inquiry, as opposed to the process of cognition, as requiring a different faculty. He prefaced his consideration of the validity of probable inference with the remarks: "Is it not that besides ordinary experience which is dependent on there being a certain physical connection between our organs and the thing experienced, there is a second avenue of truth dependent only on there being a certain intellectual connection between our previous knowledge and what we learn in that way? Yes, this is true. Man has this faculty, just as opium has a somnific virtue" (5.341). Taken by themselves, these remarks seem to imply at least two faculties of inquiry; one for gaining knowledge of objects immediately present in the environment and another for objects only mediately present. However, this implication is inconsistent not only with Peirce's later views but also with his analysis in the preceding essay. For the assumption of noninferential faculties in the process of mental

64

action was found impossible because it presupposed a cognition not determined by a previous cognition. But then in the case of a cognition that is supposed to depend on "a direct physical connection between our organs and the thing experienced," there would be an infinite number of previous cognitions just as much as in the case where the cognition was supposed to depend on "a certain intellectual connection" with previous cognitions. In both cases a single faculty of drawing inferences would be sufficient to account for the cognitions.

These misleading remarks on the faculties of inquiry are perhaps best explained by the circumstance that Peirce at this time had not fully worked out his views on the nature of man as an inquiring organism and on the relation between the processes of mental action and inquiry. His examination of the faculties of mental action led him to the view that "the word or sign which the man uses *is* the man himself" (5.314). That is, since the process of thought is taken as ultimate rather than the things which the process is ordinarily said to presuppose, both the objects of thought and the subjects who think must be explained by the process. As Peirce remarked in a footnote to this essay, "just as we say that a body is in motion, and not that motion is in a body, we ought to say that we are in thought, and not that thoughts are in us" (5.289, p. 173, n. 1). But certainly the same analysis must be applied to man as the subject who conducts inquiry. The essential characteristics of man as an inquiring organism must be given by what he is in the process of inquiry and not by anything he might be, biologically, physically, or otherwise, when regarded as a *thing* outside this process. Since every event in the process of inquiry no less than in the process of mental action must be a sign, man as an inquiring organism should be a sign. The assertion that man is a biological or physical thing in dynamic interaction with other things must be interpreted so as to take account of this fact. Such an interpretation can be given only when inquiry as a physical process taking place in the environment has been properly related to the mental process of cognition.

65

Some insight into the nature of Peirce's views at this time may be obtained from a comment he later made on these early essays regarding the point in question. In a paper of 1892 entitled *Man's Glassy Essence* he gave a somewhat different treatment of the problem and remarked in passing: "Long ago, in the *Journal of Speculative Philosophy*, I pointed out that a person is nothing but a symbol involving a general idea; but my views were, then, too nominalistic to enable me to see that every general idea has the unified living feeling of a person" (6.270). The phrase "general idea" does not occur in the original statement, and for the purpose at hand it is unnecessary to distinguish it from "symbol." The important word is "nominalistic." It has already been noticed that for Peirce, even in these early essays, any reference to a thing in itself, either as subject or as object, appeared nominalistic. His remarks about the faculties of inquiry were inconsistent with his conclusions regarding the faculties of mental action precisely in the sense that they seemed to imply both an organism and an object experienced as things in themselves undetermined by processes of thought or inquiry. The truth of the matter appears to be that Peirce's early views concerning the determination of logical subject matter by the forms of relation occurring in the process of symbolic operations committed him to views about the existential conditions of knowledge which it took him some time to develop. If term, proposition, and argument cannot be defined in logic by reference to entities or faculties outside the process of inference, a similar situation should obtain for attempts to define man as thinker or inquirer independently of the process in which he essentially exists. Peirce's early views, then, were nominalistic in so far as he failed to take full account of this situation and tended to regard man as something in himself apart from what he becomes when he participates in processes of thought or inquiry. In fact, a comparison of the wording in the earlier and later statements clearly suggests the point. In the first case, man is the subject who *uses* the sign, thereby being identical with it, while, later, man is *nothing but* a sign. Whether or not Peirce ever succeeded in explaining the process of inquiry without supposing the notion of an inquirer who in some fundamental sense remains something besides a sign will be considered below in the final chapter.

Having examined the grounds for belief in the validity of the logical laws presupposed by every inference, Peirce can proceed to the various ways a man may use inferences to obtain beliefs about the character of his environment. The central problem becomes that of relating man to his environment through the mediation of ideas in the form of beliefs. The apparent paradox in Peirce's ultimate assumption that human inquiry will continue indefinitely can be investigated more fully in the context of this problem.

central problem

III

The Methods of Obtaining Knowledge

EACH of the remaining essays in the *Search for a Method* treats specifically some aspects of the problem of determining the method best fitted to give man true knowledge of his environment. Broadly speaking, this problem may be viewed as that of analyzing the process of inquiry, as the problem in the earlier essays could be viewed as that of analyzing, first, the process of logical operations and, second, the process of mental action. The method to which Peirce was led by his search actually involves two phases: the scientific or inductive method of establishing true beliefs and the pragmatic method of making ideas clear.

1. THE METHODS OF FIXING BELIEF

A. The paper intended for Essay VII of the *Search for a Method* was entitled *The Fixation of Belief* (5, Bk. II, Paper IV) and originally appeared in the *Popular Science Monthly* (1877) as the first of six papers in a series called "Illustrations of the Logic of Science." The preliminary considerations delimit the process of inquiry by marking its beginning and end, just as the analysis in the earlier essays started by giving a similar delimitation of logical and mental processes. But the nature of man, the subject whose actions constitute the process, now assumes an importance it did not have in the earlier cases. For the terms "doubt" and "belief," which mark, respectively, the beginning and end of inquiry, seem to require for their explanation a reference to human nature, unlike the terms "premiss" and "conclusion," "substance" and "being," "sign" and "interpretant." While Peirce was thus led to refer to doubt and belief as "states of mind," he seems here deliberately to avoid the issue of whether human nature explains, or is explained by, the process of inquiry. He remarks that "in asking why a certain conclusion is thought to follow from certain premisses, . . . a variety of facts are already assumed. . . . It is implied, for instance, that there are such states of mind as doubt and belief —that a passage from one to the other is possible, the object of thought remaining the same, and that this transition is subject to some rules by which all minds are alike bound" (5.369). In short, the existence of doubt, belief, and other facts about human nature are assumed rather than explained by a logical analysis of inquiry. Peirce's next sentence, moreover, explicitly declares that he does not regard such an assumption as standing in need of justification. "As these are facts which we must already know before we can have any clear conception of reasoning at all, it cannot be supposed to be any longer of much interest to inquire into their truth or falsity." The concern of logical analysis, on the contrary, is with "those rules of reasoning which are deduced from the very idea of the process"— irrespective, presumably, of anything about the nature of doubt and belief as states of mind—and, Peirce feels, so long as inquiry conforms to these rules, "it will, at least, not lead to false conclusions from true premisses."

It was found in the preceding essays that genuine doubt could not be achieved arbitrarily and that belief was always the result of an inference. Peirce now gives a more specific characterization of doubt and belief as the beginning and end of inquiry. They are to be distinguished not only according to the different sensations which accompany doubting and believing but also according to "a practical difference" (5.371). For "our beliefs guide our desires and shape our actions," while "doubt never has such an effect." Further, "doubt is an uneasy and dissatisfied state from which we struggle to free ourselves and pass

69

into the state of belief; while the latter is a calm and satisfactory state which we do not wish to avoid, or to change to a belief in anything else" (5.372). Hence, doubt "reminds us of the irritation of a nerve and the reflex action produced thereby; while for the analogue of belief, in the nervous system, we must look to what are called nervous associations—for example, to that habit of the nerves in consequence of which the smell of a peach will make the mouth water" (5.373). Inasmuch, then, as doubt "causes a struggle to attain a state of belief," it initiates a process which may be termed "inquiry," "though," Peirce adds, "it must be admitted that this is sometimes not a very apt designation" (5.374). Since the process thus initiated can be terminated only by the production of belief, "the sole object of inquiry is the settlement of opinion" (5.375).

This manner of explaining the sole object of inquiry, Peirce declares, "sweeps away, at once, various vague and erroneous conceptions of proof" (5.375). In the first place, we cannot, as was already remarked in the preceding essays, "begin our studies with questioning everything," since inquiry can only arise when there is "a real and living doubt, and without this all discussion is idle" (5.376). Second, there is no need to assume that "a demonstration must rest on some ultimate and absolutely indubitable propositions," such as "first principles of a general nature" or "first sensations." For, "in point of fact, an inquiry, to have that completely satisfactory result called demonstration, has only to start with propositions perfectly free from all actual doubt." Finally, "when doubt ceases, mental action on the subject comes to an end; and, if it did go on, it would be without a purpose," "except," Peirce added in a note of 1903, "that of self-criticism."

Doubt and belief, whatever may be their complete explanation, thus afford the ultimate determination of when an inquiry actually begins and when a conclusion is reached. Universal doubt and absolute first principles might be justified by a theory which delimited the process of inquiry according to its subject matter, but, if reality cannot be defined except as the outcome of infinite inquiry, both the beginning and the end of finite inquiry must be specified without reference to subject matter. Peirce's note here of 1903 clearly points to the need for some theory of the nature of man, or the "self," to substantiate his analysis of inquiry as the passage from doubt to belief. The note also contains the injunction: "Insert here a section upon self-control and the analogy between Moral and Rational self-control." But it was not until about the time he wrote this direction, which apparently he never carried out, that Peirce came to regard the moral nature of man as having some essential bearing on his theory of inquiry.

B. The main portion of Peirce's essay consists in a discussion of the relative advantages and disadvantages to be found in four different methods of fixing belief—in four different ways of conducting inquiry and bringing it to a conclusion. One possible method of terminating inquiry would be that of "taking as answer to a question any we may fancy, and constantly reiterating it to ourselves, dwelling on all which may conduce to that belief, and learning to turn with contempt and hatred from anything that might disturb it" (5.377). "But this method of fixing belief, which may be called the method of tenacity, will be unable to hold its ground in practice. The social impulse is against it. . . . Unless we make ourselves hermits, we shall necessarily influence each other's opinions; so that the problem becomes how to fix belief, not in the individual merely, but in the community" (5.378). Consequently, a second method, arising from the weakness of the first, consists merely in letting "the will of the state act . . . instead of that of the individual" (5.379). An institution is created "which shall have for its object to keep correct doctrines before the attention of the people, to reiterate them perpetually, and to teach them to the young; having at the same time power to prevent contrary doctrines from being taught, advocated, or expressed." This method may be called the "method of authority" and must be allowed "immeasurable mental and moral superiority to the method of tenacity" (5.380). In fact, "for

71

the mass of mankind, . . . there is perhaps no better method than this," since "if it is their highest impulse to be intellectual slaves, then slaves they ought to remain." However, such a method is necessarily subject to considerable weaknesses in that it is restricted to finite communities. For even

in the most priest-ridden states some individuals will be found who . . . possess a wider sort of social feeling; they see that men in other countries and in other ages have held to very different doctrines from those which they themselves have been brought up to believe; and they cannot help seeing that it is the mere accident of their having been taught as they have, and of their having been surrounded with the manners and associations they have, that has caused them to believe as they do and not far differently [5.381].

Another method naturally arises to remedy the unsatisfactoriness of this second method. To the extent that the "action of natural preferences" is left "unimpeded" in the community, under the influence of such preferences, men,

conversing together and regarding matters in different lights, gradually develop beliefs in harmony with natural causes. This method resembles that by which conceptions of art have been brought to maturity. The most perfect example of it is to be found in the history of metaphysical philosophy. Systems of this sort have not usually rested upon any observed facts, at least not in any great degree. They have been chiefly adopted because their fundamental propositions seemed "agreeable to reason" [5.382].

"This method is far more intellectual and respectable from the point of view of reason than either of the others which we have noticed" (5.383). However, a fundamental weakness of the method arises from the fact that "it makes of inquiry something similar to the development of taste," while "taste, unfortunately, is always more or less a matter of fashion, and accordingly metaphysicians have never come to any fixed agreement, but the pendulum has swung backward and forward between a more material and a more spiritual philosophy, from the earliest times to the latest."

From the deficiencies of this third approach, "which has been called the *a priori* method, we are driven, in Lord Bacon's phrase, to a true induction" (5.383). The a priori method fails "to deliver our opinions from their accidental and capricious element," in that, while the development to which it gives rise "is a process which eliminates the effect of some casual circumstances," it "only magnifies that of others." "This method, therefore, does not differ in a very essential way from that of authority." Hence, in order to satisfy our doubts, "it is necessary that a method should be found by which our beliefs may be determined by nothing human, but by some external permanency—by something upon which our thinking has no effect" (5.384). But "our external permanency would not be external, in our sense, if it was restricted in its influence to one individual"; "it must be something which affects, or might affect, every man. And, though these affections are necessarily as various as are individual conditions, yet the method must be such that the ultimate conclusion of every man shall be the same," or, as Peirce added in 1903, "would be the same if inquiry were sufficiently persisted in." "Such is the method of science," and

its fundamental hypothesis, restated in more familiar language, is this: There are Real things, whose characters are entirely independent of our opinions about them; those Reals affect our senses according to regular laws, and, though our sensations are as different as are our relations to the objects, yet, by taking advantage of the laws of perception, we can ascertain by reasoning how things really and truly are; and any man, if he have sufficient experience and he reason enough about it, will be led to the one True conclusion.

This fourth method, Peirce finds, shares none of the weaknesses of the others. In the first place, while "investigation cannot be regarded as proving that there are Real things, it at least does not lead to a contrary conclusion; but the method and the conception on which it is based remain ever in harmony" (5.384). Hence, "no doubts of the method . . . necessarily arise from its practice, as is the case with all the others." However, "nobody . . . can really doubt that there are Reals, for, if he did, doubt would not be a source of dissatisfaction.

73

The hypothesis, therefore, is one which every mind admits," "so that the social impulse does not cause men to doubt it." Again, "everybody uses the scientific method about a great many things, and only ceases to use it when he does not know how to apply it." Finally, "experience of the method has not led us to doubt it, but, on the contrary, scientific investigation has had the most wonderful triumphs in the way of settling opinion."

The scientific method is further differentiated from the others in that it is the only one "which presents any distinction of a right and a wrong way" (5.385). It is impossible to use the method of tenacity wrongly, since in using it one shuts himself "out from all influences," and whatever he thinks "necessary to doing this, is necessary according to that method." The method of authority cannot be misused because in this case the only test is "what the state thinks," and "the very essence" of the a priori method is "to think as one is inclined to think." But, in pursuing the scientific method, "the test" of correct use "is not an immediate appeal to my feelings and purposes, but, on the contrary, itself involves the application of the method. Hence it is that bad reasoning as well as good reasoning is possible; and this fact is the foundation of the practical side of logic."

But each of the first three methods, Peirce declares, "has some peculiar convenience of its own. The a priori method is distinguished for its comfortable conclusions," it being "the nature of the process to adopt whatever belief we are inclined to." "The method of authority will always govern the mass of mankind," and, since by means of it "uniformity of opinion will be secured by a moral terrorism to which the respectability of society will give its thorough approval," "following the method of authority is the path of peace." The method of tenacity is to be admired "most of all" for its "strength, simplicity, and directness. Men who pursue it are distinguished for their decision of character, which becomes very easy with such a mental rule" (5.386). But, whatever may be the advantages

74

of these other methods, a man "should consider that, after all, he wishes his opinions to coincide with the fact, and that there is no reason why the results of those three first methods should do so. To bring about this effect is the prerogative of the method of science" (5.387).

Peirce closes his essay with a few hortatory remarks on the importance of choosing the scientific method of fixing belief. The principal difficulty in strict adherence to the method appears to be the reluctance to give up beliefs once science has proved them false. "The force of habit will sometimes cause a man to hold on to old beliefs, after he is in a condition to see that they have no sound basis. But reflection upon the state of the case will overcome these habits, and he ought to allow reflection its full weight" (5.387). This seems but another way of stating Peirce's ultimate requirement of logic given in the earlier essay on the validity of the laws of logic. An individual who is to make logical inferences must be always ready to sacrifice his personal interests, to give up his old beliefs, as inquiry dictates. Peirce's use of "ought" here would seem to imply a close connection between moral and rational behavior and clearly to point to his later concern with analogues between the two and his view that logic is a normative science along with ethics and esthetics.

C. Without considering further at this point the extent to which Peirce's theory of inquiry entails assumptions about the intellectual and moral nature of man, some understanding of his theory may be obtained from an examination of the rationale which seems to underlie his fourfold division of the methods of fixing belief. Since Peirce himself offered no explanation as to why there should be just four methods, the obvious implication would be that he felt it was simply a matter of how many the facts in the case should disclose. However, the division is somewhat unusual, and, while almost every treatise on logic contains some consideration of scientific and unscientific ways of settling opinion, it would be difficult to find any (works influenced by Peirce excluded) which enumerated the methods of tenacity, authority, and taste as the three distinct unscientific ways. There are perhaps, then, some principles stemming from the peculiar nature of Peirce's approach to philosophy which led him to view the facts as he did and to arrive at his fourfold classification.

A comparison of the four methods of fixing belief with the four propositions listed at the beginning of Peirce's earlier essay, *Some Consequences of Four Incapacities* (see above, pp. 45–46), suggests at once some common scheme of organization for both sets. The first proposition asserts the impossibility of immediate knowledge of the self, not inferred from external facts; the first method represents the attempt to fix belief solely by what appears to the individual himself, isolated from everyone else. The second proposition denies the existence of a cognition not connected with other cognitions; the method of authority seeks to prevent an individual from holding opinions not shared by others. The third proposition declares that all reasoning is essentially a process of signification; the method of taste, or the a priori method, is distinguished from the first two primarily in its appeal to reason. Finally, Peirce's theory of reality as something independent of this or that individual's opinion was first formulated as a consequence of his fourth proposition, while an appeal to reality so conceived is precisely what distinguishes the scientific method from the others.

The argument given in the preceding chapter for an interpretation of the first three propositions as an expression of Peirce's categories may thus have an analogue applicable to the methods of fixing belief. The first method takes the individual in himself prescinded from reference to anything else; the second relates him to other individuals through the sheer force of authority; while the third allows what "seems agreeable to reason" to mediate between conflicting opinions. Peirce's statement that the latter method "does not differ in a very essential way from that of authority" refers, of course, to the fact that neither method is designed to achieve opinions which accord with reality. But there is nevertheless a considerable difference between the two methods, and, even though reason may be used by the state to supplement the force of authority, the fixation of belief in such a case is still by the coercive power of the state and quite different from the free play of reason in the individual. It should be noted, moreover, that Peirce's account of the four methods clearly suggests a historical progression.[1] The method of tenacity is the most primitive and probably the first to appear historically; the method of authority represents an advance and by its efforts to achieve unanimity attempts to overcome the chief defect of the first method; the a priori method, in turn, by its appeal to "natural preferences" in all men to accept what seems agreeable to reason counteracts in some measure restriction to the arbitrary authority of a finite community.

In these prescientific stages of inquiry the movement is thus from belief for the individual alone to belief for the community, which becomes continually more comprehensive, until at the scientific stage belief is fixed only for the unlimited community. The scientific method, as the only one completely transcending the peculiarities of finite communities, is therefore sharply differentiated from the other three; so much so, in fact, that it cannot be regarded as just another stage in the same process. There is, in other words, a discontinuity in the passage from any of the other three methods to the scientific one, as there is a discontinuity in any passage from the limited to the unlimited. Now, although Peirce in his later writings distinguished three stages in the process of scientific inquiry (abduction, deduction, and induction) and tried to explain them as expressions of his categories, he never attempted a similar explanation for his three stages of prescientific inquiry. This situation might seem to be accounted for by the fact that scientific inquiry, since it is concerned only with belief for the unlimited community, can be analyzed as a purely logical process (can have its rules "deduced from the very idea of the process") without reference to actual historical situations, while prescientific inquiry is not bound to any specific logical order but seems always dependent on the historical accidents of finite

77

communities. However, Peirce does speak as though the historical passage from the method of tenacity. to that of authority, then, of taste, and, finally, of science were an inevitable and continuous progression due to certain forces in human nature, such as the "social impulse," "instinct," and the "wish" to have one's "opinions coincide with the fact"; and the first three methods do seem suspiciously like instances of the three categories which appear in any rational process.

The problem here is crucial for Peirce's approach to philosophy in that it leads to the problem of relating rational to historical processes, or the formal to the material or existential aspects of a sign-process. Scientific inquiry, in so far as it transcends the peculiarities of finite communities, becomes identical with a purely logical process; yet, if scientific inquiry is to exist, it can only do so as the inquiry of this or that finite community. In terms reminiscent of Kant, the question arises: How, then, is scientific inquiry possible? Just as Kant argued that the human mind supplies the necessary preconditions of all experience and makes scientific knowledge possible, Peirce seems forced to argue that the human struggle from doubt to belief supplies the necessary preconditions of all inquiry and makes scientific inquiry possible. In spite of its dependence on historical accidents, prescientific inquiry should thus tend inevitably in a direction which makes the emergence of scientific inquiry a possibility. But this means that characteristics of a rational process should be discernible in the histories of prescientific inquiry. Peirce's later views on this problem were centered around his theory that science advances with the gradual refinement of instinctive beliefs through the development of self-control. This theory entails considerable revision of the present analysis, especially with reference to the prescientific methods of fixing belief. Some indication of the revision may be seen from the sentence which Peirce inserted ca. 1910 regarding the a priori method. "Indeed, as long as no better method can be applied, it ought to be followed, since it is then the expression of instinct which must be the ultimate cause of belief in all

78

cases" (5.383). This point will be discussed below (chap. vi, sec. 3, C), and it will suffice to remark now that the sentence implies an essentially new conception of the opposition between the third and fourth methods.

In short, then, both the discontinuity between the first three methods and the scientific method and the apparent categorial order and continuity in the historical progression involving all four methods point to aspects of Peirce's philosophy which are still far from their final development. It should be noticed in conclusion that the problem here in the last analysis becomes closely connected (if not identical) with the problem of relating inquiry to human nature, since the character of the latter is precisely what is needed to account for the existence of the former. Further consideration of the rationale underlying Peirce's four methods will be given in the next section, where the methods can be related to the ways of making ideas clear.

2. THE MEANING OF IDEAS

A. The paper appearing as the next essay in the *Search for a Method* is the well-known *How To Make Our Ideas Clear*, which contains Peirce's first explicit formulation of his pragmatism.[2] While the specific problem is that of stating a criterion for the meaning, as distinct from the truth, of ideas, it becomes in effect a first step in the attack on the more general problem just mentioned above. For inasmuch as belief in the truth or falsity of an idea can be subjected to the test of scientific inquiry only after the meaning of the idea has been clearly determined, the presence of clear and exact ideas in the minds of individual inquirers is an indispensable prerequisite for the existence of scientific inquiry. Peirce distinguishes three different grades of clearness with which the meaning of an idea may be apprehended and finds a progression from the first to the third grade which seems to have certain similarities to the progression through the different methods of fixing belief.

A recognition of the first two grades of clearness can be discerned in previous books on logic. Peirce concludes, however, that while "it may be acknowledged . . . that the books are right in making familiarity with a notion the first step toward clearness of apprehension, and the defining of it the second," "in omitting all mention of any higher perspicuity of thought, they simply mirror a philosophy which was exploded a hundred years ago" (5.392). Familiarity with an idea "only amounts to a subjective feeling of mastery which may be entirely mistaken" (5.389), while the distinctness which is obtained by analyzing the definitions of concepts can accomplish nothing but to set "our existing beliefs . . . in order" (5.392). Neither kind of clarity can refer ideas to an external permanency, independent of subjective feeling and beliefs already held, which would be necessary for application of the scientific method. A third grade of clearness, not remarked by previous books on logic, becomes apparent from the analysis of inquiry given in the *Fixation of Belief,* which maintained that "the production of belief is the sole function of thought." For since "the essence of belief is the establishment of a habit," and "different beliefs are distinguished by the different modes of action to which they give rise" (5.398), in order to develop the meaning of a conception it is only necessary to determine the beliefs which it occasions or "what habits it produces" (5.400). That is, "what a thing means is simply what habits it involves." Thus, "our action has exclusive reference to what affects the senses, our habit has the same bearing as our action, our belief the same as our habit, our conception the same as our belief," and, hence, "our idea of anything *is* our idea of its sensible effects" (5.401). "It appears, then, that the rule for attaining the third grade of clearness of apprehension is as follows: Consider what effects, that might conceivably have practical bearings, we conceive the object of our conception to have. Then, our conception of these effects is the whole of our conception of the object" (5.402).

B. This statement of the rule for attaining the third grade of clearness constitutes Peirce's first explicit formulation of what he later called "the pragmatic maxim." An understanding of how the maxim is related to other parts of Peirce's philosophy as he had developed it at this time may be approached by comparing the three grades of clearness with the methods of fixing belief. There seems little difficulty in interpreting the three grades as an expression of the categories. Familiarity with an idea, since it is based only on subjective feeling, pertains to the idea considered in itself as a nonrelative term. The mere analysis of a definition involves nothing but the relations of an idea to other ideas and employs only the dyadic relations *distinct from* and *identical with*. The pragmatic determination of meaning regards an idea as mediating between man and his environment and places in a triadic relation man, the environment toward which he acts, and the beliefs or habits according to which his actions are made. Fixation of belief by the method of tenacity would require only the subjective familiarity achieved by the first grade of clearness. The distinctness proper to the second grade would enable one to relate a particular idea to others already dictated by authority or the inclinations of taste and would suffice for an application of either of the remaining two prescientific methods. Any use of scientific induction, of course, would presuppose that the ideas to be tested were understood with reference to an external permanency unaffected by individual preferences. However, achievement of this third grade of clearness is in no sense a guarantee that beliefs will be fixed only by the scientific method. A man may clearly apprehend his idea of an object to mean nothing but the conceivable, practical effects the object might have and nevertheless come to a belief regarding the idea without subjecting it to the test of scientific inquiry. There is thus an important difference between the final method of fixing belief and the highest grade of clearness: the former by its very nature must refer to reality, to what is actually the case, and its practice provides a sufficient condition for the ultimate attainment of truth; the latter refers only to conceivable effects, to what is possibly the case, and its practice provides only a necessary condition for the use of the scientific method.

This difference between scientific inquiry and the pragmatic criterion of meaning affords some clue to an explanation of the fact that Peirce enumerated four methods of fixing belief and only three grades of clearness. A discontinuity between the pre-scientific and scientific methods necessarily arose because only in the second case was there a reference to reality. In general, it would seem that at this point in the development of his philosophy Peirce believed that any determination of the real lay beyond the processes which evolved the categories. Thus, in his original analysis the categories comprised the three stages intermediate between the manifold of substance and the unity of being. The formation of a proposition at the third stage did not guarantee a determination of the real, which involved a fourth step distinct from the three stages. Similarly, in the essay *Some Consequences of Four Incapacities* the relation of thought to reality provided a fourth proposition considered after the relevant aspects of the thought-process itself had been examined under three headings which reflected the categories. By analogy, then, the process of fixing belief should have three stages intermediate between the mere irritation of doubt and the final settlement of opinion by a determination of the real. But, since the clearness of ideas is independent of what is actually the case, the process in this instance should contain only the three stages which seem analyzable without suppositions concerning reality.

The question as to whether a determination of reality in some sense or other requires a fourth step beyond the categories remains a serious problem throughout Peirce's philosophy. It was remarked above in the preceding section that his conception of the opposition between the third and fourth methods of fixing belief suffered considerable alteration. But, on the other hand, in 1902 Peirce came to distinguish "a still higher grade of clearness" beyond the three he had differentiated in 1878 (cf. 5.3). The need for this fourth grade is closely connected with the development of his ontology and, hence, in some sense with a determination of the real. In this respect, Peirce's first analysis of the clearness of ideas and the fixation

82

of belief is limited by the undeveloped state of his ontology. Something of the problem as it appears at this time may be seen from the following considerations.

The concluding portion of *How To Make Our Ideas Clear* offers some applications of the pragmatic maxim. The last and most lengthy one is an application of the maxim to a definition of reality, and the result is a somewhat more elaborate statement of the views on reality Peirce had presented ten years earlier in his *Some Consequences of Four Incapacities*. At the second grade of clearness "we may define the real as that whose characters are independent of what anybody may think them to be" (5.405). But, at the third grade, we must understand that "reality, like every other quality, consists in the peculiar sensible effects which things partaking of it produce," and since "the only effect which real things have is to cause belief," the problem of defining reality becomes that of stating "how is true belief (or belief in the real) distinguished from false belief (or belief in fiction)" (5.406). Peirce concludes: "The opinion which is fated to be ultimately agreed to by all who investigate, is what we mean by the truth, and the object represented in this opinion is the real. That is the way I would explain reality" (5.407). But this explanation, as Peirce remarked, may seem open to the objection that it is "directly opposed" to the definition given at the second grade, "inasmuch as it makes the characters of the real depend on what is ultimately thought about them" (5.408). The answer to the objection is that, "on the one hand, reality is independent, not necessarily of thought in general, but only of what you or I or any finite number of men may think about it; and that, on the other hand, though the object of the final opinion depends on what that opinion is, yet what that opinion is does not depend on what you or I or any man thinks."

The important point here, as far as grades of clearness are concerned, is that reality at the third grade is treated "like every other quality" and hence as consisting in "the peculiar sensible effects which things partaking of it produce." But this supposes the more general notions of *quality* and *thing* and implies that some things have and others do not have the quality which consists in the effect of producing belief after sufficient inquiry. Aside from other serious difficulties raised by this explanation of reality, there is the general question as to whether the statement just made has any meaning at the third grade of clearness. What are the sensible effects which constitute "having a quality," or merely "being a thing," real or unreal? Peirce's fourth grade of clearness is connected with this problem, and there is of course the additional question of fixing belief with respect to these notions. The unsatisfactoriness of the analysis at this time is also apparent from the lack of any mention of existence as distinct from what Peirce here calls reality. Existence is hardly to be treated as not necessarily independent of "thought in general" and as "like every other quality." But, then, what are the sensible effects which distinguish existence and reality? Despite these difficulties, Peirce suggested at the close of *How To Make Our Ideas Clear* that his explanation of reality might be offered as "a metaphysical theory of existence for universal acceptance among those who employ the scientific method of fixing belief" (5.410).

3. THE TRUTH OF IDEAS

A. Peirce concluded his essay on how to make ideas clear with the following paragraph:

We have, hitherto, not crossed the threshold of scientific logic. It is certainly important to know how to make our ideas clear, but they may be ever so clear without being true. How to make them so, we have next to study. How to give birth to those vital and procreative ideas which multiply into a thousand forms and diffuse themselves everywhere, advancing civilization and making the dignity of man, is an art not yet reduced to rules, but of the secret of which the history of science affords some hints [5.410].

The remaining essays of the *Search for a Method* are concerned with various aspects of this general problem of reducing to rules the art of obtaining true ideas. In the course of the somewhat rambling considerations in these essays Peirce succeeded in at least touching on most of the important issues which were to occupy his later philosophic endeavors. Certain of the rather troublesome matters already encountered in his earlier writings reappear and receive more extended treatment.

The paper intended for Essay X, the *Doctrine of Chances* (2, Bk. II, chap. 6), begins by disclosing a "hint" from the history of science for crossing the threshold of scientific logic. "It is a common observation that a science first begins to be exact when it is quantitatively treated" (2.645). "It is not, however, so much from *counting* as from *measuring*, not so much from the conception of number as from that of continuous quantity, that the advantage of mathematical treatment comes" (2.646). Then, taking the hint for logic, Peirce concludes that "the science of logic quantitatively treated" is simply "the theory of probabilities" (2.647). For "the general problem of probabilities is, from a given state of facts, to determine the numerical probability of a possible fact," and since "this is the same as to inquire how much the given facts are worth, considered as evidence to prove the possible fact," "the problem of probabilities is simply the general problem of logic." Moreover, "probability is a continuous quantity, so that great advantages may be expected from this mode of studying logic" (2.648). But "unfortunately," of the various branches of mathematics, the calculus of probabilities seems to be "the only one . . . in which good writers frequently get results entirely erroneous." Peirce offers the following explanation of this situation:

This is partly owing to the want of any regular method of procedure; for the subject involves too many subtleties to make it easy to put its problems into equations without such an aid. But, beyond this, the fundamental principles of its calculus are more or less in dispute. In regard to that class of questions to which it is chiefly applied for practical purposes, there is comparatively little doubt; but in regard to others to which it has been sought to extend it, opinion is somewhat unsettled.

This last class of difficulties can only be entirely overcome by making the idea of probability perfectly clear in our minds in the way set forth in our last paper.

85

Peirce proposes, then, to cross the threshold of scientific logic by first of all making clear, through an application of his pragmatic maxim, the fundamental principles of the calculus of probabilities. The application of this maxim to the concept of probability leads to a consideration of "what real and sensible difference there is between one degree of probability and another" (2.649). Such difference seems to consist in the fact that

in the frequent employment of two different modes of inference, one will carry truth with it oftener than the other. It is evident that this is the only difference there is in the existing fact. Having certain premisses, a man draws a certain conclusion, and as far as this inference alone is concerned the only possible practical question is whether that conclusion is true or not, and between existence and non-existence there is no middle term. . . . For we found that the distinction of reality and fiction depends on the supposition that sufficient investigation would cause one opinion to be universally received and all others to be rejected [2.650].

／ In the light of this consideration Peirce was led to "define the probability of a mode of argument as the proportion of cases in which it carries truth with it" (2.650). By way of ＼further elucidation, he explained:

The inference from the premiss, A, to the conclusion, B, depends, as we have seen, on the guiding principle, that if a fact of the class A is true, a fact of the class B is true. The probability consists of the fraction whose numerator is the number of times in which both A and B are true, and whose denominator is the total number of times in which A is true, whether B is so or not. Instead of speaking of this as the probability of the inference, there is not the slightest objection to calling it the probability that, if A happens, B happens. But to speak of the probability of the event B, without naming the condition, really has no meaning at all [2.651].

Yet this definition of probability is pronounced "manifestly wrong" in the notes which Peirce appended to his paper in 1910. According to these notes, the account is correct in insisting that "probability never properly refers immediately to a single event, but exclusively to the happening of a given kind of event on any occasion of a given kind." "But," Peirce continues,

when I come to define probability, I repeatedly say that it is the quotient of the *number* of occurrences of the event divided by the *number* of occurrences of the occasion. Now this is manifestly wrong, for probability relates to the future; and how can I say how many times a given die will be thrown in the future? To be sure I might, immediately after my throw, put the die in strong nitric acid, and dissolve it, but this suggestion only puts the preposterous character of the definition in a still stronger light. For it is plain that, if probability be the ratio of the occurrences of the specific event to the occurrences of the generic occasion, it is the ratio that there *would be* in the long run, and has nothing to do with any supposed cessation of the occasions. This long run can be nothing but an endlessly long run; and even if it be correct to speak of an infinite "number," yet $\frac{\infty}{\infty}$ (infinity divided by infinity) has certainly, *in itself*, no definite value [2.661].

For the most part the issues involved in this change in Peirce's conception of probability are beyond the scope of the present study. But there is one aspect of the problem which pertains directly to his entire philosophy and perhaps at the same time provides the best explanation for this somewhat puzzling criticism of his early definition. The suggestion that the die might be dissolved in nitric acid has a parallel in an example given in the paper *How To Make Our Ideas Clear*. Peirce supposed that "a diamond could be crystallized in the midst of a cushion of soft cotton, and should remain there until it was finally burned up" (5.403). He then asked, "Would it be false to say that that diamond was soft?" His conclusion in 1878 was that there would be no falsity in "saying that all hard bodies remain perfectly soft until they are touched, when their hardness increases with the pressure until they are scratched." This "would involve a modification of our present usage of speech with regard to the words hard and soft, but not of their meanings." However, when Peirce came to reconsider the problem in 1905, he declared: "To say, as the article of January 1878 seems to intend, that it is just as an arbitrary 'usage of speech' chooses to arrange its

87

thoughts, is as much as to decide against the reality of the property, since the real is that which is such as it is regardless of how it is, at any time, thought to be" (5.457). On the contrary, the real hardness of the diamond must be said to consist in the sensible results which *would* ensue under certain circumstances. This explanation depends on Peirce's later doctrine that there are modes of being corresponding to his categories, so that the hardness of the diamond may have the reality of a law even though it is never actually tested. The destruction of the diamond before any test was made thus does not justify denying that it was really hard. Similarly, if a die were dissolved in nitric acid after a certain number of throws, the ratio of the number of sixes among the throws to the total number of throws could not be said to constitute the *real* probability which this die had of turning up a six. This situation would obtain for any finite number of throws, however large, so that the real probability can never be defined as a ratio formed from the number of throws, since this would lead to infinity divided by infinity. While in the actual practice of induction the probability must always be taken as a ratio formed from the number of occurrences examined, this ratio is not the real probability but only our estimate of it, just as the tests made on the diamond do not constitute its real hardness but only our knowledge of that hardness.[3] In accordance with this view, Peirce argued in his notes of 1910 that the real probability should be defined as a "would-be," as referring to what *would* result under certain circumstances whether or not these circumstances are ever fulfilled (2.664).

B. Further consideration of this view of probability will be given below in later chapters where it can be regarded in connection with the subsequent development of Peirce's philosophy as a whole. Besides the contention that probability never refers immediately to a single event, Peirce's notes of 1910 accept a second point, "the better of the two," made in his *Doctrine of Chances*. This is the point about the ultimate requirement of logic, already made ("still better" according to the notes) in his papers of 1868 and discussed above at the close of the preceding chapter. Despite Peirce's preference for his earliest statement, his account of 1878 is not only more detailed but actually seems to succeed in clarifying certain aspects of the problem. In some of the details the account may rely upon the "erroneous" definition of probability, and, while this reliance might have seemed to Peirce sufficient reason for preferring his more simplified statement, it need not affect the general clarification achieved by the account.

Two fundamental aspects of the problem are definitely clarified. In the first place, the status of the ultimate requirement of logic as an irrational factor, as a matter of emotion and sentiment, is made more explicit. Peirce finds "three sentiments, namely, interest in an indefinite community, recognition of the possibility of this interest being made supreme, and hope in the unlimited continuance of intellectual activity, as indispensable requirements of logic" (2.655). While this "may seem strange," he adds, "when we consider that logic depends on a mere struggle to escape doubt, which, as it terminates in action, must begin in emotion, and that, furthermore, the only cause of our planting ourselves on reason is that other methods of escaping doubt fail on account of the social impulse, why should we wonder to find social sentiment presupposed in reasoning?" The ultimate dependence of logic upon ethics in Peirce's philosophy is suggested by his further comment: "It interests me to notice that these three sentiments seem to be pretty much the same as that famous trio of Charity, Faith, and Hope, which, in the estimation of St. Paul, are the finest and greatest of spiritual gifts."

In the second place, Peirce makes some illuminating comments pertaining to the paradox which seems to arise from his position. His "realism" asserts that any assumption of an inexplicable ultimate, a final unknowable, is self-contradictory and yet seems to lead to the view that any determination of the real must presuppose an inexplicable assumption, an ultimately unknowable fact, that intellectual inquiry will continue indefinitely. After mentioning that "there can be no reasons, for thinking that the human race, or any intellectual race, will exist forever," Peirce declares, "on the other hand, there can be no reason against it" (2.654), and then he adds in a footnote: "I do not here admit an absolutely unknowable. Evidence could show us what would probably be the case after any given lapse of time; and though a subsequent time might be assigned which that evidence might not cover, yet further evidence would cover it."

This comment hardly affords a satisfactory answer to the paradox. Even if there were some conceivable means of estimating the probability that intellectual inquiry will continue beyond, say, ten, twenty, or thirty million years from now, the estimate would have no bearing on the assumption in question. To exist *forever* means to exist infinitely longer than any finite time, and the ultimate unknowability of the assumption is not diminished by evidence covering a finite period, however long. Peirce cannot claim here, as he can in those cases where the end of inquiry is the true value of a probability ratio, that some amount of finite inquiry is sure to yield an approximation of the true value. The probability that A will happen, given B, can be approximated, but not the probability that A alone will continue to happen indefinitely, regardless of the conditions.

Yet, in defense of Peirce, it must be observed that his realism does not force him to admit an unknowable in the sense he himself alleged to be "nominalistic" and self-contradictory. In the latter case, it is admitted that the *objects* of inquiry, the very things supposed to be knowable, are nevertheless, as things in themselves, ultimately unknowable. But, for Peirce, the objects have no status apart from being the outcome of inquiry and are thus ultimately knowable; it is only the fact of the infinite process of inquiry itself that remains unknowable. The paradox actually does not arise until this fact is viewed as an object as well as a precondition of inquiry. The utterly unique status of the assumption of this fact, already noted in the previous discussion as essential to any solution of the paradox, thus demands, first of all, that the fact be a precondition and not an object of inquiry. Peirce's contention that his ultimate requirement of logic is a matter of emotion and sentiment, with reasons neither for nor against it, is entirely in accord with this demand; but the position taken in his footnote that evidence is always possible for the existence of inquiry beyond any assignable date involves precisely the view which gives rise to the paradox. Further attempts by Peirce to extricate himself from the paradox must thus come from development of the former, rather than the latter, course.

C. The last four essays of the *Search for a Method* follow the conception of probability outlined in the preceding paper and are thus subject from a philosophic point of view to the criticisms given in the notes of 1910. While the first of these essays, *The Probability of Induction* (2, Bk. III, chap. 7), is of considerable importance for any discussion of Peirce's doctrine of probability, the issues with which it is mainly concerned are not those of the present study. But several points of crucial significance for Peirce's philosophy are treated in the next essay, *The Order of Nature* (6, Bk. II, chap. 1),[4] which seems by far the most important of the group for the general development of his thought.

In the first part of this essay Peirce attempts to give logico-mathematical arguments to show that "a contradiction is involved in the very idea of chance-world" (6.404). While he had dismissed the subject in 1868 by declaring that it was impossible to specify how a chance-world should be "other than self-contradictory" (see above, p. 56), he now attempts to describe such a world mathematically and to show wherein the contradiction arises. The details of the arguments are unimportant from the standpoint of his main philosophic position, but the analysis as a whole leads to a fundamental problem. Even if order and uniformity are demonstrated of every possible universe, how do they come to be ingredients of actual experience? The remainder of *The Order of Nature* is devoted to various aspects of this problem and constitutes Peirce's first explicit treatment of what he later called "cosmology" or "metaphysics."

After his consideration of order and uniformity in the realm of logical possibilities, Peirce remarks: "In order to descend from this abstract point of view, it is requisite to consider the characters of things as relative to the perceptions and active powers of living beings" (6.406). From this way of regarding the situation, the order perceived in an experience is directly proportionate to the intelligence by which that experience is apprehended. Then, "a world of chance is simply our actual world viewed from the standpoint of an animal at the very vanishing-point of intelligence," and "the interest which the uniformities of Nature have for an animal measures his place in the scale of intelligence." Any explanation of how valid inductions can occur in actual inquiry must thus take account of mind or intelligence as an indispensable factor in the process of discovery. This is apparent, Peirce believes, from the fact that "induction only has its full force when the character concerned has been designated before examining the sample" (6.413). "If the character be not previously designated, then a sample in which it is found to be prevalent can only serve to suggest that it *may be* prevalent in the whole class" (6.409). A genuine inductive inference can come only after further random samplings have been made and the character in question, now already designated, is checked for its continued prevalence. Inquiry, in other words, is a process always involving conjointly organism and environment, or mind and nature, so that the order or uniformity discovered must be the result of both factors.

Mill's principle of the uniformity of nature as an explanation of valid induction is again open to criticism. In 1868 Peirce had declared the principle vitiated because it was forced to presuppose a world without order as logically possible (see above, p. 57). From a cosmological or metaphysical standpoint, he now finds three "imperfections" in the doctrine. The basis for all three lies in the fact that Mill attempts to explain order as a characteristic of the environment alone, without reference

92

to the factor of mind or intelligence in the organism. In the first place, to assume that absolute uniformity exists in nature hardly accounts for those inferences "where the conclusion, instead of being that a certain event uniformly happens under certain circumstances, is precisely that it does not uniformly occur, but only happens in a certain proportion of cases" (6.411). When uniformity, on the contrary, is regarded as the outgrowth of inquiry resulting from the conjoint activity of organism and environment, degrees of uniformity are quite possible, and these inferences do not present a special problem. In the second place, "if the uniformity of Nature were the sole warrant of induction, we should have no right to draw one in regard to a character whose constancy we knew nothing about" (6.412). That is, to take Mill's example, though all swans observed have been white, the inference that all swans are white is invalid if the constancy of color as a generic character is unknown. The *logical* validity of certain inductions is thus made contingent upon previous *factual* knowledge. With Peirce's conception of uniformity, on the other hand, the inductive inference that all members of a collection are of a certain color when every known sample is of that color always remains logically valid, though the conclusion may be proved false by subsequent inquiry. The third imperfection comprises the "fatal disadvantage" of Mill's doctrine, as Peirce interprets it. The "conditions which really are essential to the validity of inductions" are "overlooked," with the result that nothing is made clear concerning the "proper method of induction" (6.413). For Mill's attempt to make uniformity a characteristic of the environment alone takes no account whatever of the necessity for designating the character concerned before sampling is begun.

Peirce turns next to the principle that "every event must have a cause." Unlike Mill's "uniformity of nature," this principle, as Peirce interprets and accepts it, is in no sense an assumption about the nature of reality. Its "truth" "follows immediately from the theorem that there is a character peculiar to every possible group of objects" (6.414). Peirce already referred to this theorem in the first part of his paper where he attempted to demonstrate mathematically that a chance-world is logically impossible (cf. 6.402). From the explanation he there gives the theorem is simply the analytic proposition that every class has a defining property which is possessed by all its members and by nothing else. In the realm of logical possibilities, therefore, every event has a cause in the sense that it always possesses, in common with other possible events, some property which makes it the peculiar sort of event that it is. When this principle is applied to the realm of actual inquiry, it seems equivalent to the assertion that "it is always possible to discover, by investigation sufficiently prolonged, a class of which the same predicate may be affirmed universally" (6.414). The word "cause" is to be understood here as meaning a statement of the conditions which must obtain whenever a particular sort of event occurs—the conditions which make up the property of being an event of such and such a kind. In terms common to Peirce's later analysis of the problem, this is "cause" in the sense of the *law* which the event exemplifies;[5] it is not "cause" in the sense of referring to the particular antecedent *facts* which produced a given occurrence of the event—a given exemplification of the law.

Since these antecedent facts always admit of infinite variation, there arises the crucial problem of distinguishing in the course of actual inquiry between those facts required only for particular occurrences of the event and those facts which make up the conditions of the event itself. Peirce comments on this circumstance: "That we ever do discover the precise causes of things, that any induction whatever is absolutely without exception, is what we have no right to assume. On the contrary, it is an easy corollary, from the theorem just referred to, that every empirical rule has an exception" (6.416). While there is no explanation in Peirce's essay of how this corollary follows from the theorem, the cardinal point is certainly the relation of the formal and mathematical to the empirical. The definitive property of a class can be determined with absolute certainty

94

only by accounting for every member of that class. If the members are infinite in number, the possibility of the determination can still be demonstrated mathematically, but it cannot be carried out empirically. Since the number of times an event of a given sort may actually occur can always exceed any finite number, the empirical determination must be qualified in the manner indicated by Peirce's phrase "investigation sufficiently prolonged." But as there is never assurance that any finite time is sufficiently long, no empirical rule can be regarded as holding without exception. Now, inasmuch as order in the actual universe, upon Peirce's theory, is simply an outgrowth of inquiry, this relation between the formal and empirical permits the following two assertions. (1) The universe can never be conceived as essentially disordered or as having any characteristics that must remain forever undiscovered. (2) On the other hand, at no stage in the actual pursuit of inquiry can it be maintained that everything in the universe has been subsumed under laws and that nothing real can happen according to chance.

This manner of accounting for inquiry and uniformity seems to require special assumptions in order to explain how something approaching a universally true induction can actually occur at a finite stage of investigation. If the possibilities of variation are always infinite, how can a finite consideration ever come near the final outcome? Peirce remarks: "Though there exists a cause for every event, and that of a kind which is capable of being discovered, yet if there be nothing to guide us to the discovery; if we have to hunt among all the events in the world without any scent; . . . then the discovery would have no chance of ever getting made" (6.415). His further comments indicate the intention of this last clause should be: the discovery would have little or no chance, since its realization would be entirely accidental. For he continues: "But there are certain of our inductions which present an approach to universality so extraordinary that, even if we are to suppose that they are not strictly universal truths, we cannot possibly think that they have been reached merely by accident" (6.416). After considering

95

some examples of these inductions, such as the conceptions of space and time and the law of gravitation, Peirce concludes: "It seems incontestable, therefore, that the mind of man is strongly adapted to the comprehension of the world; at least so far as this goes, that certain conceptions, highly important for such a comprehension, naturally arise in his mind; and, without such a tendency, the mind could never have had any development at all" (6.417). This adaptation of mind to nature might be explained by a theory of evolution as the result of natural selection, but Peirce here merely suggests such an explanation and makes no attempt to apply it.

The closing remarks in *The Order of Nature* are in praise of a mechanical explanation of the universe and inclined to favor the view that science and theology are hostile. "Mystical theories" are "all those which have no possibility of being mechanically explained," and Peirce declares: "To the mind of a physicist there ought to be a strong presumption against every mystical theory; and therefore it seems to me that those scientific men who have sought to make out that science was not hostile to theology have not been so clear-sighted as their opponents" (6.425).

D. In this brief treatment of metaphysical or cosmological problems Peirce succeeded in at least indicating the essential elements of the views he continued to maintain on the subject. Yet any means of integrating these elements into a consistent philosophic position is still wanting. His account of order and uniformity requires *mind* as a fundamental ingredient of the real, but there is no mention of whether this is mind as a property of an organism (and perhaps capable of mechanical explanation) or whether it is mind in some metaphysical sense. The former alternative would be difficult to square with his strictures against "nominalistic" assumptions of an ultimate subject, while the latter appears contrary to his pragmatism. What seems to be his denial of complete determinism, based on the corollary that every empirical rule has an exception, does not make explicit whether the indeterminateness lies merely in the fallibility of knowledge or in the universe itself. Problems arise with either supposition, since the universe can never be conceived as disordered, and yet reality can only be known as the outcome of finite inquiry.

The immediate link between these early metaphysical speculations and Peirce's doctrines in the papers preceding them may be found in his analysis of the mathematics of probability and the logic of induction. The self-contradictoriness of a metaphysics which is forced to entertain the possibility of a thoroughly chance-world followed immediately from that analysis. The necessity for regarding mind as an indispensable factor in any explanation of order in the actual universe could be seen from the fact that a logical requirement for valid induction was an intelligent designation of the characters concerned before sampling began. Some sort of indeterminateness in our knowledge of the actual world became inevitable because the exhaustiveness required for mathematical certainty could never be achieved in finite experience. The integration of all these factors into a consistent philosophic position would depend on the way in which the results of purely mathematical and logical analyses can be said to determine characteristics of reality. Peirce's stand on this issue in his later writings involves such complications as his distinction between logic as the "simplest mathematics" and as the normative science which prescribes rules for the attainment of truth. His theory of the categories plays of course a central role in this development of his philosophy. The last two essays of the *Search for a Method* deal with aspects of probability and induction which bear somewhat on this subject of the categories and the general relation of mathematics to reality.

Essay XIII, *Deduction, Induction and Hypothesis* (2, Bk. III, chap. 5), was originally the sixth and last paper of the series "Illustrations of the Logic of Science" and is concerned primarily with developments of Peirce's early classification of arguments. His three genera of arguments, as discussed above in chapter i, were presented as derived from the three figures

97

of the syllogism and named in the manner indicated by the title of this later essay; they were identified shortly afterward in the *On a New List of Categories* as expressions of the three fundamental forms of signification, but their relation to the figures of the syllogism remained unaltered. Peirce now regards the relation of hypothesis and induction to the second and third figures, respectively, as arising from an "artificial conception" which overlooks the fact that synthetic reasoning, unlike any syllogism properly so called, never yields a necessary conclusion (cf. 2.626–31). While the categories are not mentioned explicitly in the essay, some of Peirce's remarks on the difference between induction and hypothesis become contrary to his original statement of how the genera of arguments expressed the categories. If the three genera are interpreted by means of "an important psychological or rather physiological difference in the mode of apprehending facts," it may be said that "hypothesis produces the *sensuous* element of thought, and induction the *habitual* element" (2.643). When Peirce in his later writings related these two elements to the categories, "habit" was always given as an instance of thirdness. But in the original treatment of the genera of arguments deduction expressed a thirdness, since its premises formed a symbol of the conclusion, while those of induction gave only an index, so that it expressed a secondness. In the present treatment Peirce declares: "As for deduction, which adds nothing to the premises, but only out of the various facts represented in the premises selects one and brings attention down to it, this may be considered as the logical formula for paying attention, which is the *volitional* element of thought, and corresponds to nervous discharge in the sphere of physiology" (2.643). Inasmuch as volition was later given as an instance of secondness (cf., e.g., 1.332–34), deduction and induction have now changed places with respect to the categories they express.

Peirce's remarks here, as indicating the direction of his subsequent thought, are significant in two respects. First, the relation of the genera of arguments to the figures of the syllogism is recognized as accidental. Second, by considering these genera, which had already been related to the categories in one way, as also reflecting a "difference in the mode of apprehending facts," the possibility is pointed out for a theory which connects them with the categories in another way; and, as this possibility is developed, the consequent differences in the way of relating the genera of arguments to the categories inevitably raises questions about the ultimate function of the categories and the relative priority of logical and psychological analyses.[6]

The last essay in the *Search for a Method* is *A Theory of Probable Inference* (2, Bk. III, chap. 8), which first appeared in the Johns Hopkins *Studies in Logic* (1883). With the figures of the syllogism no longer fundamental in determining types of arguments, Peirce now becomes concerned with new forms of classification for probable inferences. He develops for the first time the notions of "probable deduction" and "statistical deduction" and regards them as specifically, though not generically, different from the syllogism. His analysis of these forms of deduction and their relation to induction presents a complicated problem which is beyond the scope of the present study. The concluding portion of the essay contains some remarks on the question of uniformity in nature and the general problem of relating mathematics to reality. One point of considerable importance stands out perhaps more prominently than in the earlier discussions. Even though a thoroughly disordered world is mathematically impossible, Peirce now admits that nevertheless some factual assumption about the universe is necessary to account for valid induction. "I grant, then, that even upon my theory some fact has to be supposed to make induction and hypothesis valid processes; namely, it is supposed that the supernal powers withhold their hands and let me alone, and that no mysterious uniformity or adaptation interferes with the action of chance" (2.749). Peirce hastens to point out that this "negative fact" "plays a totally different part" in his theory from that played by the positive facts assumed in other accounts of valid induction. Instead of claiming that inductions become valid because the universe is in fact ordered rather than disordered, Peirce's theory declares merely that, whatever may be the positive character of the universe, inductions will eventually yield truth so long as no special circumstances intervene to make the practice of induction impossible.

While Peirce's admission here may be primarily rhetorical and unimportant in itself, it clearly draws attention to a crucial but as yet unsettled issue in his general philosophic position. The assumption of the nonexistence of a *malin genie* might seem unnecessary from the standpoint of his argument of 1868 that a universe in which men were forever fated to be deceived in their inductions is logically impossible (see above, p. 59). But if the earlier argument is understood to show merely that inquiry as a *logical* process is such as eventually to disclose all factors that might temporarily cause deception, the assumption in question amounts to nothing more than the recognition that the discovery of order in the actual universe supposes inquiry as an *existential* process. The issue to be settled is simply that of determining how far order in the universe can be explained cosmologically or metaphysically without postulating the existence of inquiry. The question has a unique significance for Peirce's philosophy, of course, since reality has so far been given no status apart from being the outcome of inquiry.

4. CONCLUSIONS FROM THE SEARCH FOR A METHOD

As remarked at the close of the preceding chapter, the first six essays of the *Search for a Method* (the last of which was published in 1869) gave rise to certain problems which required further investigation before anything like a complete statement of Peirce's philosophy could be given. It was suggested that these problems could be grouped conveniently under three main headings: first, the relation of the formal to the material or factual conditions of valid induction; second, the dependence of ontology on logic and metaphysical questions, such as the relation of mind to reality; and, finally, the nature of man as an inquiring organism. The extremely close connection between

100

these three groups of problems as well as the treatment which Pierce has given them up to this point in the development of his philosophy may be indicated in the following summary considerations.

The next six essays of the *Search for a Method* were published eight to nine years after the preceding ones, and in the intervening years Peirce's principal work was in the field of formal logic, especially the logic of relatives. In his paper of 1870 on this topic the formal validity of the syllogism is exhibited as depending on the transitive character of certain relations (cf. 3.66 and 3.148–49), and the question thus arises as to the precise sense in which logical principles can be explained formally in themselves apart from their function in the actual process of inquiry. Despite his work in formal logic before he wrote the remaining essays, Peirce can hardly be said to have settled this question in the latter part of his *Search for a Method*, although some further complications of the problem are clearly indicated. In the essays dealing with probability, logic and mathematics were seen to be intimately connected, and, aside from explaining the nature of this connection, Peirce is left with the question whether the ultimate explanation of mathematics is to be found in its purely formal character or in the manner of its evolution in the actual course of inquiry.

In the subsequent development of his philosophy, Peirce came to regard mathematics generally and formal logic, or "the simplest mathematics," as comprising an independent discipline whose essential feature lies in the unique character of its observations. Peirce had, in fact, expressed at least the basic idea of this position as early as 1869, though he did not incorporate it in the essays of his *Search for a Method*. In his "Lectures on British Logicians," delivered at Harvard in 1869, he remarked in Lecture I:

Now it is plainly not an essential part of this [the scientific] method in general that the tests were made by the observation of natural objects. For the immense progress which modern mathematics has made is also to be explained by the same intense interest in testing general propositions by particular cases—only the tests were applied by means of particular demonstrations. This is observation, still, for as the great mathematician Gauss has declared—algebra is a science of the eye, only it is observation of artificial objects and of a highly recondite character [1.34].

This passage suggests an explanation of mathematics with reference to its subject matter, to what is observed, rather than to the manner in which mathematical forms arise in the evolution of human inquiry. While the suggestion seems in general accord with the approach to logic adopted in the first essay of the *Search for a Method*, where the principles for the classification of arguments were to be found in the operations of substitution performed on the premises laid down, Peirce's concern in the later essays with the actual process of inquiry seems to have inclined him toward the other form of explanation. In this sense, logico-mathematical forms would be explained as the expression of habits developed in the inquiring organism. The paper of 1880 *On the Algebra of Logic* represents Peirce's most thoroughgoing attempt to work out such an explanation, and his comment of 1903 on the first two parts of this paper reflects clearly his later position that pure mathematics is not to be explained ultimately with reference to "the general laws of nervous action." His comment is: "The whole of these two parts is bad, first, because it does not treat the subject from the point of view of pure mathematics, as it should have done; and second because the fundamental propositions are not made out" (3.154, n. 1). This does not mean, of course, that an explanation of logico-mathematical forms as arising from the habits of the human organism is simply wrong but only that a paper which professes to give "the reasons of the fundamental formulae" of logical algebra must not adopt this point of view.

Both these explanations of logic are certainly involved in the cosmology sketched in *The Order of Nature*. If the presence of order in the universe is to be asserted without special assumptions as to the course of nature, then the logico-mathematical principles required for the demonstration that a completely disordered world is self-contradictory must themselves be independent of anything that may have actually happened in the universe. Yet, in accord with Peirce's pragmatic definition of reality, it would seem that the principles of logical induction must be in some way indigenous to the process of actual inquiry if the order in the universe can be called real. For, in so far as inquiry does not follow the rules of induction, there can never be the agreement necessary to establish any determination of reality. The dependence of ontology on logic and metaphysical problems, such as that of accounting for order in the universe and of relating mind to reality, would thus seem to require for their final resolution some means of interrelating the purely formal character of mathematics and logic with the nature of man as an inquiring organism. As suggested in *The Fixation of Belief*, ethical and biological characteristics of man are both involved; the rules of logic provide norms which man ought to follow as well as being habits which he may naturally develop in the course of inquiry. The apparent paradox arising from Peirce's ultimate assumption that human inquiry will continue indefinitely clearly points to the priority of the ethical factor, since only in this sense did it seem at all possible to avoid a contradiction. The assumption viewed ethically as an ultimate sentiment or hope may not itself constitute an object of inquiry in the sense that man's biological nature does. But then there is also the problem, apparent in *How To Make Our Ideas Clear*, of a criterion of meaning as well as of truth. When meaning was restricted in accordance with the pragmatic maxim to the third grade of clearness, it appeared difficult to give a meaningful account of ontology; and, similarly, an ethical as opposed to a biological account of man would seem hardly feasible with strict adherence to Peirce's first statement of a pragmatic criterion of meaning. However, Peirce had first to work out his metaphysical conception of mind as a factor manifested in natural phenomena and to develop its consequences for the problem of chance and necessity before he became concerned with revising his criterion of meaning and considering the need for a priority of ethics.

PART II

IV

Scientific Metaphysics

THE most extensive single treatment of metaphysical problems in the Collected Papers is to be found in a series of five essays which originally appeared in The Monist, 1891–93. While the principal doctrines of metaphysics which Peirce continued to hold are presented here in some form, most of them underwent considerable alteration in his later writings. In fact, as Peirce later worked out his position, even the character of metaphysics as a scientific discipline is not adequately appreciated in these essays. For they give no consideration to philosophic problems that are prior to those of scientific metaphysics and suffer from an attempt to accomplish too much by an observational method too narrowly conceived. Yet in so far as Peirce left no subsequent work on metaphysics which systematically goes over all the problems again, but only indicated his revisions from time to time in writings on various aspects of the problems, these five essays afford perhaps the best introduction to a study of his metaphysics.

The first three sections of the present chapter constitute an examination of these essays in their order of publication. References are given both to Peirce's earlier and to Peirce's later writings for clarification of the issues. The final section of the chapter turns to the status of metaphysics among the various parts of philosophy recognized in Peirce's classification of the sciences.

1. THE CONSTRUCTION OF A PHILOSOPHY
OBJECTIVE IDEALISM AND TYCHISM

A. In the first essay, The Architecture of Theories (6, Bk. 1, chap. 1), Peirce proposed "to make a systematic study of the conceptions out of which a philosophical theory may be built, in order to ascertain what place each conception may fitly occupy in such a theory, and to what uses it is adapted" (6.9). As the title of the paper suggests, this proposal stems from a conviction that Kant was fundamentally right in holding that philosophic "systems ought to be constructed architectonically." Peirce feels that previous philosophers did not begin their attempts to construct a system with an adequate grasp of all the elementary conceptions requisite for the architecture of philosophy and that the fruits of their labors have thus remained subject to one or the other of two limitations. There have been the "one-idea'd philosophies," which have resulted when a single idea "which has been found interesting and fruitful has been adopted, developed, and forced to yield explanations of all sorts of phenomena" (6.7). Such philosophies have been "not so much results of historical evolution, as happy thoughts which have accidentally occurred to their authors." On the other hand, "the remaining systems of philosophy have been of the nature of reforms, sometimes amounting to radical revolutions, suggested by certain difficulties which have been found to beset systems previously in vogue" (6.8). Yet these revolutionary philosophies have only "partially" rebuilt the house because their repairs "have generally not been sufficiently thorough-going," nor have they taken "sufficient pains . . . to bring the additions into deep harmony with the really sound parts of the old structure" (6.8).

This summary estimation of the achievements of past philosophies and the proposal for improving the situation suggest a pattern already remarked in Peirce's thought. Each of the "one idea'd" systems stands essentially by itself, the result of a happy accident on the part of its author, and unrelated to other systems through the historical evolution of ideas. While its claim to being systematic would presuppose that its ideas could be grasped with the second grade of clearness, it would seem as a whole analogous to the first grade. For its principal characteristic as a system would seem to consist in pushing forward a

single, familiar idea as an explanation for "all sorts of phenomena." Each of the revolutionary philosophies, on the contrary,
stands essentially related to others which it seeks to reform and
is thus part of a historical evolution. In so far as its distinguishing mark as a system consists in the oppositions it draws between various sets of ideas, it would seem analogous to the
second grade of clearness. Finally, the "systematic study" which
Peirce himself proposed to make of the basic conceptions necessary for an adequate philosophy supplies the most likely analogue to the third grade. For not only is each conception to be
related to others so that its "place" in the system may be determined, but also the "uses" to which the conception is adapted
must be ascertained.

It does not seem important to urge the point that Peirce actually followed his categories, as they are manifested in his three
grades of clearness, in this discussion of the ways in which philosophic systems have been and ought to be constructed. The
observations he makes here are not incorporated in his more
extensive analyses of previous systems in the history of philosophy. It is important, however, to notice that Peirce now con-
ceives of philosophy as an enterprise which must begin by taking its basic conceptions from other sciences. These conceptions include methods as well as principles, and the architectonic task of philosophy seems tantamount to fashioning all
human knowledge into a single edifice. All principles susceptible of explanation must be explained, and, once ideas have
been made clear, their truth must be tested scientifically in order to achieve a fixation of belief. Peirce was thus led in The
Architecture of Theories to end with rather extravagant claims
for his "cosmogonic" philosophy of "objective idealism." "That
idea has been worked out by me with elaboration. It accounts
for the main features of the universe as we know it—the characters of time, space, matter, force, gravitation, electricity, etc.
It predicts many more things which new observations can alone
bring to the test. May some future student go over this ground

again, and have the leisure to give his results to the world" (6.34).

B. While his proposed systematic study of basic conceptions in philosophy would at best involve "a complete survey of human knowledge," since "the adequate treatment of this single point would fill a volume," Peirce decides instead to "endeavor to illustrate" his "meaning by glancing at several sciences and indicating conceptions in them serviceable for philosophy" (6.9).

The "first step taken by modern scientific thought" was "the inauguration of dynamics by Galileo" (6.10), and the development of this science, "by Huygens and others, led to those modern conceptions of *Force and Law*, which have revolutionized the intellectual world" (6.11). The analysis which Peirce now gives of these conceptions is quite different from his later treatment. He here regards laws as simply "uniformities" and as "precisely the sort of facts that need to be accounted for" (6.12). Thus, "that a pitched coin should sometimes turn up heads and sometimes tails calls for no particular explanation; but if it shows heads every time, we wish to know how this result has been brought about. Law is par *excellence* the thing that wants a reason." The reason, of course, would consist in an explanation of the force which brought about the uniform action of the coin. In general, this amounts to specifying certain facts from which the facts to be explained follow as a logical consequence.[1] There is thus in this context no ultimate distinction between *force* and *law*, since both are always sets of facts, differing only as antecedent and consequent. When Peirce came to distinguish these a few years later, he developed the notion of "force without law or reason, *brute* force" (1.427), and, in this sense, law appears to be the same as reason rather than that which par excellence requires a reason. Law, in other words, becomes thirdness rather than secondness.[2]

Peirce hopes to accomplish two apparently different things in the explanation he here seeks of law. On the one hand, a reason is to be given for our knowledge of the law—for the cir-

110

cumstance that our minds were led to apprehend it—and, on the other hand, the rise of the law itself as a fact of the universe is to be accounted for. In some cases, as with the simple laws of dynamics, it seems possible to have entirely separate explanations of these factors. For example, since "a body left to its own inertia moves in a straight line, and a straight line appears to us the simplest of curves," though "in *itself* no curve is simpler than another" (6.10), our apprehension of the law of inertia could be explained by our tendency to regard its action as simple and "natural." It would then be a further question why the law in the first place came to be a fact of the universe. Yet the process of explanation cannot stop here, for it must still be asked why our minds came to regard this law as simple and natural, however the law may itself have become a fact of the universe. In answer to this, it could be said that "our minds having been formed under the influence of phenomena governed by the laws of mechanics, certain conceptions entering into those laws become implanted in our minds, so that we readily guess at what the laws are." But this means, in other words, that our minds are nothing but further facts or laws in the universe and that a final explanation of facts or laws in general will account for those special ones which constitute our affinity with certain other facts of nature.

The program, in short, calls for a theory of evolution which will account for everything in the universe. But to account for laws by evolution "supposes them not to be absolute, not to be obeyed precisely. It makes an element of indeterminacy, spontaneity, or absolute chance in nature" (6.13). The point is not elaborated here, and Peirce seems content to indicate from a cursory sketch of theories of evolution current at the time that chance as well as law is a conception of science serviceable for philosophy.

A third conception is discovered by glancing at psychology, where it is found that "the one primary and fundamental law of mental action consists in a tendency to generalization." "Feeling tends to spread; connections between feelings awaken

111

feelings; neighboring feelings become assimilated; ideas are apt to reproduce themselves. These are so many formulations of the one law of the growth of mind" (6.21). But the "cloudiness" of these "psychological notions may be corrected by connecting them with physiological conceptions" (6.22). When this has been done, the tendency to generalization becomes a tendency to take habits, and the physiological analogue of the law of mental action becomes "the law of habit." This law

exhibits a striking contrast to all physical laws in the character of its commands. A physical law is absolute. What it requires is an exact relation. . . . On the other hand, no exact conformity is required by the mental law. Nay, exact conformity would be in downright conflict with the law; since it would instantly crystallize thought and prevent all further formation of habit. The law of mind only makes a given feeling *more likely* to arise [6.23].

It might seem, then, that there are two basically irreducible types of law among the facts of the universe. A philosophy framed in accordance with this view Peirce describes as "a doctrine often called *monism*,[3] but which I would name *neutralism*" (6.24). Of the remaining possibilities, the position which regards "the psychical law as derived and special, the physical law alone as primordial . . . is *materialism*"; and the one which regards "the physical law as derived and special, the psychical law alone as primordial . . . is *idealism*." Since the first position renders both types of law primordial, Peirce feels that it is "sufficiently condemned by the logical maxim known as Ockham's razor." The force of this condemnation depends of course on the fact that one of the remaining possibilities is satisfactory. The second position Peirce considers "quite as repugnant to scientific logic as to common sense," "since it requires us to suppose that a certain kind of mechanism will feel, which would be a hypothesis absolutely irreducible to reason—an ultimate, inexplicable regularity; while the only possible justification of any theory is that it should make things clear and reasonable." The third position, however, appears satisfactory, since physical laws seem explicable as habits. Accordingly, "the one intelligible

112

theory of the universe is that of objective idealism, that matter is effete mind, inveterate habits becoming physical laws" (6.25).

In the final paragraphs of *The Architecture of Theories*, Peirce glances at two other sciences to illustrate conceptions serviceable for philosophy. Mathematics, he explains, "is very instructive" in its manner of generalization (6.26). Thus, in the geometry of perspective, "generalization is not bound down to sensuous images," so that one may, for example, "talk of the parts of lines at an infinite distance as points." Similar instances of such generalization are taken from theories of measurement and space. In addition to this conception of generalization, mathematics also affords the notion of continuity, which has great importance for philosophy. The notion is merely mentioned here, but not illustrated, as it ought to be, Peirce says, if he had "more space" (6.31). While he insisted throughout his later writings that true generality is but a rudimentary form of continuity, his failure here to associate the two conceptions in any way indicates clearly he had yet to make a careful analysis of thirdness.

Logic is the last science considered as a source of philosophic conceptions, though among its "many principles . . . which find their application in Philosophy," only one is noted (6.32). This is the principle that yields the categories, which are characterized as "conceptions so very broad and consequently indefinite that they are hard to seize and may be easily overlooked." "To illustrate these ideas," Peirce "will show how they enter into those we have been considering." He does this merely by listing some triads formed from conceptions prominent in science, the most important of which seems to be that of chance, law, and the tendency to take habits.

While the categories, even in this brief illustration of them, appear to be conceptions that afford principles of order rather than materials, Peirce gives no indication that such a distinction should be made. He begins the next paragraph by remarking, "Such are the materials out of which chiefly a philosophical theory ought to be built, in order to represent the state of

113

knowledge to which the nineteenth century has brought us" (6.33). A metaphysics "constructed from those conceptions" "would be a Cosmogonic Philosophy."

It would suppose that in the beginning—infinitely remote—there was a chaos of unpersonalized feeling, which being without connection or regularity would properly be without existence. This feeling, sporting here and there in pure arbitrariness, would have started the germ of a generalizing tendency.... Thus, the tendency to habit would be started; and from this, with the other principles of evolution, all the regularities of the universe would be evolved. At any time, however, an element of pure chance survives and will remain until the world becomes an absolutely perfect, rational, and symmetrical system, in which mind is at last crystallized in the infinitely distant future.

The remaining four essays of the series comprise in effect a collection of footnotes to this sketch of a cosmogonic philosophy. Although they purport to deal with the principal factors needed in developing such a metaphysics, they draw no fundamental distinction between those conceptions such as that of generalization, which reflect a method of looking at the universe, and those, such as that of the tendency to habit, which are the results of observation of the universe. In the analysis suggested by Peirce's glance at psychology, the tendency to generalization was a cloudy notion to be clarified by reference to its outward manifestation, its physiological analogue, which was the tendency to take habits. The same point of view is apparent in the circumstance that our apprehension of a scientific law as well as the status of the law itself as a fact of the universe is to be explained ultimately by a theory of evolution. In short, it seems as though Peirce is here trying to regard the activities of the architect as part of the architecture—to include the precepts of construction among the materials to be arranged in the building.

C. The second essay of the present series, *The Doctrine of Necessity Examined* (6, Bk. I, chap. 2), undertakes "to examine the common belief that every single fact in the universe is precisely determined by law" (6.36). Peirce takes the doctrine

114

quite literally as precluding even the minutest element of chance at any time in the course of the universe, past, present, or future. "Thus, given the state of the universe in the original nebula, and given the laws of mechanics, a sufficiently powerful mind could deduce from these data the precise form of every curlicue of every letter I am now writing" (6.37).

The first set of arguments against this position are designed to show that "the principle of universal necessity cannot be defended as being a postulate of reasoning" (6.43). In essence, the arguments constitute a recapitulation of points already made in the essays of the *Search for a Method.* The logical validity of induction can be accounted for by the nature of the process of random sampling for predesignated characters without a special postulate about the uniformity of the actual universe. Peirce does not mention here the point he urged so strongly in his earlier essays, that since "a contradiction is involved in the very idea of a chance-world," a postulate of the uniformity of nature is absurd because it assumes that uniformity distinguished one possible world from another (see above, pp. 56–57, 91). When Paul Carus in 1893 suggested that this point was inconsistent with Peirce's later views on the reality of chance, Peirce replied that "this is in entire harmony with my present position" (6.609) and cited a sentence at the close of his *The Architecture of Theories* to support his contention: "It [Peirce's philosophy] would suppose that in the beginning—infinitely remote—there was a chaos of unpersonalized feeling, which being without connection or regularity would properly be without existence" (6.33). While this does say that a thoroughly chance-world would be nonexistent, it seems to present a rather striking difficulty. How can the present logically consistent universe of science have evolved from a nonentity, from a logical impossibility, even if the beginning were infinitely remote? Perhaps an indication of Peirce's answer was given earlier in his reply to Carus:

Everybody is familiar with the fact that chance has laws, and that statistical results follow therefrom. Very well: I do not propose to

115

explain anything as due to the action of chance, that is, as being lawless. . . . But I only propose to explain the regularities of nature as consequences of the only uniformity, or general fact, there was in the chaos, namely, the general absence of any determinate law [6.606].

But this amounts to characterizing the original chaos as simply a state of utter random in which everything conceivable would have an equal chance of happening. Such a state comes very close to what Peirce had called in 1878 "the simplest order" (5.345). The only difference would seem to be that, while the latter is limited to a universe in which everything conceivable would continue to happen with equal frequency, the former includes among the things conceivable a tendency for certain characters to start appearing with greater frequency than others —a tendency, in other words, to take habits. It is necessary, of course, to assume an infinite amount of time before such a tendency would be sure to turn up among the infinite number of conceivable things, but Peirce has assumed a "beginning infinitely remote."[4] The difficulty is rather in explaining why the primordial state so characterized "would properly be without existence." For it does possess the regularity prescribed by the laws of chance, while, according to Peirce's position of 1878, a "chance-world" was necessarily nonexistent only when it was specified as beyond the laws of chance and hence self-contradictory. There must be some way of distinguishing between possibility, existence, and law, and in these terms Peirce later came to speak of his cosmic evolution as giving rise to three universes.

The next set of arguments are directed against the position that the principle of universal necessity may be "proved to be true, or at least rendered highly probable, by observation of nature" (6.43). Instead of maintaining, as he did in The Order of Nature, that the principle that "every empirical rule has an exception" can be demonstrated mathematically (see above, p. 94), Peirce rests his case here against the "necessitarians" entirely on empirical considerations. "For the essence of the necessitarian position is that certain continuous quantities have certain exact values. Now, how can observation determine the value of such a quantity with a probable error absolutely *nil?* To one who is behind the scenes . . . the idea of mathematical exactitude being demonstrated in the laboratory will appear simply ridiculous" (6.44). While this statement must be slightly modified in order to deal with continuous quantities that are "discontinuous at one or at two limits," this in no way affects the argument against necessity, since the absolute evaluation of these limits by observation is never possible (cf. 6.45).

In the last section of the essay Peirce outlines the principal features of his own doctrine, which he found "convenient to christen *tychism* (from τύχη, chance)" (6.102), and develops a point-for-point contrast with the necessitarian view. The main accomplishment is perhaps a clarification of the issues as Peirce saw them at this time. It seemed possible from the discussion of the problem in *The Order of Nature* that the absence of complete determination in every empirical rule was only the result of the inevitable fallibility of finite inquiry rather than an expression of reality, which could only be defined as the outcome of unlimited inquiry. But this possibility is now ruled out as nothing but a corollary of the theory Peirce is opposing. For the necessitarian will hold that "chance is only a name for a cause that is unknown to us" and that sufficient inquiry can always show that what is called "chance" is really necessity (6.54). This is, moreover, as Peirce interprets it, equivalent to asserting that "all the arbitrary specifications of the universe were introduced in one dose, in the beginning, if there was a beginning, and that the variety and complication of nature has always been just as much as it is now" (6.57). Tychism, on the contrary, holds that "the diversification, the specification, has been continually taking place" (6.57) and that hence "pure spontaneity or life" is "a character of the universe" (6.59). "I account for all the variety and diversity of the universe," Peirce continues, "in the only sense in which the really *sui generis* and new can be said to be accounted for."

Tychism is in complete accord with the philosophy of objective idealism sketched in the preceding essay, while necessitarianism demands a materialistic cosmology, since it "cannot logically stop short of making the whole action of the mind a part of the physical universe" (6.61). The argument against materialism (that it assumes an ultimate and inexplicable regularity) applies, then, to those who accept the principle of universal necessity. Objective idealism, on the other hand, makes "use of chance chiefly to make room for a principle of generalization, or tendency to form habits, which," it holds, "has produced all regularities" (6.63).

2. SYNECHISM: MIND AND MATTER

A. The third essay, *The Law of Mind* (6, Bk. I, chap. 5), is concerned with "the next step in the study of cosmology," which "must be to examine the general law of mental action" (6.103). The architectonic conception for the analysis is "the idea of continuity," and the resulting doctrine is called "synechism" (from συνεχής, "continuous"). While continuity in Peirce's later analyses is taken as the primary expression of thirdness, the point is of course not mentioned in the present essay or in any of the others in the series.

After remarking that his early essays on the faculties of knowledge were in effect an attempt to develop synechism, Peirce declares, "I am now able to improve upon that exposition, in which I was a little blinded by nominalistic prepossessions" (6.103). It was suggested above at the close of chapter ii that these tendencies toward nominalism centered around the issue of whether the thought-process in any sense presupposed the existence of individual things, either as subjects or as objects. Peirce does not explain here how he was blinded by nominalism in his earlier writings, and his only explicit remarks on such a position later in the essay indicate that nominalism in opposition to synechism regards consciousness as a chain of separate and distinct events inexplicably connected by relations of similarity and contiguity (cf. 6.105). But it seems hardly possible to find anything like this position in Peirce's previous analysis, and he now dismisses it as absurd in a summary of his argument. "First, then, we find that when we regard ideas from a nominalistic, individualistic, sensualistic way, the simplest facts of mind become utterly meaningless. That one idea should resemble another or influence another, or that one state of mind should so much as be thought of in another, is, from that standpoint, sheer nonsense" (6.150). The only clue as to what Peirce at this time regarded as nominalistic in his early papers seems to be the passage already quoted above at the close of chapter ii from *Man's Glassy Essence*, the next essay in the present series: "My views were, then, too nominalistic to enable me to see that every general idea has the unified living feeling of a person" (6.270). The nominalistic bias would thus be the tendency to regard a person as somehow unique and not quite the same as a general idea.

Peirce begins his consideration of this problem in *The Law of Mind* by remarking that "recent observations of double and multiple personality" have made it clear that "personality is some kind of coördination or connection of ideas" (6.155). Moreover, according to the principle of synechism, "a connection between ideas is itself a general idea," and "a general idea is a living feeling." Thus, "personality, like any general idea, is not a thing to be apprehended in an instant. It has to be lived in time; nor can any finite time embrace it in all its fullness. Yet in each infinitesimal interval it is present and living, though specially colored by the immediate feelings of that moment. Personality, so far as it is apprehended in a moment, is immediate self-consciousness" (6.155). It must also be recognized that each personality involves "a teleological harmony in ideas" and that this "is more than a mere purposive pursuit of a predeterminate end; it is a developmental teleology" (6.156). A personality as "a general idea, living and conscious now, . . . is already determinative of acts in the future to an extent to which it is not now conscious."

In this manner the thought-process itself with its clusters of feelings and general ideas affords the basis for explaining what

119

each man is as a thinking subject; a nominalistic approach, on the contrary, would seek to explain thought as an attribute of such a subject. A thoroughgoing realism would demand not only that "every person is a kind of general idea" but also the converse of this proposition. For any attempt to draw a sharp distinction between general ideas which are persons and those which are not would disrupt the continuity of the thought-process. Nor can this continuity be broken by an ultimate division between mind and matter, or ideas and their external causes. Synechism must hold that "an idea can only be affected by an idea in continuous connection with it," and hence, with respect to the external causes of ideas, "feelings are communicated to the nerves by continuity, so that there must be something like them in the excitants themselves" (6.158). Matter is thus "not completely dead, but is merely mind hidebound with habits." Finally, even an ultimate separation of one mind from another is excluded by such analysis. For, in virtue of its continuity with matter, mind possesses spatial extension. "Since space is continuous, it follows that there must be an immediate community of feeling between parts of mind infinitesimally near together. Without this, I believe it would have been impossible for minds external to one another ever to become coördinated, and equally impossible for any coördination to be established in the action of the nerve-matter of one brain" (6.134).

Peirce felt that this explanation of mind and personality "is forced to accept the doctrine of a personal God" (6.162) but that, in doing so, it encounters a difficulty. Because of the continuity of minds, synechism "in considering communication" "cannot but admit that if there is a personal God, we must have a direct perception of that person and indeed be in personal communication with him." Yet, "if that be the case, the question arises how it is possible that the existence of this being should ever have been doubted by anybody." The only answer Peirce says he can offer at this time is that "facts that stand before our face and eyes and stare us in the face are far from being, in all cases, the ones most easily discerned."

120

Elucidation of this answer is given in Peirce's later treatment of the problem, which will be considered below in the last section of the present chapter, but some indication as to what he now regarded as a direct perception of God appears in his reply to Carus. "The manifold diversity or specificalness, in general, which we see whenever and wherever we open our eyes, constitutes its [the universe's] liveliness, or vivacity. The perception of it is a direct, though darkling, perception of God" (6.613). In a short piece entitled *What Is Christian Faith?* published in the same year, this direct perception of the deity is characterized as "that experience with which religion sets out" and is supposed to be just as credible as one's perception of his own personality (6.436).

B. A comparison of Peirce's analysis here with that of his early essays should be of some help in forming an estimation of what he accomplished in *The Law of Mind*. The charge that his early efforts were tainted with nominalism may be balanced against the derogatory remarks he made later concerning his second exposition of synechism. A brief discussion of the notion of continuity (1906) begins with the remark: "I feel that I ought to make amends for my blundering treatment of Continuity in a paper entitled 'The Law of Mind' " (6.174). In another passage on continuity a few years later (1911), Peirce refers to "perhaps the crudest of my struggles with such subjects, a paper (regretted as soon as published) entitled 'The Law of Mind' " (6.182). Neither of these references is accompanied by an explanation of the blunders and crudities in the earlier treatment, and the positive characterization of continuity in both cases seems too cursory to afford any hints. The most likely guess is perhaps that the failure of *The Law of Mind* to associate continuity in any definite way with thirdness seemed to Peirce to infect the entire analysis. This would make the central issue that of the role of continuity in a system of philosophy and would suggest that this role is not primarily that of being a manifestation in the universe of the law of mind.[5]

In some respects the early papers of 1868 seem more in accord with this suggestion. The thought-process was characterized there principally as a process of signification, and every thought was a sign interpreted in another thought. *The Law of Mind*, however, makes no mention of thought as signification, and this fact together with the prominence here of "consciousness" rather than "thought," and "idea" rather than "cognition," may be taken as symptomatic of a fundamental difference in approach. The former analysis constituted an examination of the faculties of knowledge and was therefore concerned with the cognitive factors of mental action. But repeated application of the three references involved in any sign provided the means for distinguishing the various aspects under which any thought-sign might appear, such as feeling, sensation, and understanding. The ordering principles were thus the categories derived from logic, and the continuity of the process was presupposed in any application of these principles. The later analysis, on the other hand, attempts to find continuity in the data of psychology and is chiefly concerned with thought as consciousness rather than as an expression of knowledge. The term "idea" more than "cognition" seems capable of including an aspect of feeling, and "general idea" as a "cluster of feelings" emphasizes a connection between intellection and the stream of consciousness more than do "sign" and "symbol." To speak of one idea as "affecting another" rather than of one thought as being "interpreted in another" as in a sign again emphasizes the element of feeling over that of understanding.

Immediately after his reference ca. 1911 to *The Law of Mind* quoted above, Peirce continued: "William James, in one of his last talks with me, expressed the opinion that that paper was, perhaps, the best I had ever written. I mention this in the hope that it may lead to somebody's using what truth there may be in it, in new and far better treatment of the continuity of time and consciousness. My notion is that we directly perceive the continuity of consciousness" (6.182). This clearly suggests an explanation of continuity as a constitutive part of experience and appears to represent the approach taken in *The Law of Mind*. But when consciousness is regarded as a succession of thought-signs to be analyzed by the formal principles governing any process of signification, continuity would enter only as a regulative principle.

The latter point of view is in accord with the attitude Peirce finally developed toward his synechism. In an article on the topic for Baldwin's *Dictionary of Philosophy and Psychology* (1902), he explained: "Synechism is not an ultimate and absolute metaphysical doctrine; it is a regulative principle of logic, prescribing what sort of hypothesis is fit to be entertained and examined" (6.173). But the fact that continuity might be directly perceived in certain phenomena of immediate consciousness does not afford the basis for an explanation of its role as a precept of construction.[6] Peirce's castigations of his paper of 1892 may thus have been directed against an attempt to account for continuity only with reference to psychological data.[7] To be sure, there is a brief section (6.144–46) in *The Law of Mind* headed "Mental Law Follows the Forms of Logic," but the concern here is merely to show that the three genera of arguments have analogues in psychological phenomena. The section seems little more than a restatement of the point already made in the paper of 1878, *Deduction, Induction, and Hypothesis*, that these three genera may be interpreted by means of "an important psychological or rather physiological difference in the mode of apprehending facts" (2.643). There is no suggestion that the forms of signification which these genera reflect are fundamental for ordering the thought-process. In fact, in a passage just before the section in question Peirce reverted to the traditional notions of "subject and predicate" and abandoned his former "sign and interpretant." "We can now see what the affection of one idea by another consists in. It is that the affected idea is attached as a logical predicate to the affecting idea as subject. So when a feeling emerges into immediate consciousness, it always appears as a modification of a more or less general object already in the mind" (6.142). While it is true that Peirce had decided some years earlier in his formal logic that the relation of subject to predicate was essentially the same as that of antecedent to consequent and sign to interpretant, he makes no use of the point here. His analysis in *The Law of Mind*, then, reflects the tendency already noted in *The Architecture of Theories* to fuse regulative principles with what is to be observed by inquiry.

C. The fourth essay of the series, *Man's Glassy Essence* (6, Bk. I, chap. 9), undertakes "to elucidate, from the point of view chosen, the relation between the psychical and physical aspects of a substance" (6.238). Broadly speaking, the procedure is the inverse of that in the preceding essay. Peirce here begins with an analysis of matter and ends by arguing that it is continuous with mind. But the continuity proclaimed seems to be that between mechanical and physiological action instead of that between matter and consciousness or feeling.

Peirce propounds in the essay a "molecular theory of protoplasm" as a possible explanation of habit. The action of protoplasm described in the theory differs essentially from other "mechanical examples of actions analogous to habit" in that it "involves no forces but attractions and repulsions strictly following the law of energy" (6.261). In fact, Peirce declares, "the explanation is even too satisfactory to suit the convenience of an advocate of tychism. For it may fairly be urged that since the phenomena of habit may thus result from a purely mechanical arrangement, it is unnecessary to suppose that habit-taking is a primordial principle of the universe" (6.262). The only answer to this seems to be the main argument already advanced in favor of tychism. Without the assumption of such a primordial principle growing out of an original chaos, the laws of mechanics would remain inexplicable uniformities and could not be accounted for by evolution. The continuity between mechanical and physiological action is thus established by this assumption which regards mechanical laws as inveterate habits. The relevance of Peirce's theory of protoplasm would thus be to show the intimate connection, approaching complete identity, between the two kinds of action.

But, then, how is this continuity of actions the same as that between matter and consciousness or feeling? Peirce's reply is clearly indicated in his remarks: "Wherever chance-spontaneity is found, there in the same proportion feeling exists. In fact, chance is but the outward aspect of that which within itself is feeling" (6.265). Now the basis for maintaining that chance is the outward aspect of feeling might seem to be the pragmatic maxim, understood to mean that ideas are to be made clear by reference to externally observable effects. Yet this is hardly Peirce's intention. The closest he comes to such an application of the maxim is in *The Architecture of Theories* where he remarks that "the cloudiness of psychological notions may be corrected by connecting them with physiological conceptions," and, in this context, "feeling may be supposed to exist wherever a nerve-cell is in an excited condition" (6.22). The analysis in the present essay might then be taken as a refinement of such a position, in so far as it makes the meaning more definite by specifying that chance deviations in the more or less mechanical reactions of the nerve-cell constitute the externally observable aspect of consciousness or feeling. The only difficulty with this interpretation is simply that Peirce does not seem to regard the problem as primarily one of making ideas clear. Thus, he explains near the end of the essay:

Viewing a thing from the outside, considering its relations of action and reaction with other things, it appears as matter. Viewing it from the inside, looking at its immediate character as feeling, it appears as consciousness. These two views are combined when we remember that mechanical laws are nothing but acquired habits, like all the regularities of mind, including the tendency to take habits, itself; and that this action of habit is nothing but generalization, and generalization is nothing but the spreading of feelings [6.268].

The problem, then, is not that of making certain ideas clear but rather that of exhibiting a certain identity between two apparently different types of phenomena, both of which are unquestionably real aspects of the universe. The continuity between mechanical and physiological action is merely that between various sets of feelings viewed under a different aspect.

Precisely because of this essential identity between the two aspects, any mechanical reaction, any bit of matter, is also a feeling, and any general idea or cluster of feelings is also characterizable in material terms, even as a distribution of molecules, since "all mind more or less partakes of the nature of matter" (6.268). The external and internal points of view, with this approach to the problem, are thus to be combined as more or less complementary. But with the pragmatic maxim applied in the way suggested above, the internal would become the cloudy, subjective, and unscientific and the external alone would be acceptable. Peirce's remark about the cloudiness of psychological conceptions probably reflects his interest, manifest in the present essay, to go as far as possible toward explaining mind in material and even mechanical terms; but it is hardly to be taken as a general precept of method which would pronounce unscientific the internal point of view that was presupposed throughout most of The Law of Mind.

It will be noticed, moreover, that, with the analysis Peirce is following, these two points of view do not give rise to the epistemological issue of private versus public observation. For any formulation of this issue must presuppose individual minds not in continuous connection with one another, which would be impossible according to synechism and would lead to the "nominalistic" assumption of ultimate individuals. The external and internal views must be taken as representing different aspects of every point in the universe rather than different perspectives from an isolated point. The pragmatic maxim in this context will never take the form simply of an injunction to clarify ideas by reference to the publicly observable. As stated in Peirce's original formulation of the maxim, the reference should be to effects that "might conceivably have practical bearings," or, in other words, that might be encountered in the actual course of inquiry. There is a passage near the beginning of The Law of Mind which, while clearly from the internal point of view, seems just as clearly an application of pragmatism. "What distinct meaning can attach to saying that an idea in the past in any way affects an idea in the future, from which it is completely detached? A phrase between the assertion and the denial of which there can in no case be any sensible difference is mere gibberish" (6.106). In other words, if the continuity of consciousness is ignored and each idea is said to acquire its own character in complete detachment from all others, an inquiry into the nature of consciousness could encounter nothing to confirm or disconfirm the assertion that one idea affects another.

3. AGAPASM AND EVOLUTION

A. Peirce's failure to deal separately with the precepts of construction in his architecture of philosophy is perhaps most serious in the fifth and last essay, *Evolutionary Love* (6, Bk. I, chap. 11). Aside from a single mention of Ockham's razor in the first essay (6.24), Peirce has explicitly acknowledged only one regulative principle which he has been following in the construction of his cosmogonic philosophy. This principle, which might well be called Peirce's "hope for further explanation," is that *no fact, no regularity, can be accepted as ultimate and inexplicable.* From the prominence given the principle, both in the essays themselves and in the reply to Carus, it certainly appears to be the leading one for the whole project. The application of the pragmatic maxim considered just above is actually, in its context, a subsidiary argument designed to show the absurdity of the opposing position. Peirce remarked immediately after the passage quoted, "I will not dwell further upon this point, because it is a commonplace of philosophy" (6.106). His own position is then presented as following from the actual continuity of consciousness rather than from pragmatism. Objective idealism seemed at first to depend on the fact that physical laws could be explained as special cases of the mental law or law of habit, but not vice versa, and on the principle forbidding inexplicable ultimates. Ockham's razor then figured as another form of the petition for further explanation and was the basis for excluding neutralism. When it seemed from Peirce's theory of protoplasm that habits might in turn be explained by mechanical laws, the deciding factor in favor of tychism and a primordial habit-taking tendency was again the hope for further explanation.

A theory of evolution which would account for all facts, all laws and regularities in the universe, and at the same time presuppose only an absolute chance, an irregularity which "calls for no explanation" (cf. 6.612), would seem to be the final fulfilment of Peirce's hope. In the present essay he classifies theories of evolution current at the time into three groups. Those of Darwin and Lamarck represent the first and third groups, respectively, while those of Nägeli, Kölliker, and Weismann are mentioned as representatives of the second. The three groups are of course manifestations of the categories, and the Lamarckian theory with a new interpretation as evolution by the action of love (called *agapasm*, from ἀγάπη, "love") performs the essential function of thirdness and mediates between the other two. The categorial scheme is pushed even further, and two varieties of the second type of theory are distinguished and three of the third (6.307).

Some insight into the nature of Peirce's undertaking here may be achieved by comparing it with the analysis in his essay of 1869 on the validity of the laws of logic. Just as the latter was an attempt to explain the grounds for belief in the logical laws presupposed by all explanations, the present analysis seems like an effort to account for the natural origin of all the laws of nature. The former endeavor ended in a seemingly paradoxical situation (see above, pp. 61 ff.). The logical validity of induction was explicable only if a logically inexplicable assumption—one for which there could be no reasons—was granted. It seems easy to construct a similar paradox for the second analysis. All the laws of nature are explicable by evolution from an original chaos if the natural laws explaining this evolution are presupposed as inexplicable. Carus urged precisely this point against Peirce: "How little after all we can escape the determination of law as being a feature of the world will be seen from the fact, that the explanation for the evolution of law is presented by Mr. Peirce as being itself a law, i.e. a formula describing a regularity supposed to obtain in facts."[8]

Peirce did not refer to this statement in his reply, but it seems fairly clear from his other comments that he must have felt there was no paradox here because his theory of evolution enjoyed a unique status among laws of nature. The principal factor common to this analysis and that of the grounds of logical validity is of course the hope for further explanation, and this hope originally appeared as a corollary of Peirce's realism and his pragmatic definition of reality. Carus argued that this definition also showed the necessity for assuming at the start some inevitable regularities in the course of nature. "If the ultimate conclusion of every man concerning reality shall be the same, there must be some truth in the idea of necessity. If there is an opinion 'fated to be ultimately agreed to,' we are confronted in our representation of reality with something inevitable."[9]

When Peirce replied to this charge, he began by professing surprise that anyone should have construed his definition in such fashion. He referred to his former insistence that there can be reasons neither for nor against his ultimate assumption that intellectual inquiry will continue indefinitely and that the community will reach an ultimate conclusion for every question. "All that we are entitled to assume," he reiterated, "is in the form of a *hope* that such conclusion may be substantially reached concerning the particular questions with which our inquiries are busied" (6.610). The comments which follow throw an essentially new light on the interrelations of realism, tychism, and evolution. Peirce continued: "Such, at least, are the results to which the consideration of the doctrine of probability brings my mind irresistibly. So that the social theory of reality, far from being incompatible with tychism, inevitably leads up to that form of philosophy. Socialistic, or as I prefer to term it, agapastic ontology . . . is a natural path by which the nominalist may be led into the realistic ways of thought." Realism is then characterized as "a doctrine which declares general truths to be real —independent of the opinions of any particular collection of minds—but not to be destined, in a strictly universal, exact, and sure acceptation, to be so settled, and established." This doctrine, moreover, will lead the "agapastic ontologist" to tychism, since "to assert that general truths are objectively real, but to deny that they are strictly universal, exact, and certain, is to embrace the doctrine of absolute chance."

The fundamental point here, which was not brought out in any of the five essays, is that the evolution of natural laws is in the final sense identical with the evolution of scientific inquiry. For, in accordance with the pragmatic definition of reality, the only way a law can become real is to be established by inquiry. Inasmuch as the process of inquiry is always from the vague to the more definite, and yet laws are never confirmed as "strictly universal," chance as much as law is a real product of inquiry and may be specified as that out of which laws evolve. In this context Peirce's hope for further explanation is merely another form of his ultimate assumption of logic, that intellectual inquiry will continue indefinitely.

But this way of looking at the problem involves more than the addition of a fundamental point not made in the essays—it entails an altogether different type of analysis. Mind is now given the role of architect and inquirer, and precepts of construction rather than anything observed by inquiry must supply the ultimate principles. Any account of the evolution of scientific inquiry, when mind is viewed as determining the course of inquiry instead of remaining just another natural object, seems impossible without introducing logical and ultimately moral considerations. Mind as inquirer is essentially active, striving toward a goal which it ought to pursue; and the process of its activity is essentially rational, ordered by the logical norms it must follow if its goal is to be achieved. But, on the other hand, mind as a natural object may be explained entirely in biological terms, and its activities in the process of inquiry are but one phase of the struggle for existence in accordance

130

with some such principle as that of natural selection or the transmission of acquired characteristics.

Peirce's agapasm seems very much like an attempt to work both views of mind into a single theory of evolution. He characterizes the Darwinian theory by the moral precept, "Every individual for himself, and the Devil take the hindmost" (6.293), while he describes Lamarckian evolution as coinciding with "the action of love" (6.300), which "is fully summed up in the simple formula we call the Golden Rule" (6.288). Since "love cannot have a contrary, but must embrace what is most opposed to it, as a degenerate case of it," Lamarck's theory expanded into agapasm can thus embrace Darwinian and other types of evolution as special cases (6.304–5). Whatever Peirce may have accomplished by this fusion of biological and moral considerations, it is perhaps the reason why he felt it unnecessary to answer Carus' objection that in the end his agapasm only accounted for natural laws by assuming further natural laws. For in giving rise to moral precepts and embracing opposed theories, agapasm has hardly the same status as other laws of nature, if indeed Peirce thought of it as a law of nature at all. But, then, in its final result Peirce's attempt to explain natural laws seems to reduce to the same assumption as his earlier account of the validity of logical laws. In so far as the evolution of inquiry is in accordance with the proper "logical sentiments" and men hope for further explanation by identifying themselves with an unlimited community of inquirers, the validity of induction is assured, and the reality of the laws of nature can be accounted for.

B. The fact that Peirce never used the term "agapasm" or any of its derivatives after his reply to Carus in 1893 (at least in writings contained in the *Collected Papers*) seems fair indication that this doctrine was the least satisfactory of any advanced in the present series of essays. Although his conceptions of tychism and synechism suffered considerable alteration, his treatment of them at this time was at any rate satisfactory enough to justify retention of the names. The great difficulty

131

with agapasm is the endeavor to include entirely diverse views of mind and also of inquiry in a single account, but before proceeding with this point it seems well to turn briefly to Peirce's later views on evolution.

While his interest in explaining the laws of nature by evolution continues unabated throughout his later writings, Peirce seems to have given up the attempt to accomplish this by a theory which professed to be an assimilation, achieved by a classification that suggests his categories, of evolutionary theories current at the time. The last effort in the *Collected Papers* to distinguish three principal types of evolution manifested in the theories of Darwin and others (and the threefold classification was altered somewhat with each effort) is given in *Lessons from the History of Science*, ca. 1896 (1.103–9).[10]

In his later writings Peirce still seems to talk about evolution in three fundamentally different senses, but he does not himself explicitly enumerate them, and they in no way reflect three different contemporary theories, or even three aspects of a single theory as distinguished by his categories. In the first sense, evolution is conceived as one of the special sciences, although its precise place among them seems difficult to determine. It is given once along with geology as one of the "Retroductive Inquiries, or the Explanatory Sciences" (5.578). But its one characteristic Peirce seems most certain about is that it involves action by final causation (1.204, 1.269, 2.86), and factors like that of natural selection would constitute the efficient causation whereby the end is brought about. Thus, "natural selection is the theory of how forms come to be adaptive, that is, to be governed by a *quasi* purpose. It suggests a machinery of efficiency to bring about the end" (1.269). Peirce did not elaborate this point, but it certainly seems to imply that evolution as a part of the special sciences is a study of the means by which the process is carried on, and in this sense it presupposes a philosophic explanation of ends. While illustrating instances where questions of natural science depend on philosophy, Peirce remarked: "In biology, besides the old logico-metaphysical dispute

132

about the reality of classifications, the momentous question of evolution has unmistakable dependence on philosophy" (1.249). The other two senses in which Peirce later spoke of evolution seem to concern this dependence on philosophy.

With respect to the two views of mind mentioned above, a consideration of final causation would be necessary only when mind is viewed as inquirer, and in this case both logical and moral considerations seem to be involved. Peirce's second way of regarding evolution is an attempt to isolate the logical factor by assuming it to be objective rather than normative and culminates in what he called his "objective logic,"[11] or "logic of events." In its broadest sense, this entails a view of the cosmos as an ordered and rational process evolving toward definite ends. It is in general accord with the view of cosmic evolution presented in *The Architecture of Theories*, where agapasm was not mentioned. The study, as Peirce finally came to speak of it, presupposes three modes of being corresponding to his categories, and the being of the ends is that of thirdness. This being, properly conceived, affords the basis for explaining the rational character of the process without making it one of absolute necessity, since the reality of thirdness is that which is destined to come about on rational grounds and yet does not happen by necessity. Peirce explained in 1906, "in addition to actuality and possibility, a *third* mode of reality must be recognized in that which, as the gipsy fortune-tellers express it, is 'sure to come true,' or, as we may say, is *destined*" (4.547). He then elaborated in a footnote:

I take it that anything may fairly be said to be *destined* which is sure to come about although there is no necessitating reason for it. Thus, a pair of dice, thrown often enough, will be sure to turn up sixes sometime, although there is no necessity that they should. The probability that they will is 1: that is all. *Fate* is that special kind of *destiny* by which events are supposed to be brought about under *definite circumstances* which involve no necessitating cause for those occurrences.

The laws of nature may thus have the reality of thirdness and be destined to make their appearance in the actual evolution of events, although this appearance is not necessitated and there is still an element of real chance in the universe.

In 1898[12] Peirce characterized the objective logic of Hegel as the view that "the whole universe and every feature of it, however minute, is rational, and was constrained to be as it is by the logic of events, so that there is no principle of action in the universe but reason" (6.218). This view, Peirce maintained, is the result of "a logical slip," and "the conclusion reached is manifestly at variance with observation." It seems well to quote his explanation of this in full:

> It is true that the whole universe and every feature of it must be regarded as rational, that is as brought about by the logic of events. But it does not follow that it is *constrained* to be as it is by the logic of events; for the logic of evolution and of life need not be supposed to be of that wooden kind that absolutely constrains a given conclusion. The logic may be that of the inductive or hypothetic inference.
>
> This may-be is at once converted into must-be when we reflect that among the facts to be accounted for are such as that, for example, red things look red and not blue and *vice versa*. It is obvious that that cannot be a necessary consequence of abstract being.
>
> The effect of this error of Hegel is that he is forced to deny [the] fundamental character of two elements of experience which cannot result from deductive logic. What these elements are will appear in the sequel.

These elements, of course, are Peirce's categories of firstness and secondness, and, when they are taken into account, the necessitarian position of Hegel which seems to recognize only the kind of thirdness which consists in deductive necessity must be abandoned in favor of a view which allows for real chance—the logic of evolution becomes inductive and hypothetic rather than deductive. But, in this analysis, the scheme presented in the essays of 1891–93 is radically altered. Laws constitute thirdness rather than secondness, and tychism becomes part of the doctrine that the logic of events is not that of deductive rationalization but rather that of probable inference regulated by the principle of synechism.[13]

134

This brief survey of Peirce's conception of evolution as objective logic may suffice to show that evolution so regarded is far more in accord with his aim of explaining the laws of nature than anything which might be found literally in the hypotheses of natural selection and the inheritance of acquired characteristics. Yet it is also necessary, for Peirce's aim, to assume that some force is operating to bring about the logic of events. Evolution in the sense of hypotheses of efficient causation can explain the means which the force uses in its operation but not the force itself. Within the context of objective logic, this force becomes that of final causation viewed objectively and would appear to be ultimately that of God conceived as continually creating the universe. But in Peirce's pragmatic scheme, any reality, even that of God, must be ultimately accounted for as the result of perception and inquiry. This circumstance leads to a third view of evolution in which the ultimate force is moral and the logic of the process is normative rather than objective. In speaking of evolution in this third and moralistic sense, Peirce remarked that "in its higher stages, evolution takes place more and more largely through self-control" (5.433). Just before this, he had explained that "the ideas 'justice' and 'truth' are, notwithstanding the iniquity of the world, the mightiest of the forces that move it" (5.431).

Such consideration of evolution in moral terms occurs for the most part in writings dated later than 1900, where Peirce is concerned chiefly with explaining the philosophy he felt was entailed by his own conception of pragmatism. It is in this context that the reality of natural laws as well as the logical validity of induction comes to depend on Peirce's ultimate assumption of an unlimited community of inquirers, expressed as a moral sentiment embodying the hope for further explanation. The point will be developed below in the next two chapters, but the issue should be sufficiently clear by now to remark that in virtue of his definition of reality Peirce's metaphysics must finally be supported by his theory of inquiry, and not vice versa.

C. While Peirce claimed to have derived the three types of

evolution distinguished in his *Evolutionary Love* from scientific hypotheses already developed by others, his analysis in this essay clearly reflects the three senses in which he later spoke of evolution. Thus, in discussing the second type of evolution (called anancasm, from ἀνάγκη, "necessity"), Peirce mentions not only the theories of Nägeli, Kölliker, and Weismann as examples but also the "Hegelian philosophy" (6.305). The common element here would seem to depend on the fact that Peirce regards the theories in question as requiring a deductive logic of events similar to Hegel's objective logic. The difference between the two species of anancasm is not that varieties of the former claim to be part of natural science while the latter is the outgrowth of a rationalistic philosophy but rather that, of the two possible kinds of dyadic relations in Peirce's categorial scheme, the purportedly scientific theories represent one and Hegel's philosophy the other. The "anancastic development of thought" may proceed "by causes either external to the mind, such as changed circumstances of life, or internal to the mind as logical developments of ideas already accepted, such as generalizations" (6.307).[14] But, on the other hand, "tychastic evolution," which Peirce identified with the Darwinian theory, seems incompatible with any logic of events. For the "tychastic development of thought . . . will consist in slight departures from habitual ideas in different directions indifferently, quite purposeless and quite unconstrained whether by outward circumstances or by force of logic." Agapasm alone seems capable of combining a logic of events with chance variations, but only when the consideration becomes moralistic and is based on the gospel of love rather than on the scientific evidence for Lamarckian evolution.

In order to disentangle the naturalistic, logical, and moral factors in this analysis, it must be recalled first of all that, while reality has been defined as the product of inquiry, this applies only to inquiry that has been rightly conducted. The fact that certain rules of procedure have actually been followed in the history of inquiry is no guarantee of their logical correctness. But then the reality of scientific laws can be accounted for by evolution only if there are causes which impel inquiry to follow right rules. If the process is viewed objectively, the actual development of inquiry becomes part of the course of events and is governed by whatever real laws determine the logic of events. These laws might be assumed to be expressions of the architectural activities of mind (divine or human) or of some natural factor like the responses of an organism to a changed environment. Either assumption would result in exactly the sort of paradox that Carus urged against Peirce—laws would be explained as real only by assuming that further laws are real.[15] In order to avoid this situation, the logic of inquiry must be viewed normatively rather than objectively. The evolution of laws will then rest on the assumption that moral sentiments, such as the hope for further explanation, rather than certain laws already taken as real, direct the course of inquiry. In these terms, the scientific hypotheses of evolution which Peirce attempted to embrace in his agapasm should be restricted to a concern with efficient causation, while the philosophy of Hegel becomes an attempt to explain the objective logic of evolution with mind assumed as the architect. When the normative and objective views of inquiry are thus distinguished and there is no attempt to fuse regulative principles with what is discovered by inquiry, the gospel of love espoused by agapasm has nothing to do essentially with the hypothesis of Lamarckian evolution but is rather another expression of Peirce's doctrine that the success of inquiry depends on certain moral sentiments, which he had already declared in 1878 "to be pretty much the same as that famous trio of Charity, Faith, and Hope" (2.655).[16]

4. METAPHYSICS AS A PART OF PHILOSOPHY

A. The conception of metaphysics which Peirce developed in the light of his re-examination of pragmatism seems well summarized in a statement ca. 1906:

There are certain questions commonly reckoned as metaphysical, and which certainly are so, if by metaphysics we mean ontology, which as soon as pragmatism is once sincerely accepted, cannot logically resist settlement. These are for example, What is reality? Are necessity and contingency real modes of being? Are the laws of nature real? Can they be assumed to be immutable or are they presumably results of evolution? Is there any real chance, or departure from real law? But on examination, if by metaphysics we mean the broadest positive truths of the psycho-physical universe—positive in the sense of not being reducible to logical formulae—then the very fact that these problems can be solved by a logical maxim is proof enough that they do not belong to metaphysics but to "epistemology," an atrocious translation of *Erkenntnislehre* [5.496].

In his *Minute Logic* of 1902 Peirce mentions "epistemology" as another name for the branch of logic called "speculative grammar," a discipline which considers, "for example, in what sense and how there can be any true proposition and false proposition, and what are the general conditions to which thought or signs of any kind must conform in order to assert anything" (2.206). Pragmatism as the criterion of significant assertion would be the logical maxim resulting from this study which supplies the basis for ontology.

Peirce sometimes used the phrase "ontological metaphysics" to characterize an undertaking whose absurdity he thought was exposed by his pragmatic maxim. Thus, in 1905 he began an explanation of the *raison d'être* of pragmatism:

It will serve to show that almost every proposition of ontological metaphysics is either meaningless gibberish—one word being defined by other words, and they by still others, without any real conception ever being reached—or else is downright absurd; so that all such rubbish being swept away, what will remain of philosophy will be a series of problems capable of investigation by the observational methods of the true sciences . . . [5.423].

When this passage is interpreted in the light of the one quoted above, it certainly is not meant to imply that questions of ontology are either meaningless or absurd. The gibberish results from an improper method rather than from posing pseudo-problems, and the correct procedure for ontology is not the observational one of the positive sciences but the kind of logical or epistemological analysis which leads to pragmatism.

Ontological metaphysics arises from a confusion of ontology with metaphysics in the sense of "the broadest positive truths of the psycho-physical universe" and results in an attempt to solve the problems of the latter by methods other than those of the positive sciences. When the rubbish created from this confusion is swept away by pragmatism, philosophy conceived as metaphysics distinct from ontology becomes a series of problems to be solved by empirical methods.

However, it is easy to become confused as to what Peirce meant by this observational method of scientific metaphysics. According to his "detailed classification of sciences" in the *Minute Logic*, all sciences, even mathematics, are in some sense observational. What is called "philosophy" in this scheme includes much more than metaphysics distinct from ontology; it is given as having "three orders" in its "first subclass, that of *necessary philosophy*."[17] The first of these orders is phenomenology; the second, normative science, including logic (and hence ontology); and, the third, metaphysics (1.279–82). Yet at the beginning of the classification, Peirce speaks of philosophy generally as a science "which deals with positive truth, indeed, yet contents itself with observations such as come within the range of every man's normal experience, and for the most part in every waking hour of his life" (1.241). Now the expression "positive truth" here can hardly mean "positive in the sense of not being reducible to logical formulae," as there is no indication Peirce meant to exclude logic from this characterization of philosophy. In his lectures on pragmatism in 1903, he explained "positive science" in a manner which seems to accord with the usage here:

By a *positive* science I mean an inquiry which seeks for positive knowledge; that is, for such knowledge as may conveniently be expressed in a *categorical proposition*. Logic and the other normative sciences, although they ask, not what *is* but what *ought to be*, nevertheless are positive sciences since it is by asserting positive, categorical truth that they are able to show that what they call good really is so; and the right reason, right effort, and right being, of which they treat, derive that character from positive categorical fact [5.39].

The only science not positive in this sense is the "Conditional or Hypothetical Science of *Pure Mathematics*" (5.40).

A crucial factor in distinguishing the broad and narrow use of "positive truth" would seem to be the attitude taken toward reality. Ontology as established by normative logic can show through an application of the pragmatic maxim how reality ought to be defined, but in this capacity it can show nothing of the actual character of reality. Metaphysics, on the other hand, when it is conceived as a science apart from ontology can presuppose this definition and, like physics and the other special sciences, show something of the actual character of reality by discovering truths of the psycho-physical universe. The great difference between this and ontology is that any inquiry into what reality actually is must proceed in accordance with the formulae already established by logic, so that the truths it seeks are never those reducible to such formulae. Thus, in his classification in the *Minute Logic*, Peirce characterized metaphysics, as distinct from logic and phenomenology, as a science "whose attitude toward the universe is nearly that of the special sciences (anciently, *physics* was its designation), from which it is mainly distinguished, by its confining itself to such parts of physics and of psychics as can be established without special means of observation. But these are very peculiar parts, extremely unlike the rest" (1.282). The attitude of metaphysics toward the universe would be nearly that of the special sciences because it uses the formulae of valid inference to determine the actual character of reality, and it differs from these sciences only in that, like other branches of philosophy, it does not require special means of observation. In the narrow sense of "positive," as Peirce used the term in 1905–6, metaphysics would be "the highest of the positive sciences" (5.423),[18] since it is concerned with the most general positive truths of the psycho-physical universe; while in the broad sense of this word, which he preferred in 1902–3, Peirce could say that phenomenology is "the most primal of all the positive sciences" (5.39).

B. The interrelations of phenomenology, normative science,

and metaphysics, together with related problems such as the status of ontological propositions and their claim to positive truth, will be considered below in the next two chapters. The remainder of the present chapter will be concerned with explicating some aspects of scientific metaphysics and the character of its observational method. The nature of God as a real object—as something in the actual universe—constitutes one of the principal problems of metaphysics in this sense. Peirce had already declared in *The Law of Mind* that the only observation needed to establish the reality of God was of "facts that stand before our face and eyes and stare us in the face" (6.162), yet if the hypothesis of God's reality is to be part of scientific metaphysics, it should be subject to the same logical analysis as any scientific hypothesis. Peirce's treatment of this problem may be taken as an illustration of his metaphysical method stretched to its limits.

In a late paper (1908) entitled *A Neglected Argument for the Reality of God* (6, Bk. II, chap. 3), Peirce begins by explaining "certain lines of reflection which will inevitably suggest the hypothesis of God's Reality" (6.465). This reflection consists in something called "the Pure Play of Musement" and allows the "Muser" to let his thoughts roam where they will throughout "the three universes of experience," following no principle but "the law of liberty." As a result of this musement, "the idea of God's Reality will be sure sooner or later to be found an attractive fancy, which the Muser will develop in various ways" (6.465).

While this may seem a particularly unscientific way of approaching the hypothesis of God's reality, there is a subtlety in the argument that is easily overlooked. Peirce remarked at the end of the paragraph in which he explained what he meant by "musement":

One who sits down with the purpose of becoming convinced of the truth of religion is plainly not inquiring in scientific singleness of heart, and must always suspect himself of reasoning unfairly. So he can never attain the entirety even of a physicist's belief in electrons, although this is avowedly but provisional. But let religious

141

meditation be allowed to grow up spontaneously out of Pure Play without any breach of continuity, and the Muser will retain the perfect candour proper to Musement [6.458].

This is perfectly consistent with Peirce's contention that the success of inquiry depends ultimately on the moral sentiments of the inquirers. If a physicist, for example, inquired into the nature of electrons with a desire to enhance his personal fame eclipsing his hope for further explanation, he should "always suspect himself of reasoning unfairly." But one's conception of God is very apt to be so inseparably bound up with his own feelings of personal security that the subject becomes extremely difficult to approach with scientific detachment. Moreover, since the hypothesis in this case "supposes an infinitely incomprehensible object" (6.466), it seems impossible to reject any particular type of experience as totally irrelevant. Peirce's approach to the problem by starting only with musement, far from being particularly unscientific, thus seems to be an attempt to state what conditions would be necessary if something like scientific detachment is to be achieved.

When the hypothesis of God's reality is subjected to logical analysis, the musement which leads to the suggestion that there is one creator of all the universes of experience seems to constitute the first or "retroductive" ("abductive") stage of inquiry. Peirce remarks three peculiarities which distinguish this from ordinary retroductive inferences. "In the first place, the Plausibility of the hypothesis reaches an almost unparalleled height among deliberately formed hypotheses" (6.488). This plausibility seems so impressive that "there is great danger that the investigation will stop at this first stage, owing to the indifference of the Muser to any further proof of it." Yet it must be admitted, Peirce feels, that "this very Plausibility is undoubtedly an argument of no small weight in favor of the truth of the hypothesis."

The second peculiarity, however, seems to render the hypothesis incapable of scientific verification in the ordinary sense. Peirce concedes:

142

Although it is a chief function of an explanatory hypothesis (and some philosophers say the only one) to excite a clear image in the mind by means of which experiential consequences of ascertainable conditions may be predicted, yet in this instance the hypothesis can only be apprehended so very obscurely that in exceptional cases alone can any definite and direct deduction from its ordinary abstract interpretation be made [6.489].

Peirce does not indicate what the exceptional cases are and emphasizes instead the impossibility of predicting the conduct of an omniscient and omnipotent being, an *Ens necessarium*. But, then, "the effects of the second peculiarity of the hypothesis are counteracted by a third, which consists in its commanding influence over the whole conduct of life of its believers" (6.490). It is not easy to see how this circumstance, if granted, can afford a scientific test of the hypothesis and counteract its being unverifiable in the ordinary sense. About all that can be gathered from Peirce's further remarks on the matter here is that the issue somehow depends on his pragmatism. He declared a few pages earlier in his paper that for a pragmatist the "ultimate test" of the hypothesis "must lie in its value in the self-controlled growth of man's conduct of life" (6.480).

The point to be urged in favor of the cogency of Peirce's analysis is that the preceding sentence expresses what must be the ultimate test of any scientific hypothesis. The successful prediction of experimental consequences affords a test of truth precisely because without demanding such prediction the path of inquiry would be blocked—there would be no possibility of objectively determining the adequacies of given hypotheses and advancing to further truth. But this amounts to saying that the final test lies in the value of the given hypothesis in the self-controlled growth of man's conduct of life or, more particularly, of inquiry.[19] For the final aim of each inquirer is never the verification of this or that hypothesis but rather the truth which is pursued by the unlimited community. The ultimate test of a hypothesis should thus be specified as its value in the advancement of inquiry, and, while in most cases this value would be nil if the hypothesis afforded no successful predictions, this does not mean that the ultimate test can be specified as the success of certain predictions apart from the advancement of inquiry. The hypothesis of God's reality, taken as Peirce seems to intend it, possesses the unique characteristic that, while it may yield no successful predictions, it can nevertheless have considerable value in advancing the growth of inquiry. A man who accepts this hypothesis is led to see that "nothing has any kind of value in itself—whether aesthetic, moral, or scientific—but only in its place in the whole production to which it appertains; and that an individual soul with its petty agitations and calamities is a zero except as filling its infinitesimal place" (6.479). In other words, the man may be led to see the need of sacrificing his own interests for those of an unlimited community—to acquire the sentiments of faith, hope, and charity, the moral prerequisites of scientific inquiry demanded by Peirce's pragmatism.[20]

The hypothesis of God thus comes close to being another form of Peirce's ultimate assumption that intellectual inquiry will continue indefinitely. But there remains the great difference that, in being a scientific hypothesis and claiming support from inquiry, the former must presuppose the latter. The uniqueness of the hypothesis is apparent in the circumstance that belief in God, while being in one sense a belief in the reality of a particular object, is also a belief about the origin and development of the whole universe—of all three universes of experience corresponding to Peirce's categories. There can be but one object of reality supposed to stand in this way to all reality, and hence but one hypothesis which can be tested by its value in the self-controlled growth of inquiry without yielding predictions as to any specific character of reality. Yet, in so far as the reality of God is a scientific hypothesis, the belief to which it gives rise must remain "provisional," along with all other scientific beliefs (cf. 6.485). In this way the ultimate assumption—the moral sentiment—about the indefinite continuation of inquiry remains prior even to the hypothesis of God. In short, Peirce's scientific

144

metaphysics must rest on his logic and ethics as they determine his theory of inquiry.

Further understanding of Peirce's hypothesis of God may be obtained by considering it briefly under three headings: (i) the sense in which the hypothesis may be misused and result in blocking the way of inquiry; (ii) the sense in which it may be made consistent with Peirce's contention that we have a direct perception of God; and (iii) the relation of the hypothesis to other parts of Peirce's metaphysics, especially his theory of evolution.

(i) The criticism in a fragment ca. 1893 of Leibniz's doctrine of pre-established harmony affords a good illustration of what Peirce regarded as an improper use of the hypothesis of God. In this passage, with the important exception of a critical reference to nominalism, Peirce speaks very much like a positivist and may seem prima facie a long way from the position that God's reality can be supported by scientific evidence. Leibniz's theory of pre-established harmony is being considered as an explanation of the interrelations between mind and matter.

The fault of this explanation is the capital fault which attaches to all nominalistic explanations, namely that they merely restate the fact to be explained under another aspect; or, if they add anything to it, add only something from which no definite consequences can be deduced. A scientific explanation ought to consist in the assertion of some positive matter of fact, other than the fact to be explained, but from which this fact necessarily follows; and if the explanation be hypothetical, the proof of it lies in the experiential verification of predictions deduced from it as necessary consequences. Leibnitz's explanation merely comes to this, that the motions and changes of state of atoms are relative to one another, because God made them so in the beginning. But nothing can be deduced from this theory, since it is impossible for man to predict what God might see fit to do. This stamps the theory as one of those to which Auguste Comte applied the epithet *metaphysical*, that is, unverifiable. To accept it as sufficient would be to block the road of inquiry [6.273].

Now the fact of interaction between mind and matter, while it may concern the broadest aspects of the psycho-physical universe, is nonetheless but one fact among others. Its explanation

145

must therefore be sought in further facts, such as those which reveal the laws of matter to have the character of habits. To say that a given fact is so because God made it that way affords no explanation of the fact in its particularity, distinct from other facts, and the procedure is nominalistic in that it makes the particularity ultimate and inexplicable. Leibniz's theory thus seems an illustration of what Peirce later called the meaningless gibberish of ontological metaphysics—a fact is said to be so because it is so. Tautological statements might be appropriate in the logical analysis laying the foundations of ontology, but they have no place in scientific metaphysics. Yet Peirce could not, like a thoroughgoing positivist, deny any scientific meaning to the hypothesis of God and remain consistent with his own conception of reality and the realism which it implied. For if the ultimate test of any hypothesis lies in its value in the self-controlled growth of inquiry, the hypothesis of God may have value when it is not misapplied and taken as an explanation for the particularity of given facts—when it is not treated as a hypothesis which should yield definite predictions.

(ii) Some of Peirce's remarks about a direct perception of God seem even more than his "prope-positivism" to be at variance with the possibility of treating the hypothesis scientifically. The problem posed in *The Law of Mind*, far from that of unearthing a neglected argument for the reality of God, was that of explaining how anyone could doubt His reality, since a direct perception of the deity could be found in facts that stare us in the face. At times, Peirce even speaks as if a proof of God's reality were impossible. In his reply to Carus in 1893, he remarked that "we cannot tell what God would do, nor penetrate his counsels. We see what He *does* do, and nothing more. For the same reason one cannot logically infer the existence of God; one can only know Him by direct perception" (6.613). The main point here would seem to be the one already discussed, that the hypothesis of God cannot be tested, in the ordinary sense, by the predictions it yields. The further point is then the question of how the idea of God arises. A fragment on the

146

"knowledge of God" *ca.* 1896 emphasizes that the idea must
come from direct experience and not from reasoning.

Where would such an idea, say as that of God, come from, if not
from direct experience? Would you make it a result of some kind of
reasoning, good or bad? Why, reasoning can supply the mind with
nothing in the world except an estimate of the value of a statistical
ratio, that is, how often certain kinds of things are found in certain
combinations in the ordinary course of experience. . . . No: as to God,
open your eyes—and your heart, which is also a perceptive organ—
and you see him [6.493].

The contrast intended here is hardly meant to imply that direct experience and inference are in all respects mutually exclusive, as Peirce never renounced his position of 1868 that
every modification of consciousness is an inference. Yet there is
certainly a vast difference between an idea comprising an estimate of a statistical ratio and one which would ordinarily be
called a perception of direct experience. Even if two such ideas,
considered simply as modifications of consciousness, differ only
in the degree of prominence in consciousness which attends the
inference, an adequate analysis should supply some means of
distinguishing sharply between them. In order to achieve this
requirement, it is necessary to turn to Peirce's categories as
modes of being. In a paper *ca.* 1906 he explained with reference
to the question, "Do you believe in the existence of God?"

I will also take the liberty of substituting "reality" for "existence."
This is perhaps overscrupulosity; but I myself always use *exist* in its
strict philosophical sense of "react with the other like things in the
environment." Of course, in that sense, it would be fetishism to say
that God "exists." . . . I define the *real* as that which holds its characters on such a tenure that it makes not the slightest difference
what any man or men may have *thought* them to be, or ever will
have *thought* them to be . . . [6.495].

In these terms, the only way we may logically infer the existence of something is by means of hypotheses that yield definite predictions. "Existence" is not a qualifying predicate, since
it occurs in consciousness only as a sense of reaction and never
as a perceived quality. An idea that consists in an estimate of

147

the frequency with which certain combinations of qualities are found together in existence is then to be sharply distinguished from a modification of consciousness that comprises a quality or a sense of reaction. The basis for the distinction, however, must be sought in the categories of being which the modifications express and not in the character which they have as events in the thought-process. In the latter case, by virtue of the continuity of the process, all the events have more or less the character of an inference. The idea of God thus arises from direct experience rather than from reasoning, in that it does not express thirdness in the sense of constituting an estimate of a statistical ratio. Yet, as Peirce contended in the fragment ca. 1896, it must always be inquired whether an idea presented in direct experience has a real object or not, since "hallucinations, delusions, superstitious imaginations, and fallacies of all kinds are experiences, but experiences misunderstood" (6.492). In other words, though they appear as objects of immediate experience, they are the results of inference, and their fallacious character arises from an error in reasoning.

The ordinary means of correcting such an error would be to proceed in accordance with the categories and form predictions as to what qualities will be forced into consciousness with the brute reaction of secondness when certain other qualities have already been so encountered. Since this procedure cannot be followed in the case of the idea of God, Peirce was led to say that the existence of God could never be logically inferred. But in so far as this idea in some vague sense seems to force itself upon anyone who "opens his heart" and attends to facts that stare him in the face, it seems correct to say that God is directly perceived. Yet it would clearly contradict Peirce's conclusions of 1868 to maintain that this perception constituted an immediate intuition of God; the perception must be explained as somehow the result of an inference. The paper ca. 1906 attempts such an explanation by insisting, first, on the difference between saying that God exists and that God is real and, second, on the view of "critical common-sensism" that, while belief in God is forced upon man by instinct, it is nonetheless the result of a kind of "uncriticized inference" even if it cannot be called reasoning (cf. 6.497). In this way, a belief in the reality of God is like all other first premisses which man cannot bring himself to doubt and must regard as part of immediate experience but not as infallible and beyond criticism. Yet this explanation does not constitute an argument for the reality of God. Peirce concluded this part of his paper by remarking that "all I have been saying is not preparatory to any argument for the reality of God. It is intended as an apology for resting the belief upon instinct as the very bedrock on which all reasoning must be built" (6.500). The article of 1908 on the "neglected argument" is then a critical examination of an instinctive belief and in this sense is not inconsistent with holding that God is known by direct perception.

(iii) When Peirce's conception of God is related to other parts of his scientific metaphysics, rather serious difficulties seem unavoidable. He remarked near the close of his paper of 1908:

Among the many pertinent considerations which have been crowded out of this article, I may just mention that it could have been shown that the hypothesis of God's Reality is logically not so isolated a conclusion as it may seem. On the contrary, it is connected so with a theory of the nature of thinking that if this be proved so is that. Now there is no such difficulty in tracing experiential consequences of this theory of thinking as there are in attempting directly to trace out other consequences of God's reality [6.491].

The theory of thinking referred to here is presumably the synechistic view of the continuity between different personalities. It surely cannot mean the pragmatic analysis of thought, which depends on a maxim of logic and was also mentioned repeatedly throughout the article.

The difficulty, however, is that, if the reality of God is logically connected with an experimentally verifiable theory of thinking, it would seem that God must have existence as well as reality. That is, if the direct perception of God is a phenomenon

149

which can be accounted for in the same way as one's perception of his own personality and of others around him (cf. 6.436 [1893]), it would seem to follow that God's personality must exist and interact with others.[21] Perhaps the only answer Peirce has for this problem is indicated by his frank admission earlier in the article on the neglected argument that "an infinite being is not tied down to any consistency" (6.480). But the answer appears more forceful as stated in the paper ca. 1906, where it is not specified that God is an infinite being. Immediately after declaring that it would be fetichism to say that God exists, though one may say that He is real, Peirce explained that difficulties inevitably arise when one attempts to render the vague concept of God too precise. For "every concept that is vague is liable to be self-contradictory in those respects in which it is vague," and "no concept, not even those of mathematics, is absolutely precise" (6.496). The specification that God is an infinite being is thus already an attempt to render the concept too precise and ends in the view that God is a self-contradictory being. And, a fortiori, an endeavor to argue that if God's personality can in a sense be perceived in the same way as other personalities, then a precise account of His existence can be given, must end in fetichism and absurdity. Peirce may thus have intended his synechistic theory of thinking to show no more than that the hypothesis of God's reality is not an absolutely isolated conclusion and that it receives some vague support from certain psychological experiments concerning the nature of personality. But then his phrase "if this be proved so is that" seems a bit too strong.

The most serious difficulties seem to arise in connection with Peirce's attempts to use the hypothesis of God in a theory of cosmic evolution. It should be remarked, first of all, that, of the three senses in which Peirce came to speak of evolution, this hypothesis might be of use only with respect to objective logic. A scientific account of the means by which evolution proceeds, as that given by the theory of natural selection, could hardly be said to need the hypothesis, even though Peirce did seem to regard such an account as subject to correction by what he thought he had established through his logic of events.[22] On the other hand, he never spoke of God as a final cause, as identical with the *summum bonum*, the ultimate goal of evolution in the moral sense. This would have to be the case in so far as no object of scientific inquiry, not even God, can be made prior to the theory of inquiry as part of normative science.

The role of God in the logic of events would seem to be that of a creator, not only as one who started the process but as one who continually keeps it going. In the paper ca. 1906, Peirce remarked that he believed God "not so much *to have been* as to be now creating the universe," and cited his *Monist* articles of 1891–93 for further reference (6.505). This view is of course in accord with the continual manifestation of God's personality in direct experience, as proclaimed in *The Law of Mind*. It would seem to be in this sense that the hypothesis of God possesses such great plausibility as an abductive inference which postulates a supreme creative force continually shaping the natural course of events.

Peirce's final remarks in the *Collected Papers* on the manner in which cosmic evolution would proceed from an original chaos are contained in a paragraph near the close of his article of 1908 on the neglected argument. He does not claim here, as he did in his reply to Carus in 1893, that the regularities of nature are to be explained as consequences of an original uniformity which consisted in nothing but the general absence of any determinate uniformity. He now professes to be imagining, "in such vague way as such a thing can be imagined, a perfect cosmology of the three universes" (6.490). The primordial chaos, then, "must represent a state of things in which the three universes were completely nil," and this does not mean a state of pure random in the statistical sense, in which everything conceivable would have an equal chance of taking place.

We cannot ourselves conceive of such a state of nility; but we can easily conceive that there should be a mind that could conceive it, since, after all, no contradiction can be involved in mere non-existence. A state in which there should be absolutely no super-order whatsoever would be such a state of nility. For all Being involves some kind of super-order. For example, to suppose a thing to have any particular character is to suppose a conditional proposition to be true of it, which proposition would express some kind of super-order, as any formulation of a general fact does.

This state of nility clearly seems to be nothing but the self-contradictory. A condition of pure random would have a kind of super-order which would allow at least conditional propositions of the sort, that if A and B are any two characters, they have an equal chance of turning up. Peirce does not indicate how we can easily conceive of a mind that could conceive of this state of nility which appears to us as self-contradictory. Perhaps he intends some subtlety in his remark that "after all, no contradiction can be involved in mere non-existence." This would be true only if "non-existence" means the logically possible but not actual. Earlier in the paragraph Peirce remarked in reference to God as *Ens necessarium*: "A disembodied spirit, or pure mind, has its being out of time, since all that it is destined to think is fully in its being at any and every previous time. But in endless time it is destined to think all that it is capable of thinking" (6.490). Now our own thinking is definitely limited by the fact that we have our being in time, and Peirce seems never to have altered his position of 1868 that to say that we always think through a time is but another way of saying all thought is in signs (5.253). Since time is continuous, we can always conceive that something may be thought through less and less time or that more and more may be thought in a single interpretant. Then, as a limiting case, we could say that a mind which did not think through a time would be one whose entire thought is wholly contained in any specifiable moment of time. In so far as it does not think through a time, its thought would not be limited by the laws of signs,[23] and we at least could not say that it would be impossible for it to conceive of a state of nility absolutely devoid of super-order.

This may be reading too much into Peirce, and at any rate

the main point seems sufficiently clear without going into the difficulties raised by this forced interpretation. Since the three universes would include everything conceivable, the ultimate beginning of their evolution must be something inconceivable. It cannot even be specified as a temporal or logical beginning, since both time and the logic of events are conceivable. As early as 1898, Peirce came to regard "time and logic" as results of evolution (6.200). God alone seems to have the unique property of being at least vaguely conceivable and yet exempt from evolution, although in so far as He is manifest in experience, God too might be said to evolve. Yet even if we can conceive of a divine mind which can conceive of the primordial nility, it is difficult to see what this contributes to a theory of cosmic evolution. In the paper ca. 1906 Peirce remarked with reference to divine omniscience, "We cannot so much as frame any notion of what the phrase 'the performance of God's mind' means. Not the faintest! The question is gabble" (6.508). The next paragraph on divine omnipotence ends: "But we only wildly gabble about such things" (6.509).

However difficult it may be to conceive of God in a fashion that would materially aid a perfect cosmology of the three universes, this circumstance does not affect Peirce's philosophy as a whole. Logic is not supposed to be a result of evolution in any sense that would make a scientific account of the character of reality prior to the rules of inquiry. The logic which evolves is of course not to be taken normatively but objectively like time, as something by which events are ordered. God, like the primeval nothingness, stands in this context only as a hypothesis which may be demanded by a particular type of inquiry. The failure to make anything but the vaguest sort of sense out of the hypothesis is merely a comment on the sad state of the inquiry, and, while the hope for further explanation may be severely shaken, it is not entirely destroyed. Peirce was forbidden to accept an agnostic attitude toward any question by this supreme hope in the form of a regulative principle of his normative logic. In fact, it was in the name of this very principle that he accused other philosophers of falling into the meaningless gibberish of ontological metaphysics and blocking the road of inquiry. If his own discussions of God sometimes became gabble, inquiry was blocked neither by offering the gabble as sound explanation nor by giving up to the despair of agnosticism.

It was noticed above in the preceding sections of this chapter that Peirce's evolutionism in the last analysis became moralistic and centered around the self-controlled growth of inquiry. The final test of the hypothesis of God's reality was found in evolution in this sense which calls for normative rather than objective logic. Scientific metaphysics, like all other phases of scientific inquiry, must thus depend finally on the prior branches of philosophy—on phenomenology, normative science, and ontology as it arises from logic.

V

The Order of the Sciences

WHEN Peirce spoke in the 1890's of erecting "a philosophical
edifice that shall outlast the vicissitudes of time," he declared
that the "first step toward this is to find simple concepts applicable to every subject," and listed as examples of such con-/
cepts in previous philosophy Aristotle's "matter and form, act
and power" (1.1). But the attempt to determine these concepts,
even with the help of the categories, led Peirce to regard his
edifice as involving a hierarchy of distinct sciences, with the various sciences effecting different determinations of fundamental
concepts. The need for such an ordering of the sciences has already become apparent in the consideration of metaphysics, and
the aim of the present chapter is to examine the order with
particular reference to the sciences coming before metaphysics.
In the lectures of 1903 on pragmatism, Peirce referred to three
modes of being corresponding to his categories as performing a
function in his philosophy similar to that of matter, form, and
entelechy in the Aristotelian system (1.22–23). While modes of
being are properly metaphysical conceptions, it was only with
the help of prior sciences that Peirce was able to justify them
as the simple concepts on which to erect a philosophic edifice.

Throughout the present chapter the word "science" will be
taken as referring only to what Peirce regarded as "theoretical
science." His conception of "practical science" will be considered in chapter vi. The ordering of the sciences itself belonged
to what he called "theoretical science of review" as opposed to
"theoretical science of discovery," so that in the strict sense the
concern here is with what Peirce said under the former heading,

which includes the philosophy of science (cf. 1.182). While he spoke of a "classification of the science of review," he was careful to point out that his own account makes no attempt at such classification (1.202, 243). He has little to say specifically about the science of review, and from the examples he gives of previous endeavors to develop it (Comte's *Philosophie positive* and Spencer's *Synthetic Philosophy*) his own attempt seems appropriately regarded simply as his pragmatic philosophy applied to the problem of ordering the sciences.

1. PHENOMENOLOGY, SPECULATIVE GRAMMAR, AND ONTOLOGY

A. The manner in which metaphysics depends on prior sciences for principles of ontology and rules of inquiry, as well as the relations which mathematics, phenomenology, and logic bear to each other and to metaphysics, is clearly indicated in two papers written about three years after the series in *The Monist* of 1891–93 considered in the preceding chapter. These papers are *The Regenerated Logic* (1896; 3, Paper XV) and *The Logic of Mathematics; an Attempt to Develop My Categories from Within* (ca. 1896; 1, Bk. III, chap. 4). The concern here will not be to examine these papers in any detail but to consider them, in the light of later writings, only with respect to their importance as providing means for integrating the various parts of Peirce's philosophy. The difficulties which he encountered in his earlier papers in *The Monist* came in large part from his failure to deal separately with the regulative principles presupposed by his metaphysics, and the two papers in question appear to represent his first attempt to remedy this defect.

The second of the papers is concerned to a great extent with what Peirce later called "phenomenology," a term which appears in none of the writings in the *Collected Papers* before the *Minute Logic*, 1902. The late appearance of this term in the development of Peirce's system may be accounted for in part at least by the tendency, already remarked in the first statement of the categories, for phenomenological considerations to become subsumed under either those of mathematics or those of logic. Such tendency can be seen from a consideration of the opening statements of the second paper, where Peirce remarks:

> Although the present paper deals with mathematics, yet its problems are not mere mathematical problems. . . . The questions which are here to be examined are, what are the different systems of hypotheses from which mathematical deduction can set out, what are their general characters, why are not other hypotheses possible, and the like. These are not problems which, like those of mathematics, repose upon clear and definite assumptions recognized at the outset; and yet, like mathematical problems, they are questions of possibility and necessity. What the nature of this necessity can be is one of the very matters to be discovered [1.417].

It is specified that mathematics never has occasion to appeal to logic for guidance in its reasoning, since "no disputes about reasoning arise in mathematics which need to be submitted to the principles of the philosophy of thought for decision." Mathematics "performs its reasonings by a *logica utens* which it develops for itself, and has no need of any appeal to a *logica docens*" (1.417). This statement is clarified by the position, referred to briefly in the *Regenerated Logic*, that "mathematical thought" is "*diagrammatical* or *iconic*" (3.429).

Peirce's later writings contain considerable treatment and development of this view of mathematical reasoning, which, as noted abvove at the close of chapter iii, he had remarked in a general way as early as 1869. A clear summary statement of the view occurs in the section on the classification of sciences in the *Minute Logic*. Mathematics is a science "which does not undertake to ascertain any matter of fact whatever, but merely posits hypotheses, and traces out their consequences." "It is observational, in so far as it makes constructions in the imagination according to abstract precepts, and then observes these imaginary objects, finding in them relations of parts not specified in the precept of construction. This is truly observation, yet certainly in a very peculiar sense; and no other kind of observation would at all answer the purpose of mathematics" (1.240).

157

The rules for such iconic reasoning can be supplied only by the precept of construction and are thus generated by the reasoner as he constructs that about which he is to reason. The very activity of the mathematician, in other words, creates a kind of logic in use, or *logica utens*, which is sufficient for mathematics. This could not be the case if the subject matter were other than the hypothetical possibilities contained in the diagrams which the mathematician himself creates. For, if a scientist were observing anything independent of his own creation and wished to reason about it, he would have to presuppose certain formal characteristics already established as holding for all possible creations. Before he could reason, for instance, that if A is less than B and B is less than C, then A is less than C, he would have to assume that this form of reasoning is valid for any A, B, and C whatever. In short, he would have to justify his own *logica utens* as having the universality claimed for a *logica docens*. But in mathematical observation the relative lengths of A, B, and C would be a result of the way in which a particular sort of diagram was supposed to have been constructed, and there would be no need to assume a principle of reasoning that applied to anything beyond what is contained in such a diagram. The *logica utens* in this case is thus limited to the constructions actually assumed by the mathematician and does not need justification as having the universality required of a theory of logic—a *logica docens*.[1] While mathematics can achieve conclusions about the formal properties of all imaginable objects—all objects capable of being represented in a diagram—it cannot by itself justify these conclusions for all observable objects.

A justification for the universality and necessity of mathematical forms with respect to objects regarded simply as observable and not merely as represented in a diagram involves a consideration of characteristics which belong to observation as such, irrespective of whether it purports to be of something real or imaginary. Peirce declared in the essay *The Logic of Mathematics; etc.*:

158

This much, however, is indisputable: if there are really any such necessary characteristics of mathematical hypotheses as I have just declared in advance that we shall find that there [are], this necessity must spring from some truth so broad as to hold not only for the universe we know but for every world that poet could create. And this truth like every truth must come to us by the way of experience. No apriorist ever denied that. The first matters which it is pertinent to examine are the most universal categories of elements of all experience, natural or poetical [1.417].

It is this examination that constitutes precisely what Peirce called a few years later "phenomenology," a science which would seem to be differentiated from pure mathematics in that it considers the formal elements present in any experience whatsoever and is not limited to observing the formal elements of imaginary constructions. However, the problems arising from such consideration, "like mathematical problems," "are questions of possibility and necessity," and, as Peirce remarked ca. 1904, "phaneroscopy [i.e., phenomenology] has nothing at all to do with the question of how far the phanerons [i.e., the appearances] it studies correspond to any realities" (1.287). The line of demarcation between phenomenology and mathematics is thus a difficult one to draw and one which inevitably involves the relation of these two sciences to logic.

The close connection between mathematics and logic is the subject of considerable discussion in the *Minute Logic*. In the section on the classification of sciences Peirce remarked: "The hypotheses of mathematics relate to systems which are either finite collections, infinite collections, or true continua. . . . The study of finite collections divides into two suborders: first, that simplest kind of mathematics which is chiefly used in its application to logic, from which I find it almost impossible to separate it; and secondly, the general theory of finite groups" (1.283). Logic, then, is intimately associated with the simplest mathematics, which is specified in "An Outline Classification of Sciences," 1903, as that to which all other branches of mathematics must have recourse (cf. 1.185). Chapter iii of the *Minute Logic* is devoted entirely to a consideration of this simplest mathematics, which can be identified with formal logic. "Mathematical logic is formal logic. Formal logic, however developed, is mathematics. Formal logic, however, is by no means the whole of logic, or even its principal part. It is hardly to be reckoned as a part of logic proper. Logic has to define its aim; and in doing so is even more dependent upon ethics, or the philosophy of aims, by far, than it is, in the methodeutic branch, upon mathematics" (4.240).

The first two branches of the simplest mathematics are called, respectively, "dichotomic" and "trichotomic" mathematics (cf. 4.250 ff. and 4.307 ff.). With regard to the latter, "the most fundamental fact about the number three is its generative potency" (4.309), since, as Peirce always contended, all polyadic relations can be treated as combinations of triadic relations. This contention seems to refer only to the elements necessary for diagraming relations in a system of graphs. Peirce's usual explanation for the sufficiency of three elements seems to amount to the following. Monads can be represented by a spot with one tail, as "X—," and dyads, by a spot with two tails, as "—R—." But with these two elements alone nothing higher than dyads can be represented, as "—R—S—" is only a combination of two dyads formed by "joining the ends of two tails." In order to picture a triad, a Y-shaped node, or spot with three tails, is required. Yet this third element is sufficient for representing all higher polyads (cf. 1.346 ff., 4.309 ff.). The "generative potency" of the number three is thus analogous to the fact that "a road with only three-way forkings may have any number of termini, but no number of straight roads put end on end will give more than two termini. Thus any number, however large, can be built out of triads; and consequently no idea can be involved in such a number, radically different from the idea of three" (1.363).[2] The fundamental requirement for diagraming polyadic relations, in other words, is that a given spot can in some way be connected with any number of termini in a single diagram, and this can always be satisfied by a sufficient number of three-way forkings.

Euler's diagrams comprise an outstanding example of dichotomic mathematics, but the "worst" fault (4.367) of his system is that it affords "no means of exhibiting reasoning, the gist of which is of a relational or abstractional kind. It does not extend to the logic of relatives" (4.356, article in Baldwin's *Dictionary of Philosophy and Psychology* [2d ed.], 1911). Consequently, the system is of interest primarily for "non-relative deductive logic, that is, the doctrine of the relations of truth and falsity between combinations of non-relative terms" (4.370). Yet because of the essential importance of truth and falsity as a dualism, "trichotomic mathematics is not quite so fundamentally important as the dichotomic branch" (4.308). "For how is the mathematician to take a step without recognizing the duality of truth and falsehood? . . . Trichotomic mathematics will therefore be a 2×3 affair, at simplest." Dichotomic mathematics, then, provides the formal structure for ordinary syllogistic, just as trichotomic mathematics performs a similar service for the logic of relatives. Hence, the two branches of the simplest mathematics present in diagrammatic thought the formal reasoning employed by any logical analysis, so that while these branches considered in themselves are properly mathematical, yet as formally identical with syllogistic and the logic of relatives they can be called "formal logic." Such mathematics is to be differentiated from logic proper only in the sense that the latter arises when the former is regarded as the basis for a general analysis of signs and is not restricted to icons.

The close affinity between phenomenology and logic arises from the circumstance that both sciences are dependent upon the same branch of mathematics, and, since this branch may be called either the simplest mathematics or formal logic, Peirce could always refer to his categories of phenomenology as an "outgrowth from formal logic" (5.469). Phenomenology or phaneroscopy, as an attempt to discern the common elements in all that is observable, need presuppose nothing from a prior science except an analysis of the formal characteristics which apply to all imaginable objects. Such analysis is precisely what is

161

given by trichotomic mathematics, or that branch of the simplest mathematics which constitutes the formal structure of the logic of relatives. Since every observable object can be diagramed in the imagination, this analysis yields formal properties which apply to all observable objects—not, however, in their immediate character as phenomena, but only in the sense in which objects possess the formal properties of their icons, or as the parts of a country exhibit the relations shown on the map of that country.[3] Inasmuch, then, as phenomenology "treats of the universal Qualities of Phenomena in their immediate phenomenal character" (5.122 [lectures on pragmatism, 1903]), it may be regarded as the science which considers the formal relations revealed by mathematical observation of icons as subsisting between the qualities which constitute the objects of the icons, or the phenomena themselves.

It is thus, presumably, that phenomenology is to show the universality and necessity of mathematical forms with respect to whatever is observable. But only when Peirce introduced normative sciences into his scheme did he come to speak of phenomenology as a separate science, and it then appeared as a necessary step in the transition from the simplest mathematics to the normative science comprising logic proper—to the formation of a *logica docens*. The one thing which is perfectly clear in Peirce pronouncements on the subject is simply that he did come to regard phenomenology as a necessary antecedent to normative science, and mathematics, in turn, as the one science upon which phenomenology must depend (cf., esp., 5.37–40). The details of this interrelation are by no means clear, and Peirce never claimed to have worked them out to any extent.

One fundamental point which has not been emphasized so far is the great importance of the notion of a sign. Peirce's original presentation of the categories centered ultimately around this notion, and his subsequent labor to make the logic of relatives in some essential way triadic undoubtedly reflects his preoccupation with the nature of a sign. But it is not until logic

162

proper, which Peirce also called "semiotic" (cf., e.g., 2.227 ff.), that the processes analyzed are actually those of signification. It would thus seem that, in so far as the simplest mathematics and phenomenology are prior to semiotic, they should provide some justification for regarding all thought as a process of signification. From this point of view, these two prior sciences together show that every object of thought—every appearance in consciousness—must express the three fundamental forms of relation corresponding to the three references of a sign. The simplest mathematics presents the triadic pattern itself as arising from the nature of diagrammatic representation, while phenomenology endeavors to establish the same pattern as indigenous to all observation. With these points granted, every phenomenon may be regarded as a sign, and the analysis in its next phase becomes normative by relating values like those of reality and illusion to the sign-phenomena.

Peirce's conclusion of 1868 that every modification of consciousness is an inference and hence that all thought is in signs was supported largely by showing that it was in accord with the facts of psychology and physiology. But this evidence is made inconclusive by his later insistence that logic should not rest on psychology (cf., e.g., 2.43, 50–51). The main issue seems clear enough. Psychology, like all other sciences which investigate the actual character of reality, must presuppose a *logica docens*, a theory of logic which prescribes rules for the inquiry after truth and cannot itself be made the basis for such a theory. The manner in which logic depends not only on mathematics and phenomenology but also on the prior normative sciences of ethics and esthetics is a further complication which will be considered below in the last section of this chapter. There remains, however, a kind of affinity between logic and psychology apparent in the circumstance that the first branch of logic itself, which affords the most general principles that are properly designated logical principles, may also be called "epistemology" (cf. 2.206).

B. In Peirce's later writings this first division of logic proper, speculative grammar, is also referred to as stoicheiology[4] (5.446

[1905]; 4.9 [ca. 1906]). In the paper *Regenerated Logic* it is described as the study which considers "those properties of beliefs which belong to them as beliefs, irrespective of their stability. For it must analyze an assertion into its essential elements, independently of the structure of the language in which it may happen to be expressed" (3.430). Such a study, according to the *Minute Logic*, "properly antecedes" critic (2.206), the second division of logic, "which, setting out such assumptions as that every assertion is either true or false, and not both, and that some propositions may be recognized to be true, studies the constituent parts of arguments and produces a classification of arguments," and "is often considered to embrace the whole of logic" (2.205). Speculative grammar is thus a study of the elements or first principles which are presupposed by the analysis commonly referred to as logic. There is explicit indication in the *Regenerated Logic* that the definition of truth or reality is given by speculative grammar. Peirce remarked in reference to Schröder's *Logic* that "only an introduction of one hundred and twenty-five pages rapidly examines the speculative grammar" (3.431), and concerning the contents of this introduction: "As to an inquiry presupposing that there is some one truth, what can this possibly mean except it be that there is one destined upshot to inquiry with reference to the question in hand—one result, which when reached will never be overthrown? Undoubtedly, we hope that this, or *something approximating to this*, is so, or we should not trouble ourselves to make the inquiry" (3.432).

These statements are in complete agreement with Peirce's later ones remarked in the preceding chapter (pp. 137–39), where it appeared that the principles of ontology are to be established by maxims of speculative grammar. Inasmuch as the problems of ontology were characterized as those which could not "logically resist settlement" once pragmatism is "sincerely accepted" (5.496), it also appeared that pragmatism is a maxim of speculative grammar. The nearest approach to an explanation in the *Collected Papers* of how pragmatism acquires this status

164

occurs in a passage in the opening chapter of the *Minute Logic*. In a section entitled "Clearness of Ideas" Peirce remarks:

After the thorough and careful discussion of all the above matters, involving many nice questions, including the one concerning which logicians are today disputing more than any other, many volumes having been devoted to it, I mean that of the nature of the proposition, and after every opinion has received its respectful hearing, we will come at last to the problem of Clearness, than which none in logic is more practically vital. I treated this subject in 1877, and enunciated a maxim, the acceptance of which constitutes the position called Pragmatism, a question which has of late years largely occupied philosophers. My opinion remains substantially the same now as then; but all those years have not passed without my learning something. I can now define the proposition more accurately, so as to close the door against those who would push the doctrine much further than I ever intended . . . [2.99].

The next section is entitled "Abduction, Deduction, and Induction" and begins with the sentence: "Critical logic is then to be taken up" (2.100).

Peirce's statement later in the *Minute Logic* that speculative grammar examines "in what sense and how there can be any true proposition and false proposition, and what are the general conditions to which thought or signs of any kind must conform in order to assert anything" (2.206), clearly implies that the problem of the nature of the proposition falls within this first branch of logic (cf. 5.29). Pragmatism, then, as a method for obtaining clearness of ideas, the development of which is subsequent to an analysis of the conditions of assertion, becomes the culmination of the stoicheiology of logic. The circumstance that Peirce in all his later expositions of pragmatism published in the *Collected Papers* referred to the doctrine as a "maxim of logic," without specifying in which of the three branches of logic it was to be included, is perhaps explained by the fact that none of these expositions was given in a context which involved a detailed consideration of logic itself.[5] The mere identification of pragmatism as a maxim in one of the three branches of logic, unaccompanied by an exposition of each of these branches in its

165

relation to the other two, would in no way contribute directly to a clarification of the doctrine. The reference to pragmatism in the *Minute Logic* is the only instance in the *Collected Papers* in which the context would warrant such identification, and, if Peirce had completed the project outlined in the opening chapter of that work, he undoubtedly would have made the place of pragmatism as a maxim of logic far more explicit.

C. The generality and certainty of speculative grammar as an epistemological analysis affording the principles of logic, as well as its affinity with psychology, are clearly described in a passage in the *Regenerated Logic*:

Now, the only sound psychology being a special science, which ought itself to be based upon a well-grounded logic, it is indeed a vicious circle to make logic rest upon a theory of cognition so understood. But there is a much more general doctrine to which the name theory of cognition might be applied. Namely, it is that speculative grammar, or analysis of the nature of assertion, which rests upon observations, indeed, but upon observations of the rudest kind, open to the eye of every attentive person who is familiar with the use of language, and which, we may be sure, no rational being, able to converse at all with his fellows, and so to express a doubt of anything, will ever have any doubt [3.432; cf. 2.227].

Speculative grammar thus involves a type of analysis and observation quite similar to that used in mathematics and phenomenology and would seem to be differentiated from these last two sciences primarily by the fact that it regards the processes analyzed by them as actual processes of signification.

Peirce asserted at the beginning of the *Regenerated Logic* that we must "appeal for our logical principles to the science of mathematics" (3.427), and he continued:

This double assertion, first, that logic ought to draw upon mathematics for control of disputed principles, and second that ontological philosophy ought in like manner to draw upon logic, is a case under a general assertion which was made by Auguste Comte, namely, that the sciences may be arranged in a series with reference to the abstractness of their objects; and that each science draws regulating principles from those superior to it in abstractness, while drawing data for its inductions from the sciences inferior to it in abstractness.

This conception of a hierarchy of the sciences is considered more at length in the *Logic of Mathematics; etc.*, and the relation between logic and scientific metaphysics is described as follows:

> Metaphysics consists in the results of the absolute acceptance of logical principles not merely as regulatively valid, but as truths of being. Accordingly, it is to be assumed that the universe has an explanation, the function of which, like that of every logical explanation, is to unify its observed variety [1.487].

The logical principles referred to here would seem to be those arising from "the logical categories of the monad, the dyad, and the polyad or higher set" (1.452), which Peirce has discovered in the preceding part of the paper. These three concepts, of course, come ultimately from the simplest mathematics, and the analysis which first makes them categories generative of logical principles is that of speculative grammar.

The transition from logic to metaphysics, and from metaphysics to the special sciences, can be explained in terms of the types of laws applying to experience:

> The laws of fact divide themselves at the outset into those which must be true if there be any true answer to every question that has a meaning, or, as we say, into laws *logically* necessary and laws *logically contingent*. To this division another is intimately connected. Namely, of laws logically contingent the most universal are of such a kind that they must be true provided every form which by logical necessity must be thought of a given subject is also a form of its real being. Calling this kind of necessity, metaphysical necessity, we may divide laws logically contingent into laws *metaphysically necessary* and laws *metaphysically contingent* [1.483].

This last group is composed of those laws which are "such as are not necessarily involved in the literal extension to being of the necessary laws of logical truth" (1.488). By further division, it is possible to proceed to laws of physics, dynamics, and of the other special sciences.[6]

167

Order of Sciences

math
Phenomenology
Logic
metaphysics
Special Sciences

The order of the sciences may thus be viewed as constituting a single line of sciences which begins with mathematics as the most abstract and runs through logic and metaphysics to the special sciences. In accord with the later development of Peirce's philosophy, phenomenology must be inserted between mathematics and logic. The relation of the simplest mathematics to phenomenology would then seem to parallel that of speculative grammar to metaphysics; in both cases, the latter science regards the purely formal principles of the first science as applying to elements of experience. However, the relation is not exactly parallel, since both the simplest mathematics and phenomenology are entirely within the realm of possibility and necessity, so that neither science discriminates between appearance and reality, while metaphyics is a science of reality, and its laws, even those that are metaphysically necessary, are logically contingent. It is possible only upon the assumption that the formal principles or categories of speculative grammar afford truths of being. The continuity of the line of sciences is thus broken by the necessity for this assumption involved in the passage from logic to metaphysics. The movement from the simplest mathematics through phenomenology to logic is continuous in that none of these sciences has occasion to assume that the objects of its investigation are reality and not appearance. Similarly, the movement from metaphysics through the special sciences is continuous in that all the sciences profess to be treating of reality and that each science receives regulative principles from the more abstract sciences above it and observational data from the more special ones below it. The assumption required by the passage to metaphysics, then, breaks the continuity in the line of sciences but divides it into two distinct realms, the movement in each of which is continuous.

This line of sciences in Peirce's system may be called the "ontological line" in that, while its order is determined by the degree of abstractness of the objects of scientific investigation, its one fundamental division arises from the establishment of ontological principles. With respect only to this way of viewing the sciences, the break in continuity might seem to occasion no difficulty, since the assumption involved may be justified as one necessary if there is to be any science of reality. Peirce seems to have taken this attitude when he remarked concerning the passage from logic to metaphysics: "Accordingly, it is to be assumed that the universe has an explanation, the function of which, like that of every logical explanation, is to unify its observed variety" (1.487). But, when the whole of his logic is taken into account, the justification of this assumption involves one of the principal problems of critic, the second branch of logic. For the assumption in one sense is equivalent to supposing that the real character of the universe can be determined by induction, and the problem thus becomes that of explaining the possibility of true inductions.

The situation here is a reflection of one already remarked above in chapter iii concerning Peirce's early views on the categories and the methods of fixing belief and making ideas clear. A determination of the real constituted the fourth step in a process which had already been divided into three stages corresponding to the categories. Thus, in the paper of 1867, a determination of the real was not guaranteed by the formulation of a proposition at the third stage in the passage from substance to being. A similar case held for the relation between thought and reality in the essays on the faculties of knowledge, and the continuity in the progression through the different methods of fixing belief was interrupted by the transition to the fourth method, the only one which could fix belief by reference to reality. It was suggested that there were only three grades of clearness for ideas, because no determination of reality, but only possibility, was involved. The break in the continuity of the ontological line seems quite analogous in that it occurs at precisely the point where the transition is made from mere possibility to reality.

Yet, if the analogy is to be complete, the three sciences prior to metaphysics should express the categories. This would relate mathematics, phenomenology, and logic as firstness, secondness,

169

and thirdness. But such a scheme does not appear anywhere in the *Collected Papers*, and on many counts it is clearly at variance with Peirce's descriptions of these sciences. It is important to remember that this first arrangement of the sciences in a single line in accordance with degrees of abstraction represents the earliest attempt (1896) in the *Collected Papers* to deal with the problem of classifying the sciences. Phenomenology was not at this time named as a separate science, and, although its problems were to some extent recognized, they were only characterized as "like those of mathematics" but "not mere mathematical problems" (1.417). Logic, moreover, was not specified as being one of the normative sciences. When these changes are made in the classification of sciences presented in 1902–3, the problem of justifying the assumption connnecting the two segments of the ontological line becomes in one sense identical with that of explaining the validity of induction, and the sciences are connected by the categories in a fashion that restores the continuity of the whole line.

In the lectures on pragmatism of 1903, Peirce suggested the following scheme:

> Phenomenology treats of the universal Qualities of Phenomena in their immediate phenomenal character, in themselves as phenomena. It, thus, treats of Phenomena in their Firstness [5.122].
>
> Normative Science treats of the laws of the relation of phenomena to ends; that is, it treats of Phenomena in their Secondness [5.123].
>
> Metaphysics, as I have just remarked, treats of Phenomena in their Thirdness [5.124].

The previous remark about metaphysics was that it "endeavors to comprehend the Reality of Phenomena. Now Reality is an affair of Thirdness as Thirdness, that is, in its mediation between Secondness and Firstness" (5.121). Mathematics as the one purely hypothetical science is prior to and falls outside the scheme of these three most universal positive sciences (cf. 5.39–40), which constitute the "three grand divisions" of philosophy (5.121). The most difficult part of this arrangement is perhaps the characterization of <u>normative science as a secondness,</u> and Peirce's first comment after presenting the scheme was: "If, then, Normative Science does not seem to be sufficiently described by saying that it treats of phenomena in their secondness, this is an indication that our conception of Normative Science is too narrow" (5.125).

The description of normative science which follows this remark in the lecture does not explicitly show how such science relates to secondness. Yet, however obscure may be the details, the general features of Peirce's philosophy which led him to this view of the sciences seem fairly clear. <u>Speculative grammar defines reality pragmatically as the ultimate end of inquiry, and the critic of arguments purports to show that induction carried on sufficiently far is sure to attain this end. But this leads finally through speculative rhetoric to the moral problem about the hope for the indefinite continuation of inquiry and involves the other normative sciences. Throughout the consideration, phenomena as merely presented are opposed to ends which ought to be pursued. Metaphysics as the science which endeavors to comprehend the reality of phenomena can be viewed as mediating between this opposition in that it considers phenomena only as determined by inquiry and hence in effect interprets what is immediately presented as an end in some sense achieved.</u> This point requires Peirce's doctrine that every modification of consciousness is an inference and will be clarified by the consideration given in the next chapter of the sense in which a perceptual judgment "shades into" an abductive inference.

In this context Peirce can no longer hold to his earlier view that a determination of the real is a fourth step in a process beyond the three which reflect his categories.[7] The break in the continuity of the ontological line is not to be healed by an assumption that the universe has an explanation—or that the character of reality can be determined. The explanation for the validity of induction afforded by normative logic leads to the view, already expressed in Peirce's early discussions of induction, that no assumption about the explicability of reality is needed to justify induction, because it is impossible to conceive of a universe whose true character could not eventually be ascertained by induction. The acceptance of principles of logic "not merely as regulatively valid, but as truths of being" (1.487), becomes in this context the same as the passage from a consideration of phenomena in opposition to ends to that of phenomena characterized only as ends—as the outcome of inquiry. But Peirce's ontology, then, merges with his theory of induction.

2. INDUCTION AND PROBABILITY

A. Peirce's later considerations of the validity of induction for the most part constitute a development and elaboration of his earlier analysis. According to the *Minute Logic*, where Peirce is outlining the material to be examined by "Critical Logic,"

the discussion of probability naturally brings us to the interesting question of the validity of induction. I undertake to demonstrate mathematically that the validity of Induction, in the proper sense of the term, that is to say, experimental reasoning, follows, through the lemmas of probabilities, from the rudiments of the doctrine of necessary consequences, without any assumption whatever about the future being like the past, or similar results following similar conditions, or the uniformity of nature, or any such vague principle. I shall set forth the reasoning in strict accuracy of form; and I defy anybody to find a flaw in it. The importance of the question for every man is tremendous [2.102].

The manner in which these promises would have been fulfilled had Peirce completed the *Minute Logic* may be inferred from his subsequent remarks on the subject in other writings. According to his articles in Baldwin's *Dictionary* (Vol. II), there are three types of probable inference.[8] The first constitutes what may be called "probable deduction," which falls within that branch of deductive logic called "the doctrine of chances," and which covers "all the ordinary and legitimate applications of the mathematical doctrine of probability" (2.785). This kind of

172

probable inference is, by the definition of it, necessary inference. But necessary inference may be applied to probability as its subject-matter; and it then becomes, under another aspect, probable inference. If of an endless series of possible experiences a definite proportion will present a certain character (which is the sort of fact called an objective probability), then it necessarily follows that, foreseen or not, approximately the same proportion of any finite portion of that series will present the same character, either as it is, or when it has been sufficiently extended [2.785].

That is, upon the assumption of a real or objective probability such as that the frequency of heads in a series of tosses of a coin is $\frac{1}{2}$, it necessarily follows that approximately the same number of tosses in any finite series will either turn up heads half the time or will do so when sufficiently extended.

This type of probable inference "is governed by precisely the same principle as the inductive inference, but applied in the reverse way," since what is here inferred is in the case of an inductive inference a premiss, and conversely. For "it is not here true that the relation of the facts laid down in the premisses to the fact stated in the conclusion, which makes the former significant of the latter, requires the recognition of the conclusion" (2.785). An inductive inference, then, begins with a frequency observed in a finite series and proceeds to the conclusion that a real probability of such-and-such a value exists, or, in other words, it "simply evaluates an objective probability" (2.775). The characters whose occurrences constitute the frequency in question must be "predesignated," or "specified in advance of, or, at least, quite independently of, any examination of the facts" (2.789), since otherwise the entire procedure would provide no confirmation of the existence of an objective probability. Induction is thus a kind of probable inference "whose business consists in testing a hypothesis already recommended" (2.755), that is, in evaluating and confirming the existence of an objective probability already assumed to hold in respect to certain designated characters. An inductive inference, consequently, as the reverse of probable deduction, requires a recognition of the conclusion in that the characters involved in

173

the observed frequency stated in the premisses are determined by the hypothesis which is to be established by the conclusion.

The third kind of probable inference is "*presumption*, or more precisely, *abduction*," and its function is to furnish "the reasoner with the problematic theory which induction verifies" (2.776). This "is the only kind of reasoning which supplies new ideas, the only kind which is, in this sense, synthetic" (2.777).[9] Hence,

> it appears that there is a mode of inference in which the conclusion is accepted as having some chance of being true, and as being at any rate put in such a form as to suggest experimentation by which the degree of its truth can be ascertained. The only method by which it can be proved that a method, without necessarily leading to the truth, has some tolerable chance of doing so, is evidently the empirical, or inductive, method. Hence, as induction is proved to be valid by necessary deduction, so this presumptive inference must be proved valid by induction from experience [2.786].

This statement agrees with Peirce's declaration in the *Minute Logic* that the validity of induction follows from the doctrine of necessary consequences. The order of procedure in critical logic would thus be first to establish the doctrine of chances, or the calculus of probabilities, by means of necessary deduction, and then to demonstrate from this the validity of induction, which in turn justifies abductive inference. This is precisely the order outlined in the *Minute Logic*. The most lengthy statement in the *Collected Papers* of the way in which the validity of induction follows from necessary deduction occurs in a passage in the lectures on pragmatism of 1903:

> Induction consists in starting from a theory, deducing from it predictions of phenomena, and observing those phenomena in order to see how nearly they agree with the theory. The justification for believing that an experiential theory which has been subjected to a number of experimental tests will be in the near future sustained about as well by further such tests as it has hitherto been, is that by steadily pursuing that method we must in the long run find out how the matter really stands. The reason that we must do so is that our theory, if it be admissible even as a theory, simply consists in

supposing that such experiments will in the long run have results of a certain character. But I must not be understood as meaning that experience can be exhausted, or that any approach to exhaustion can be made. What I mean is that if there be a series of objects, say crosses and circles, this series having a beginning but no end, then whatever may be the arrangement or want of arrangement of these crosses and circles in the entire endless series must be discoverable to an indefinite degree of approximation by examining a sufficient finite number of successive ones beginning at the beginning of the series. This is a theorem capable of strict demonstration. The principle of the demonstration is that whatever has no end can have no mode of being other than that of a law, and therefore whatever general character it may have must be describable, but the only way of describing an endless series is by stating explicitly or implicitly the law of the succession of one term upon another. But every such term has a finite ordinal place from the beginning and therefore, if it presents any regularity for all finite successions from the beginning, it presents the same regularity throughout. Thus the validity of induction depends upon the necessary relation between the general and the singular. It is precisely this which is the support of Pragmatism [5.170].[10]

This purely mathematical justification of induction makes no reference to the actual character of objects of inquiry, so that an inductive inference "does not depend upon any assumption that the series will be endless, or that the future will be like the past, or that nature is uniform, nor upon any material assumption whatever" (2.784). The reference to "the necessary relation between the general and the singular" would thus involve nothing more than the mathematical propositions which demonstrate that single members of an endless series necessarily express a general law of succession. The objective probability which induction in the long run is fated to evaluate is precisely this sort of general law and may be said to be simply "the ratio of frequency of a specific to a generic event *in the ordinary course of experience*" (2.777) (Peirce's italics). This statement agrees with Peirce's definition of 1910 when it is understood as meaning the ratio which *would be* found in the long run of experience rather than one which has actually been found, since the probability as a real law does not consist in a ratio formed from any number of occurrences (see above, pp. 86–89).

According to an article on "Validity" by Peirce and Mrs. C. Ladd-Franklin in Baldwin's *Dictionary*, validity is "the possession by an argumentation or inference of that sort of efficiency in leading to the truth, which it professes to have" (2.779). Since induction professes to do nothing more than "to commence a proceeding which must in the long run approximate to the truth" (2.780), its validity is demonstrated when it is shown that such a procedure does so approximate to the truth. It is thus important to recognize that induction is valid only as a means of approximating the true value of an objective probability and that it is not to be understood as lending "a probability to its conclusion." For "it is nonsense to talk of the probability of a law, as if we could pick universes out of a grabbag and find in what proportion of them the law held good. Therefore, such an induction is not valid; for it does not do what it professes to do, namely, to make its conclusion probable" (2.780).

Thus, induction can test the abductive inference that the direction of the flow of heat from one body to another is determined by the temperatures of the respective bodies by showing approximately in what proportion of cases heat flows of itself from a body of low temperature to one of high, and this proportion constitutes an objective probability the statement of which would be the law of entropy. While the fact that this proportion continually remains equivalent to zero confirms the hypothesis that the direction of the flow is determined by the temperatures, it indicates nothing whatsoever about the probability of the law arising from this confirmation. For inasmuch as the law is nothing but the expression of a probability, to speak of the probability of the law would be to speak of the probability of a probability, which is absurd.

The calculus of probabilities, consequently, has nothing to do with measuring the extent to which scientific knowledge falls short of certainty. In the notes of 1910 to the *Doctrine of*

Chances, Peirce wrote: "I shall in these notes endeavor to mark the three ways of falling short of certainty by the three terms *probability, verisimilitude* or *likelihood,* and *plausibility*" (2.662). The latter pertains only to abductive inference and means that a theory that "has not yet been subjected to any test, although more or less surprising phenomena have occurred which it would explain if it were true, is in itself of such a character as to recommend it for further examination or, if it be *highly* plausible, justify us in seriously inclining toward belief in it, as long as the phenomena be inexplicable otherwise" (2.662). "Likelihood" pertains to an inductive inference, that is, to a theory "which is not yet proved but is supported by such evidence that if the rest of the conceivably possible evidence should turn out upon examination to be of a *similar* character, the theory would be conclusively proved" (2.663). Peirce added: "Any numerical determination of likelihood is more than I can expect." Finally, probability may be explained as a kind of habit "quite analogous to any *habit* that a man might have" (2.664). This characteristic applies only to probable deduction and falls short of certainty in a totally different sense from that of plausibility or likelihood. For the uncertainty now arises from the actual character of the premisses and not from the fact that further evidence might show the inference to be false. One can infer the actual behavior of a die from an objective probability in a manner analogous to the way in which one can infer the actual behavior of a man from his habits; the inference is never as to what certainly will happen on a given occasion but only as to what certainly would happen in the long run.

B. Peirce's demonstration of the validity of induction, whatever may or may not be its mathematical merits, makes the assumption that the universe has an explanation unnecessary only if a prior assumption be granted, namely, that the inductive method is practically possible as a means of inquiry. For inasmuch as the demonstration is professedly purely mathematical, it permits only the assertion that, if inquiry can proceed by valid induction, then the universe will ultimately be explained, irrespective of what is independently assumed about its uniformity or lack of uniformity. While there is no need to suppose that a series of experiments must be endless in order to obtain the true value of an objective probability, it is nevertheless impossible to have any assurance whatsoever that this value actually has been obtained from any finite number of experiments, no matter how large. Peirce's final analysis of induction and probability has thus failed to avoid the necessity for an appeal to faith or hope in the indefinite extension of human inquiry in order to render the universe explicable. As noticed above in chapters ii and iii, the notes added in 1910 to the *Doctrine of Chances*, the last remarks on probability appearing in the *Collected Papers*, open with a reaffirmation of this faith: "No man can be logical whose supreme desire is the well-being of himself or of any other existing person or collection of persons" (2.661). Induction, then, as merely commencing a procedure which in the long run is sure to lead to the truth, is practically possible as a means of inquiry only in terms of an unlimited community of scientists capable of carrying on inquiry indefinitely. There is never any absolute assurance that an end obtained by finite inquiry affords even a close approximation to the true value of an objective probability.

When Peirce's order of sciences is considered only with respect to the arrangement in the ontological line as it involves speculative grammar and the demonstration of the validity of induction, there is no way of avoiding the paradox that everything real becomes explicable only at the price of an inexplicable assumption about the real continuation of inquiry. It has already been remarked in the discussion of this paradox in Peirce's early writings that any attempt to mitigate its force must come by developing the unique status of the assumption as a precondition of inquiry, as a matter of emotion and sentiment with reasons neither for nor against it. Something of this sort seems to have been one of the main objectives which Peirce hoped to accomplish by regarding logic proper as a normative science dependent on ethics and esthetics. The final phase in the consideration of his order of the sciences must thus be centered around this dependence of logic on prior normative sciences.

3. SPECULATIVE RHETORIC AND OBJECTIVE LOGIC

A. The dependence of logic on prior normative sciences should be most obvious in the third branch of logic, since it is precisely this branch which is concerned with relating principles of logic to human action. The name usually applied to this study in the *Collected Papers* is "speculative rhetoric," although "methodeutic" is used almost as frequently. In the sketch of "Proposed Work in Logic" in the opening chapter of the *Minute Logic*, the study is described as searching for "a *method of discovering methods.*" "This can only come from a theory of the method of discovery. In order to cover every possibility, this should be founded on a general doctrine of methods of attaining purposes, in general; and this, in turn, should spring from a still more general doctrine of the nature of teleological action, in general" (2.108). Every consideration of method is thus by no means confined to speculative rhetoric, but, on the contrary, it is only because various methods are developed by other sciences that speculative rhetoric as a study of methods in general is possible. Mathematics as independent of all other sciences develops its own methods; phenomenology needs only mathematics to aid in developing its peculiar method, and speculative grammar and critical logic can develop the pragmatic and inductive methods which are employed by all the sciences that investigate the character of reality. General methodeutic would then be an examination of all these methods as various prescriptions for kinds of teleological action and would in turn depend on prior normative sciences for a general doctrine of teleological action.

But unfortunately there is no explicit treatment of speculative rhetoric in the *Collected Papers*, and the brief outline presented in the *Minute Logic* affords the clearest indication of how Peirce conceived what he called a year later (1903) "the highest and most living branch of logic" (2.333). However, something more

179

of the character of this study may be seen from a consideration of objective logic, since the latter seems directly dependent on methodeutic. In fact, in his earlier views concerning objective logic (see above, chap. iv, n. 11) Peirce identified it with this third branch of logic proper. In the paper *The Logic of Mathematics; etc.* (ca. 1896), he described logic "in its broader sense" as treating

also of the laws of the evolution of thought, which since it coincides with the study of the necessary conditions of the transmission of meaning by signs from mind to mind, and from one state of mind to another, ought, for the sake of taking advantage of an old association of terms, be called *rhetorica speculativa*, but which I content myself with inaccurately calling *objective logic*, because that conveys the correct idea that it is like Hegel's logic [1.444].

When he wrote this, Peirce evidently had not yet come to regard logic as a normative science and thus to distinguish an objective from a normative account of the evolution of thought. When such distinction is made, the former account may be identified as an objective view of the process governed by normative methodeutic.

After his sketch of speculative rhetoric or methodeutic in the *Minute Logic*, Peirce opened the next section with the remarks:

With Speculative Rhetoric, Logic, in the sense of Normative Semeotic, is brought to a close. But now we have to examine whether there be a doctrine of signs corresponding to Hegel's objective logic; that is to say, whether there be a life in Signs, so that—the requisite vehicle being present—they will go through a certain order of development, and if so, whether this development be merely of such a nature that the same round of changes of form is described over and over again whatever be the matter of the thought or whether, in addition to such a repetitive order, there be also a greater life-history that every symbol furnished with a vehicle of life goes through, and what is the nature of it [2.111].

Peirce offers an apology to those who would "pooh-pooh" an idea of this sort, but he concludes:

If a reader who has thought it worth while to listen to what I have had to say upon normative logic finds objective logic too remote from his interests to care to listen to any discussion of it, I shall fully approve his allowing the leaves of my chapter upon this subject to remain uncut. But my own position is different. It lies directly in the path of my duty to consider the question critically [2.111].

A brief consideration of objective logic as part of Peirce's scientific metaphysics was presented above in the preceding chapter and centered around the different views of evolution. In this outline in the *Minute Logic*, Peirce is concerned with the relations between normative and objective logic rather than with the development of the latter for metaphysics. The central point of the discussion becomes that of justifying the basic assumption necessary for the establishment of objective logic. This assumption lies at the very foundation of Peirce's philosophy, since it turns directly on the question of modes of being. "The mere hypothesis" that there is such a real thing as a symbol, Peirce remarks at the outset, "involves the idea of a different mode of being from that of existential fact" (2.115). "This mode of being," he continues, "seems to claim immediate recognition as evident in the mere idea of it. One asks whether there is not a fallacy in using the ordinary processes of logic either to support it or to refute it."

The paragraphs in the *Minute Logic* which follow this last remark can hardly be called clear, and it will be well to review the issue before turning to Peirce's further discussion. It has been frequently remarked that in his early writings (including *The Monist* papers of 1891–93), modes of being are not distinguished. The words "being" and "existence" seem to be virtual synonyms for "reality," defined as the ultimate outcome of inquiry. In the discussion of the validity of induction in 1869, Peirce referred to his first statement of this definition as showing that "being at all is being in general" (5.349; see above, pp. 58–59). In the more lengthy presentation of the definition in *How To Make Our Ideas Clear* he suggested that it could serve as the basis for a "metaphysical theory of existence" (5.410); and in *Man's Glassy Essence* he remarked: "I long ago showed that real existence, or thing-ness, consists in regularities" (6.265). The attempt to make individual existence and the reality of general laws separate modes of being seems to have been made first around 1896. In a fragment ca. 1894, Peirce referred to his categories as "a table of conceptions drawn from the logical analysis of thought and regarded as applicable to being" (1.300), but it was not until this paper ca. 1896 that he used the phrase "modes of being."[11] In the paper *The Logic of Mathematics; etc.* (ca. 1896), Peirce declared that "existence is that mode of being which lies in opposition to another" (1.457) and referred to Duns Scotus as the philosopher "who first elucidated individual existence" (1.458). However, only two modes of being are distinguished, individual facts and general laws or real possibilities. "As *general*," Peirce argued, "the law, or general fact, concerns the potential world of quality, while as *fact*, it concerns the actual world of actuality" (1.420). In this context, then, generals partake of both modes of being, so that Peirce still speaks of generals as existing (1.422–24). "Reality" is used interchangeably with "being" (1.487).

B. The *Minute Logic* seems to mark the first attempt to distinguish a third mode of being in addition to potentiality and actuality.[12] In the paragraph which follows his suggestion that there would be "a fallacy in using the ordinary processes of logic either to support or refute" the hypothesis that there is a different mode of being from that of existential fact, Peirce remarks:

What are the modes of being? One might antecedently expect that the cenopythagorean[13] categories would require three modes of being. But a little examination will show us that they could be brought into fairly presentable accordance with the theory that there were only two, or even only one. The question cannot be decided in that way. Besides, it would be illogical to rely upon the categories to decide so fundamental a question. The only safe way is to make an entirely fresh investigation [2.116].

Peirce does not indicate here how his categories could be made to accord with the view that there are only one or two modes of being, but then his paper ca. 1896 had argued for three categories of elements of phenomena and had recognized only two modes of being, while prior to this his theory of the categories had been advanced with the assumption that there was but a single mode of existence or reality. The essentially new factor in the present outline which entails "an entirely fresh investigation" is the view that logic is a normative science, with the result that the ultimate criterion of meaning must be with reference to the final end of action, the *summum bonum*, rather than to practical effects which are actually encountered in experience. The following passage, which is a continuation of the one quoted above, marks the first appearance of the *summum bonum* as a technical term in Peirce's philosophy.

In such abstract questions, as we shall have already found, the first step, often more than half the battle, is to ascertain what we mean by the question—what we possibly can mean by it. We know already how we must proceed in order to determine what the meaning of the question is. Our sole guide must be the consideration of the use to which the answer is to be put—not necessarily the practical application, but in what way it is to subserve the *summum bonum*. Within this principle is wrapped up the answer to the question, what being is, and what, therefore, its modes must be. It is absolutely impossible that the word "Being" should bear any meaning whatever except with reference to the *summum bonum*. This is true of any word. But that which is true of one word in one respect, of another in another, of every word in some or another respect, that is precisely what the word "being" aims to express.

The general import of this would seem to be simply that, in order to designate an object of scientific inquiry, a meaning must be specified with reference to the end of inquiry. While in most cases this may be achieved simply by taking the meaning as identical with the conceivable practical application, such identification never gives the ultimate character of the meaning, which must be taken in relation to the final end of inquiry. The situation is the same as that noted above in the preceding chapter (pp. 142–43) in discussing Peirce's arguments for the reality of God. The final test of any hypothesis was found to consist in its value in the self-controlled growth of inquiry, since the ultimate aim of each inquirer could never be identified with the testing of this or that hypothesis but had to be taken rather as the truth pursued by the unlimited community. The determination of the meaning of "being" thus seems analogous to the test of the hypothesis of God's reality. Just as this hypothesis seemed to possess the unique property of yielding no definite predictions and still having a value in the advancement of inquiry, the term "being" seems to have no meaning that can be determined with reference to one practical application as distinct from another and yet is not meaningless in relation to the final end of inquiry. The test of God's reality, in other words, could only be specified in terms so general as to apply to the test of any reality, and similarly the meaning of "being" can only be specified so generally as to state what would be true of the meaning of any word whatsoever.

In the final paragraph of his sketch of "Proposed Work in Logic," Peirce states that the three modes of being are "elements of coöperation toward the *summum bonum*" (2.118). While he does not elaborate the statement, something of its meaning may be ascertained from the account of "being" given above. But it will be necessary first to review at some length certain aspects of Peirce's original definition of reality. When in 1878 he gave this definition as resulting from an application of the pragmatic maxim, he did not regard the application as essentially different from any other.[14] The eventual acceptance of ? certain opinion by all who investigate seemed to be just as much a conceivable practical effect as any result of an experiment in the laboratory. The hypothesis that an opinion expresses reality seemed to be no different philosophically from the hypothesis, for instance, that a given object is hard. For just as the meaning of the latter consists in the practical consequences of not being scratched by certain substances, so the meaning of the former consists in those of not being rejected by anyone who investigated sufficiently far. Among other things, this view leads to the difficulty that, if a particular object is assumed to have been destroyed before it was investigated, there seems to be no basis for saying that any opinions about the object could have expressed reality. Moreover, since Peirce's analysis of probability and induction makes the eventual acceptance of an opinion which effects a determination of reality a long-run affair that is never sure to have taken place at any specified time, the only things that are sure to be real are those which can be investigated through an indefinitely long period.

There seems to be no way of getting around this difficulty without first insisting that the realities which science seeks are of the nature of real laws or objective probabilities. But then it is also necessary to maintain that there is something objective in the here and now of immediate experience if hypotheses are ever to be tested. In the views which he held until sometime after *The Monist* papers of 1891–93, Peirce seems to have believed that the continuity of experience prevented any absolute distinction between the here and now and what would be discovered. There is a single continuum of existence or reality in which nothing can be made out as absolutely determinate and individual. According to the papers of 1868–69, there is no immediate intuition of reality, but every modification of consciousness is an inference, so that "being at all is being in general" (5.349). The three categories of phenomena, "feelings," "sensations of reaction," and "general conceptions," as explained in *The Architecture of Theories* (6.18–20), are three different phases in the determination of a single reality. The feelings and sensations in what seems to be here and now are always understood by general conceptions that refer to the future, and every determination of reality is in the form of a law prescribing something of the character of those general conceptions which will arise as interpretations of feelings and sensations that are just in the future.

But this position still affords no means of distinguishing the real from what will be determined by experience. There is still no basis for saying that a diamond which was assumed to have been destroyed before being touched was really hard (see above, pp. 87–88). When Peirce returned to this problem in his paper ca. 1896, his analysis centered around qualities and the subjects in which they are present. He defined a quality as "a mere abstract potentiality" and explained that "general" is "another word for the same thing" as quality (1.422). Further, a quality "is not anything which is dependent, in its being, upon mind, whether in the form of sense or in that of thought. Nor is it dependent, in its being, upon the fact that some material thing possesses it. That quality is dependent upon sense is the great error of the conceptualists. That it is dependent upon the subject in which it is realized is the great error of all the nominalistic schools" (1.422). Peirce offers arguments to refute the conceptualists and nominalists, and advances his own doctrine of scholastic realism as the only tenable position. A quality or general has a real being as a possibility or potentiality quite apart from its existence, which "depends on its subject having a place in the general system of the universe" (1.424). With respect to the case of the diamond, then, the hardness can be said to be real as a potentiality even though its existence in this particular diamond can never be confirmed.

The occasion for maintaining a theory of real possibility seems to have come originally from Peirce's work in the philosophy of mathematics. In a letter to William James, dated March 18, 1897, Peirce wrote:

Is possibility a mode of being? Good. . . . I reached this truth by studying the question of possible grades of multitude, where I found myself arrested until I could form a whole logic of possibility,—a very difficult and laborious task. You would not have reached it that way. You must have some short cut, which I am curious to know more about.[15]

The paper of 1897 entitled *Multitude and Number* (4, Bk. I, Paper VI) seems clearly to represent in part at least the fruit of the labors to which Peirce was referring in this letter. A doctrine of real possibility is proclaimed early in the paper:

We have to note the precise meaning of saying that a relation of a given description exists. A relation of the kind here considered

186

has been called an *ens rationis*; but it cannot be said that because nobody has ever constructed it—perhaps never will—it exists any the less on that account. Its existence consists in the fact that, if it were constructed, it would involve no contradiction [4.176].[16]

It would appear to be such considerations as this that led Peirce to try to work out the notion of real possibility as distinct from individual existence in more or less the terms of traditional metaphysics and epistemology, as he did in his paper *The Logic of Mathematics; etc., ca.* 1896.[17] Perhaps he was already looking for the "short cut" he assumed that James had. Apparently Peirce received no help from James in the undertaking, at least so far as can be judged from the correspondence between them.[18] While in the *Minute Logic* Peirce spoke continually of three rather than two modes of being, in the part he finished of this work he never got around to giving a clear statement of what he meant by a third mode in addition to possibility and actuality. In a paper of 1906 he explained his third mode of reality and implied in his manner of statement that he came to recognize it as a separate mode after he had already argued for the first two.

In other places, I have given many other reasons for my firm belief that there are real possibilities. I also think, however, that, in addition to actuality and possibility, a *third* mode of reality must be recognized in that which, as the gipsy fortune-tellers express it, is "sure to come true," or, as we may say, is *destined*, although I do not mean to assert that this is affirmation rather than the negation of this Mode of Reality [4.547].

A few pages later in the same paper, Peirce referred to these three modes as "modes of Being" rather than of reality (4.549),[19] although he sometimes used "reality" only for the third mode and "existence" for the second. With such usage, "reality means a certain kind of non-dependence upon thought, and so is a cognitionary character, while existence means reaction with the environment, and so is a dynamic character" (5.503, ca. 1905). Peirce went on after this statement to express doubts as to whether anybody ever believed

187

that "generals *exist*" in this sense of the word, and in another context he remarked that he would not maintain God exists in this sense (cf. 6.495 and above, p. 147).

When he characterized his third mode of being as that which is destined to come about, Peirce explained in a footnote that he meant *destined* in the sense of what is "sure to come about although there is no necessitating reason for it," as "a pair of dice, thrown often enough, will be sure to turn up sixes some time, although there is no necessity that they should" (4.547 n.). Without this third mode, there would be no way of distinguishing between mere possibilities, which are pure fiction and may never be connected with the world of actuality, and laws or habits, which are always essentially connected with some actuality. In his paper of 1908 on the reality of God, Peirce spoke of his three modes of being as giving rise to three universes and characterized the first universe as comprising

all mere Ideas, those airy nothings to which the mind of poet, pure mathematician, or another *might* give local habitation and a name within that mind. Their very airy-nothingness, the fact that their Being consists in mere capability of getting thought, not in anybody's Actually thinking them, saves their Reality [6.455].

The second universe, of course, "is that of the Brute Actuality of things and facts." The third universe comprises

everything whose being consists in active power to establish connections between different objects, especially between objects in different Universes. Such is everything which is essentially a Sign— not the mere body of the Sign, which is not essentially such, but, so to speak, the Sign's Soul, which has its Being in its power of serving as intermediary between its Object and a Mind. Such, too, is a living consciousness, and such the life, the power of growth, of a plant. Such is a living constitution—a daily newspaper, a great fortune, a social "movement" [6.455].

The main characteristic of this third mode of being would thus seem to be that of a possibility which contains the power to actualize itself—or, expressing it in another way, is destined

188

under certain conditions to be actualized.[20] The real probability of a die's turning up a six is a sign of the die's actual behavior and thereby connects a possibility with an actuality. The reason why the die eventually settles down to turning up sixes with a more or less definite frequency is simply the effect brought about by this real probability or habit which the die possesses. Any rationality discernible in the actual course of events must thus be the expression of a real habit, whether the rationality is manifested in the growth of a plant or the social and political behavior of men. By way of contrast, the real possibility, for example, of always being able to affirm of any two collections that all the elements of one may be placed in a one-to-one relation with all or part of the elements of the other has nothing to do with what will eventually take place in the world of actuality. For the reality of such a relation, Peirce declares, does not imply "an actual operation performed" (4.178). The question remains entirely within the realm of possibilities—the "airy nothings" of the first universe.[21] The reality of a daily newspaper, on the other hand, like that of a natural law, consists in its power to elicit certain responses in the world of actual fact. This does not mean that the law or the newspaper requires no individual existence for the exercise of its power. Obviously, the newspaper requires marks on paper, and the natural law requires some sort of individual bodies reacting in space and time. But that which essentially constitutes the newspaper is not the printed type but rather the habits, symbols, or words by virtue of which the print may function as it does. Similarly, the law is essentially the habit or real probability by virtue of which individual bodies react in the way they do. The hardness of the diamond as a mere quality of possible feeling would have only the reality of the first universe, though it would possess this reality even if diamonds never existed. But the hardness of an actual diamond as a law or habit more or less determining how that diamond would behave under certain conditions has the reality of the third universe, and even if the diamond were

189

destroyed before the behavior in question could· be manifested, the habit was nonetheless real.

C. Whatever may be the merits of Peirce's threefold doctrine of being, it does not accord with a strict interpretation of the original version of his pragmatic theory of reality. As long as the real is defined simply as the object of that opinion which is fated to be accepted eventually by all who investigate, the possible rather than constituting a separate mode of reality would only be something whose opposite is not established as real.[22] Inasmuch as every opinion is subject to further determination, it can never have an absolutely determinate particular for its object, so that "being at all is being in general" (5.349), and "real existence, or thing-ness, consists in regularities" (6.265). In short, different modes of being cannot be given a meaning with reference to some definite practical consequence, such as not being scratched by certain substances or not being rejected by anyone who investigates sufficiently far. Peirce's "entirely fresh investigation" proposed in the *Minute Logic*, which is to give "being" or "reality" a meaning with reference to the *summum bonum*, is thus in effect a reinterpretation of pragmatism that will render a distinction of modes of being meaningful.[23] If "being" signifies whatever there is about any word that enables it to subserve the ultimate goal of inquiry, modes of being would comprise different ways of performing this function and would therefore represent "elements of coöperation toward the *summum bonum*" (2.118).

The final discussion (*ca.* 1909) of modes of being in the *Collected Papers* begins with the remark that "all thinking is conducted in signs that are mainly of the same general structure as words" (6.338). But there are also thoughts "of the nature of those signs of which we have need now and then in our converse with one another to eke out the defects of words, or *symbols*." These "non-symbolic thought-signs" are either icons or indices, and "the substance of thoughts consists of these three species of ingredients." "The next step," Peirce continues, "consists in considering why it is that thoughts should take those three different forms" (6.339). His conclusion is that "the reason why different things have to be differently thought of is that their modes of metaphysical being are different." There is no mention of the *summum bonum* in this brief discussion, but if the account is to be given a pragmatic meaning, the only way seems to be that of maintaining that the modes of being represented by the different species of signs constitute the way in which words aided by icons and indices subserve the ultimate end of inquiry.

The initial work for a theory of modes of being would thus be given by speculative grammar, which distinguishes the three kinds of signs and provides the criterion of meaning. While this work affords the principles of ontology, it does not in itself show the validity of these principles as elements of scientific metaphysics. For even though, within the context of epistemology or speculative grammar, modes of metaphysical being appear as the reason why different things have to be differently thought of, in so far as metaphysics is a positive science of reality it must presuppose the validity of induction and hence the different ways in which words can subserve the goal of inquiry. Metaphysics itself therefore cannot give the final reason why the forms of thought appear as they do. Before stating his conclusion quoted above, Peirce declared: "The key to the solution of this question is that what we think of cannot possibly be of a different nature from thought itself. For the thought thinking and the immediate thought-object are the very same thing regarded from different points of view" (6.339). Now the pragmatic criterion of meaning surely makes the point of view of "thought thinking" the fundamental one, since it refers all reality to the goal of thought. The validity of modes of being as metaphysical principles must thus depend on the analysis which justifies the view that they are elements of co-operation toward the *summum bonum.* This carries the consideration from speculative grammar through critic and the validity of induction to speculative rhetoric, or the "general doctrine of methods of attaining purposes, in general" (2.108). After explaining in his sketch in the *Minute*

191

Logic that "being" must be understood with reference to the *summum bonum*, Peirce continued:

> Having thus worked out a tolerable conception of Being, we turn to modes of being. But these are metaphysical conceptions. Let us first inquire how the validity of *any* metaphysical conception is to be determined. For this purpose we have only to apply the principles of Speculative Rhetoric. We sketch out the method and apply it to a few metaphysical conceptions, such as Reality, Necessity, etc. In process of doing this, we discover that all such metaphysical conceptions are but determinations of the categories, and consequently form a regular system. We also find that they can be held as valid only in approximative and imperfect senses [2.117].

When this passage is considered in the light of what has already been remarked about speculative rhetoric, it would seem that the inquiry Peirce is proposing here is one which investigates the methods actually employed by metaphysics rather than one which is itself to supply the methods before metaphysics can be undertaken. The same situation would hold for all the special sciences, or the sciences of reality less general than metaphysics, so that speculative rhetoric seems to be a kind of reflective survey of scientific inquiry which reveals the normative character of logic in relation to such inquiry. It is precisely because speculative grammar makes all meaning refer to the end of inquiry that this reflective survey must be conceived at the outset as a doctrine of methods of attaining purposes. When Peirce regarded objective logic as identical with speculative rhetoric, he had not turned to the problem of reconciling modes of being with his original definition of reality. Without consideration of this problem a survey of the process of inquiry after the analysis of arguments given by critic might seem to involve nothing but an objective view of the evolution of thought. But if the pragmatic criterion of meaning is taken into account, logic must first be surveyed as a normative process before the assumption of modes of being which is required for its objective status can be adequately understood.

The two lectures of 1898 on objective logic (6, Bk. I, chaps.

7–8) were definitely prepared before Peirce had conceived of logic proper as a normative science. The contrast is thus between "our subjective logic" and "the logic of the universe . . . to which our own aspires" (6.189) rather than between normative and objective logic. Moreover, the lectures assume only the two modes of being distinguished in the paper ca. 1896, so that Peirce speaks only of two universes, "a world of ideas, a Platonic world," and "the existing universe," which, "with all its arbitrary secondness, is an offshoot from, or an arbitrary determination of," the former (6.192). There is no mention of the third universe distinguished in the paper of 1908 (6.455). The categories determine three "elements" which have to be assumed in accounting for the evolution of the two universes, but they do not provide three separate modes of being. The objective logic presented in these lectures, then, is radically different from that described in the *Minute Logic*, where the principal issue is whether signs have a distinct mode of being which is neither mere possibility nor actuality.[24] The principal characteristic of this third mode of being was seen to be that of active power to connect possibility and existence. In the second chapter of the *Minute Logic* Peirce explained this power as that of *final causation*, or "that kind of causation whereby the whole calls out its parts" (1.220). The recognition of such causation in objective logic seems inevitable if logic proper is viewed first as essentially normative, as a process directed toward an end. Speculative rhetoric is then distinct from, and a necessary antecedent to, an objective logic which moves by final causation.

The determination of three modes of being may be viewed as the final phase in the solution of the problem involved in the passage from logic to metaphysics when the sciences are arranged in an ontological line. If there are only the two universes, those of possibility and actuality, this passage from the one to the other can be made only with the help of an assumption that the actual universe has an explanation. But the general ideas or laws which comprise the third universe establish a connection between the other two and render such an assumption unnecessary.

Considered normatively, this connection depends ultimately on the hope for the indefinite continuation of inquiry, while, objectively, it results from the force of final causation—of possibilities that are destined to be actualized.[25]

4. LOGIC AND THE NORMATIVE SCIENCES

A. From the consideration of speculative rhetoric and objective logic it seems clear that logic proper must depend on prior normative sciences for a determination of the *summum bonum* if the nature and purpose of logic and the distinction of modes of being are to be fully understood. Fortunately, Peirce completed a part of the fourth chapter of the *Minute Logic*, which leaves no doubt concerning the general place of ethics in his philosophy. He declares at the outset:

The intention of this chapter is to lay the foundation for the doctrine, which will appear more and more evident as we proceed, that that truth the conditions of which the logician endeavors to analyze, and which is the goal of the reasoner's aspirations, is nothing but a phase of the *summum bonum* which forms the subject of pure ethics, and that neither of those men can really understand himself until he perceives clearly that it is so [1.575].

This statement is followed by a discussion of traits of character necessary for scientists.

At the very lowest, a man must prefer the truth to his own interest and well-being and not merely to his bread and butter, and to his own vanity, too, if he is to do much in science. This will appear in the logical discussion; and it is thoroughly borne out by examining the characters of scientific men and of great heuretic students of all kinds [1.576].

Peirce offers a résumé of biographical history to show that "excluding idle tales about pre-socratic philosophers, all history does not tell of a single man who has considerably increased human knowledge (unless theology be knowledge) having been proved a criminal" (1.576).

This consideration stems of course from the ultimate requirement of logic necessitated by Peirce's analysis of probability and

194

induction. The only means of attaining scientific knowledge is by true inductions, and, if man is to inquire in accordance with the inductive method, the ends of his actions must transcend personal interests and be identified with those of an unlimited community. Truth as the goal of scientific inquiry is thus a phase of the *summum bonum*, a phase of the final end of all human action. The crucial question, therefore, presupposed by logic and science is "What is Good?" Peirce explains:

> Now this is hardly a normative question: it is pre-normative. It does not ask for the conditions of fulfillment of a definitely accepted purpose, but asks what is to be sought, not for a reason, but back of every reason. Logic, as a true normative science, supposes the question of what is to be aimed at to be already answered before it could itself have been called into being. Pure ethics, philosophical ethics, is not normative, but pre-normative [1.577].

This inquiry into the *summum bonum*, Peirce goes on to say, contains "the true life-germ of all the truths I have to unfold" (1.578).

Since the determination of the ultimate end of all action, of "what is desirable without any reason," clearly cannot rest on any scientific analysis, as such analysis presupposes this very determination, "we must make up our minds to rely entirely upon self-questioning, with here and there perhaps some secondary aid from psychology" (1.579). But "such self-questioning produces no infallible response. On the contrary, consciousness may be set down as one of the most mendacious witnesses that ever was questioned. But it is the only witness there is; and all we can do is to put it in the sweat-box and torture the truth out of it, with such judgment as we can command" (1.580). Accordingly, Peirce proposes "to pass in review every one of the general classes of objects which anybody could suppose to be an ultimate good, and to question consciousness, first, as to whether or not each of these in turn could content us as the sole ultimate good independently of any ulterior result, and if not, whether it can be considered to be in itself a good at all, irrespective of its effects" (1.581). Peirce never completed this undertaking and perhaps gave up the idea of discovering the *summum bonum* by questioning consciousness. In his lectures on pragmatism (1903), which could have come but shortly after the above passage, he frankly admits:

It is only since 1883 that I have numbered ethics among my special studies; and until about four years ago, I was not prepared to affirm that ethics was a normative science. As for esthetics, although the first year of my study of philosophy[26] was devoted to this branch exclusively, yet I have since then so completely neglected it that I do not feel entitled to have any confident opinions about it. I am inclined to think that there is such a Normative Science; but I feel by no means sure even of that [5.129].

In another lecture in this series, Peirce described himself as "a perfect ignoramus in esthetics" (5.111), and in the second chapter of the *Minute Logic*, he listed esthetics as the third of the "pre-logical sciences" (after mathematics and phenomenology), but added, "if I am to take the word of others that there is such a science, I myself being lamentably ignorant of it, as I fear will too plainly appear" (2.120).

Yet, despite his uncertainty about esthetics, Peirce was emphatic in making it as the first of the normative sciences that upon which both ethics and logic are dependent. According to the lectures of 1903, "the logically good is simply a particular species of the morally good," and "the morally good appears as a particular species of the esthetically good" (5.130). In the sketch of "esthetics" given in these lectures, "there is no such thing as positive esthetic badness; and since by goodness we chiefly in this discussion mean merely the absence of badness, or faultlessness, there will be no such thing as esthetic goodness" (5.132). Hence, "all there will be will be various esthetic qualities; that is, simple qualities of totalities not capable of full embodiment in the parts, which qualities may be more decided and strong in one case than in another. . . . There are innumerable varieties of esthetic quality, but no purely esthetic grade of excellence."

196

The terms "good" and "bad" are thus introduced by ethics and arise from the circumstance that

an aim which *cannot* be adopted and consistently pursued is a bad aim. It cannot properly be called an ultimate aim at all. The only moral evil is not to have an ultimate aim [5.133].

Accordingly the problem of ethics is to ascertain what end is ⟨ possible. It might be thoughtlessly supposed that *special science* could aid in this ascertainment. But that would rest on a misconception of the nature of an absolute aim, which is what *would be* pursued under all possible circumstances—that is, even though the contingent facts ascertained by special sciences were entirely different from what they are. Nor, on the other hand, must the definition of such aim be reduced to a mere formalism [5.134].

It is certainly not easy to see from this characterization of esthetics and ethics how these sciences can contribute to an understanding of logic and the distinction of modes of being which marks the transition from normative to objective logic. The development of this part of Peirce's philosophy is so slight as to make any detailed consideration of his fragmentary pronouncements on its problems seem singularly unpromising. His distinction between normative and prenormative ethics, for example, is no more than mentioned, and nothing is said as to whether there is prenormative "esthetics." Peirce's own uncertainty as to how to carry out his proposal in the opening chapter of the *Minute Logic* to found logic and metaphysics on a theory of the *summum bonum* seems manifest in his strange development of the fourth chapter, where he was laboring at his proposed task. The editors of the *Collected Papers* have published only the first part of this chapter and a short digression taken from the remainder. After announcing his intention of determining ultimate goods by "questioning consciousness" and characterizing the project briefly, Peirce goes on, according to the description in the editorial footnote, "to list a number of ultimate 'ends' proposed by the early Greeks and concludes with a one-hundred-and-twenty-five-page discussion on the order, history, and contents of the Platonic Dialogues" (1.584 n.). The short digression (6.349–52) which the editors have published

197

from this last portion is in the form of a dialogue between "C.S.P." and "the stranger of Plato's *Sophist*" and was described by Peirce as an attempt to give the stranger "a little dose of his own cathartic" (6.349 n.). The dialogue is concerned with the meanings of "being," "existence," "reality," "truth," and "nothing" and indicates that Peirce had not forgotten his proposal to deal with modes of being, although he fails to mention their relation to the *summum bonum*. The discussion does not seem to contribute anything which has not already been remarked concerning his views on modes of being.

B. But even with the incompleteness of Peirce's account of esthetics and ethics, his remarks on these sciences provide some indication of the possibilities they afford for a resolution of the paradox that everything real is explicable only with an inexplicable assumption about the reality of inquiry. The phenomenological analysis of the categories shows that "not only does Thirdness suppose and involve the ideas of Secondness and Firstness, but never will it be possible to find any Secondness or Firstness in the phenomenon that is not accompanied by Thirdness" (5.90). Hence, although esthetics is concerned primarily with qualities of feeling, it also involves an intellectual element. Peirce declared:

> Ignorant as I am of Art, I have a fair share of capacity for esthetic enjoyment; and it seems to me that while in esthetic enjoyment we attend to the totality of Feeling—and especially to the total resultant Quality of Feeling presented in the work of art we are contemplating—yet it is a sort of intellectual sympathy, a sense that here is a Feeling that one can comprehend, a reasonable Feeling. I do not succeed in saying exactly *what* it is, but it is a consciousness belonging to the category of Representation, though representing something in the Category of Quality of Feeling [5.113].

Because of this intellectual element in esthetics, "to say that morality, in the last resort, comes to an esthetic judgment is not hedonism—but is directly opposed to hedonism" (5.111). Just as esthetic consciousness constitutes a representation of firstness, moral or ethical consciousness constitutes a representa-

198

tion of secondness: "every pronouncement between Good and Bad certainly comes under Category the Second; and for that reason such pronouncement comes out in the voice of conscience with an absoluteness of duality which we do not find even in logic" (5.111).

Esthetics and ethics for Peirce, then, comprise inquiries into the elements of feeling and conscience contained in the ultimate ends of human action, and such inquiries are possible only because an aspect of intelligibility is present in both kinds of elements. In so far as man pursues the inductive method because he is inclined by his feelings and commanded by his conscience to do so, rather than simply because he understands a logical exposition of the method, esthetics and ethics are precisely the studies in Peirce's scheme which should determine whether or not induction is practically possible as a mode of inquiry. It is only when truth is shown by an analysis of feelings and dictates of conscience to be an inevitable end of human action that there can be any assurance that the one method logically capable of obtaining truth will prevail in the long run in human inquiry. The paradox in question obviously breaks out again if it is maintained that esthetics and ethics are inquiries which themselves presuppose the account of truth and reality given by logic. However, this attempt to find in esthetics and ethics the ultimate basis for any determination of truth and reality does afford a dialectical answer to the paradox. For the assertion of the paradox may now be shown to assume that the normative sciences prior to logic must presuppose the definition of reality and the rules for obtaining truth given by logic, or, in other words, that the sciences which supply the presuppositions of induction are themselves inductive sciences. Inasmuch as such an assumption contradicts Peirce's ordering of the sciences, his system is saved from internal inconsistency.

In this arrangement of the parts of Peirce's philosophy, the possibility of any determination of truth and reality is thus explained by the esthetic and ethical observations of the *summum bonum* rather than paradoxically by the inductive observations which test the belief that intellectual inquiry can be indefinitely prolonged. It is doubtful, however, whether this appeal to the noninductive albeit "scientific" observations of esthetics and ethics provides an alternative to an appeal to unquestioned faith. For the results of such observations would seem indistinguishable from a kind of self-consciousness of one's faith concerning the *summum bonum*, and perhaps this is what Peirce had in mind when he spoke of "faith come to years of discretion" (2.118). In so far as mathematics is prior in the order of the sciences to esthetics and ethics, there might be a sense in which the observations in these latter sciences could employ the mathematics of induction (as in the questioning of consciousness), although such employment would not constitute induction in the logical sense of inquiry into reality. The *summum bonum* represents "what is to be sought, not for a reason, but back of every reason," or, in other words, it is itself the ultimate reason for every inquiry; and, while it is thus not directly subject to inquiry but is always presupposed, it can be exhibited as the result of reflective observation regarding the elements of feeling and conscience underlying any deliberate pursuit of truth and reailty. The circumstance that such elements regarded in themselves possess a proper intelligibility and hence in some sense fall under the forms of mathematics provides the only justification for the claim that the self-consciousness of faith resulting from esthetics and ethics constitutes a form of scientific knowledge. That is to say, the intrinsic thirdness in feeling and conscience affords a kind of objectivity or nonarbitrariness (analogous to that achieved in mathematics and phenomenology) which is presupposed in the final objectivity designated by the definition of reality.

It would seem necessary for this ordering of the sciences that mathematics and phenomenology, the two sciences prior to esthetics and ethics, have not only a *logica utens* but an *esthetica* and *ethica utens* as well.[27] Peirce admitted in the third chapter of the *Minute Logic* that the mathematician cannot "take a step without recognizing the duality of truth and false-

200

hood" (4.308), and in the lectures of 1903 he emphasized that mathematical or necessary reasoning requires self-control (cf., esp., 5.147–49). But then the first two sciences in Peirce's order must in themselves effect a kind of determination of the *summum bonum* which is to be made explicit by the three normative sciences. In this way all the sciences depend on the practice of self-control, in adherence either to principles that are developed as the inquiry proceeds or to those that are given at the outset by a prior science.

VI

Pragmatic Philosophy

THE manner in which the notion of self-control becomes in effect the focal point of Peirce's philosophy is best evidenced in his later expositions and defense of pragmatism, which he rechristened "pragmaticism" in order to have a designation free from some of the associations that had already become attached to the old name (cf. 5.414). While Peirce professed in these expositions to be defining a maxim of logic and not to be expounding a philosophy, it will be argued in the present chapter that his defense amounts to stating the case for a pragmatic philosophy. The ordering of the sciences considered in the preceding chapter becomes a central part of the case, and the full significance of the ordering is most easily presented in this context.

1. PRAGMATISM AND PERCEPTUAL JUDGMENTS

A. Peirce concluded his lectures of 1903 on pragmatism with the statement of a "maxim" for the pragmatic logician: "The elements of every concept enter into logical thought at the gate of perception and make their exit at the gate of purposive action; and whatever cannot show its passports at both those two gates is to be arrested as unauthorized by reason" (5.212). This at once suggests comparison with the assertion made in the original presentation of the categories (1867) that the concepts *substance* and *being* denote, respectively, "the beginning and end of all conception" (1.548). These two ontological concepts disappeared from the list of categories after the logic of relatives showed that the important formal elements were expressed by

202

the process of logical operations, irrespective of whether, in terms of traditional logic, the process was regarded as passing from subject to predicate (substance to being) or from premiss to conclusion. In the order of the sciences the discovery and examination of the categories required only the simplest mathematics (formal logic) and phenomenology, while pragmatism as a maxim of speculative grammar was essentially connected with the nature of assertion. Viewed with respect to this order, a maxim for making ideas clear presupposes a determination of the categories and of the ideals of conduct and is concerned properly with the conditions for significant assertion about reality. Pragmatism, then, is precisely that part of Peirce's later philosophy which takes over his early problem of connecting assertion and reality, that is, of relating subject and predicate to substance and being.

The fact that these two ontological terms as designating the beginning and end of conception are replaced, respectively, by *perception* and *purposive action* may be taken as indicative of the circumstance remarked above in the preceding chapter that Peirce's ontology and modes of being depend ultimately on normative considerations. Thus, the most important aspect for pragmatism about the passage from perception to purposive action is the fact that the process is essentially one subject to self-control. In Lecture V, "Three Kinds of Goodness," Peirce explained: "Just at this point we begin to get upon the trail of the secret of pragmatism. . . . A logical reasoner is a reasoner who exercises great self-control in his intellectual operations; and therefore the logically good is simply a particular species of the morally good" (5.130). However, if reality is to remain something independent of individual choice there must still be a part of the process which cannot be controlled by the reasoner. Peirce began his examination of perception in Lecture IV by asking:

Where then in the process of cognition does the possibility of controlling it begin? Certainly not before the *percept* is formed.
Even after the percept is formed there is an operation which seems

203

to me to be quite uncontrollable. It is that of judging what it is that the person perceives. . . . Consequently, until I am better advised, I shall consider the *perceptual judgment* to be utterly beyond control. Should I be wrong in this, the *percept*, at all events, would seem to be so [5.115] [cf. 4.540, 1905].

It follows, then, that our perceptual judgments are the first premisses of all our reasonings and that they cannot be called in question. All our other judgments are so many theories whose only justification is that they have been and will be borne out by perceptual judgments [5.116].

While perceptual judgments may always be first premisses relative to human reasoning, they clearly are not so in an absolute sense, since "what is first for us is not first in nature" (5.119). But the "premisses of nature," Peirce continues, "though they are not the *perceptual facts* that are premisses to us, nevertheless must resemble them in being premisses. We can only imagine what they are by comparing them with the premisses for us." The contrast here, of course, is that of objective with subjective rather than normative logic, and represents the point of view taken in the lectures of 1898.[1] The real logic of events is contrasted with its representation given in the reasoning of an individual person, who must start with his own perceptual judgments. When the logic becomes normative, the gap between subject and object is bridged by identifying the reasoning of the individual with that of an unlimited community, so that the first premisses of such reasoning will eventually become identical with those of nature. Yet, in order to establish this normative logic, it is essential that speculative grammar or epistemology exhibit some element of self-control with respect to perceptual judgments, since otherwise the community could not be expected to reach agreement on first premisses.

The basis for locating some element of self-control in perceptual judgments can be seen from the new analysis of the subject and predicate of a proposition afforded by the logic of relatives, which shows that these judgments involve generality. Peirce opens Lecture VI by explaining that the Logic of Relations has now reduced logic to order, and it is seen that a proposition may have any number of subjects but can have but one predicate which is invariably general. Such a proposition as "Tully is Cicero" predicates the general relation of identity of Tully and Cicero. Consequently, it is now clear that if there be any perceptual judgment, or proposition directly expressive of and resulting from the quality of a present percept, or sense-image, that judgment must involve generality in its predicate [5.151].

But, while there is generality in the predicate, the subject always refers in some way to a singular:

That which is not general is singular; and the singular is that which reacts. The being of a singular may consist in the being of other singulars which are its parts. . . . Every proposition whatsoever refers as to its subject to a singular actually reacting upon the utterer of it and actually reacting upon the interpreter of it. All propositions relate to the same ever-reacting singular; namely, to the totality of all real objects [5.152].

Even in the case of propositions referring to fictitious characters, "it becomes a real fact" that an author has imagined his heroine in a certain way, "which fact he cannot destroy by pretending or thinking that he imagined her to be otherwise" (5.152). Moreover,

it is a characteristic of perceptual judgments that each of them relates to some singular to which no other proposition relates directly, but, if it relates to it at all, does so by relating to that perceptual judgment. When we express a proposition in words, we leave most of its singular subjects unexpressed; for the circumstances of the enunciation sufficiently show what subject is intended and words, owing to their usual generality, are not well adapted to designating singulars [5.153].

When the subject of a proposition is not singular, it must be either *indesignative*, meaning that *some* singular or other "might replace this subject while the truth was preserved, while failing to designate what singular that is," or else *hypothetical*, meaning that *any* singular which fulfils certain conditions may be substituted for the subject, "without guaranteeing that there is any singular which fulfills these conditions" (5.154).

Every perceptual judgment thus in some respects uniquely determines a singular, and every proposition relates ultimately to one or more such singulars. This analysis does not conflict with the regulative principle of continuity because every singular may itself be taken as made up of singulars. "Thus heaven and earth is a singular; and its being consists in the being of heaven and the being of earth, each of which reacts and is therefore a singular forming a part of heaven and earth" (5.152). Similarly, of course, the earth may be regarded as consisting of singulars, such as the two hemispheres, and so on. The "totality of all real objects" may also be taken as a singular, and it possesses the unique characteristic of being the one singular to which all propositions are related. Now it may be difficult to conceive of a single perceptual judgment which determines such a singular, but Peirce refers to it as "the same ever-reacting singular" (5.152), and in so far as a singular is only determined by a perceptual judgment, which is always "the cognitive product of a reaction" (5.156), the analysis seems to call for a single perception of the totality of all real objects. A discussion of the point requires Peirce's doctrine that "the Immediate Object of a Percept is excessively vague" (4.539) and may be postponed until C of the next section below, where this doctrine is considered in connection with critical common-sensism. It will suffice for the present to notice that every cognition begins with the manifold of substance (in harmony with Peirce's doctrine of 1867) in that a reaction which is singular relative to the percept it produces is always necessary in order to start a process of cognition.

An existent or singular, however, is only the beginning of a perceptual judgment, just as a perceptual judgment is itself only the beginning of a process which ends in purposive action. The unity of being, which when added to the manifold of substance completes the perceptual judgment, is possible because every such judgment "must involve generality in its predicate." Because of this generality in the perceptual judgment, "the presumption is that a universal proposition can be necessarily de-

206

duced from it" (5.156). After cautioning that in saying this he "certainly never intended to be understood as enunciating any proposition in psychology" (5.157),[2] Peirce gives an illustration of such deduction from purely logical considerations. In the case of the judgment that "one event C *appears to be* subsequent to another event A," since this can only be inferred from "judgments of the same description" and since "it does not seem possible that I can have performed an infinite series of acts of criticism each of which must require a distinct effort," "it therefore appears that I must have made some judgment that one event *appeared to be* subsequent to another without that judgment having been inferred from any premiss [i.e.] without any *controlled* and *criticized* action of reasoning" (5.157). But then from the general element in this perceptual judgment, that is, from what is "implied in the meaning of subsequence, concerning which there is no room for doubt, it easily follows that whatever is subsequent to C is subsequent to anything, A, to which C is subsequent—which is a universal proposition" (5.157).

Peirce concluded this section of his lecture with the remark, "Thirdness pours in upon us through every avenue of sense" (5.157); and, in fact, the process which starts with a percept arising from reaction with a singular and ends in predicating of that percept as of a subject something involving generality seems to reflect all the important elements of Peirce's philosophy. It was in the next section of this lecture that Peirce spoke of "the validity of induction" and "the support of pragmatism" as resting on "the necessary relation between the general and the singular" (5.170). While this relation may be explained mathematically as implying merely that single members of an endless series necessarily express a general law of succession (see above, p. 175), precisely the same relation is expressed in a perceptual judgment.

According to a summary of the matter given in Lecture VII, "perceptual judgments contain general elements, so that uni- versal propositions are deducible from them in the manner in

207

which the logic of relations shows that particular propositions usually, not to say invariably, allow universal propositions to be necessarily inferred from them" (5.181). The example of such inference which Peirce offered in Lecture VI is taken from a proposition in which one subject is indesignative and the other hypothetical. It of course makes a difference which subject comes first, and "if the first general subject is indesignate, the proposition is called particular," while if it is hypothetical, "the proposition is called universal" (5.155). Hence, "there is some woman whom any Catholic you can find will adore" is a particular proposition, and from it "we can with certainty infer the universal proposition that 'any Catholic you can find will adore some woman or other'" (5.156).

The perceptual judgment, "A appears subsequent to C," may thus be analyzed as implying "There appears to be an event A to which any event appears subsequent which appears subsequent to C," and from this we may infer with certainty the universal proposition, "Whatever appears subsequent to C appears subsequent to anything A, to which C appears subsequent." Similarly, "This percept is red" implies "This percept has the same color as any red percept," and, hence, "Any red percept has the same color as this percept." In these two examples "the necessary relation between the general and the singular" lies in the fact that the singular propositions involve the predication of a transitive relation ("subsequent to" or "having the same color as") which gives the law of an endless series (the series of events appearing subsequent to a given event or the series of percepts having the same color as a given percept).

B. Peirce could thus assert that "every general form of putting concepts together is, in its elements, given in perception" (5.186). He began the seventh and last lecture by enumerating three propositions which, he declared, "seem to me to give to pragmatism its peculiar character" (5.180). (1) "Nihil est in intellectu quod non prius fuerit in sensu" (nothing is in the intellect which was not previously in sensation), where intellectus means "the meaning of any representation in any kind of cognition, virtual, symbolic, or whatever it may be," and *in sensu* is taken "in the sense of *in a perceptual judgment*, the starting point or first premiss of all critical and controlled thinking." (2) "Perceptual judgments contain general elements, so that universal propositions are deducible from them. . . ." (3) "Abductive inference shades into perceptual judgment without any sharp line of demarcation between them; or, in other words, our first premisses, the perceptual judgments, are to be regarded as an extreme case of abductive inferences, from which they differ in being absolutely beyond criticism" (5.181).

This third proposition is tantamount to the assertion that the process of forming a perceptual judgment is essentially the same as that of forming a hypothesis.

The only symptom by which the two can be distinguished is that we cannot form the least conception of what it would be to deny the perceptual judgment. If I judge a perceptual image to be red, I can conceive of another man's not having that same percept. . . . But that any man should have a percept similar to mine and should ask himself the question whether this percept be red, which would imply that he had already judged some percept to be red, and that he should, upon careful attention to this percept, pronounce it to be decidedly and clearly *not* red, when I judge it to be prominently red, *that* I cannot comprehend at all. An abductive suggestion, however, is something whose truth can be questioned or even denied [5.186].

Yet this test of inconceivability cannot be made the basis of an absolute distinction. "That which is inconceivable to us today, may prove tomorrow to be conceivable and even probable; so that we never can be absolutely sure that a judgment is perceptual and not abductive" (5.187).

The continuity between perceptual judgments and abductive inferences is of extreme importance for Peirce's entire philosophy; for if hypotheses could be necessarily deduced from indubitable perceptions and there was no danger of mistaking them for the latter, both the logic of hypotheses and the logic of induction would be superfluous. In short, the inquiry of the individual could never be merged with that of the community. It is only because one might be wrong in regarding "this per-

209

cept has the same color as any red percept" as an indubitable premiss that the universal judgment following from it must be examined as a meaningful hypothesis and tested by induction. The certainty that induction in the long run will discover the truth is the only sure way of counteracting the uncertainty that the premisses of a given hypothesis are indubitable perceptions.

Abduction as that process of logical inference which shades into a perceptual judgment is the one type of inference in critical logic which is directly connected with pragmatism and the analysis of significant assertion.

If you carefully consider the question of pragmatism you will see that it is nothing else than the question of the logic of abduction. That is, pragmatism proposes a certain maxim which, if sound, must render needless any further rule as to the admissibility of hypotheses to rank as hypotheses, that is to say, as explanations of phenomena held as hopeful suggestions; and, furthermore, this is *all* that the maxim of pragmatism really pretends to do, at least so far as it is confined to logic, and is not understood as a proposition in psychology. . . . But that pragmatism cannot interfere with induction is evident; because induction simply teaches us what we have to expect as a result of experimentation, and it is plain that any such expectation *may* conceivably concern practical conduct. In a certain sense it *must* affect *deduction.* Anything which gives a rule to abduction and so puts a limit upon admissible hypotheses will cut down *the premisses* of deduction, and thereby will render a *reductio ad absurdum* and other equivalent forms of deduction possible which would not otherwise have been possible. But . . . to affect the *premisses* of deduction is not to affect the logic of deduction [5.196].

Pragmatism is thus to supply the logic of abduction with a determination of the "goodness" or "end of an explanatory hypothesis." This end is, "through subjection to the test of experiment, to lead to the avoidance of all surprise and to the establishment of a habit of positive expectation that shall not be disappointed" (5.197). An analysis of the logical interrelations of belief, expectation, and judgment is hence a crucial task for pragmatism. In a fragment entitled "Belief and Judgment," ca. 1902, Peirce speaks at the outset as if "of theoretical beliefs, in so far as they are not practical, we may distinguish between those which are expectations, and those which are not even that" (5.539). However, it would seem that Peirce meant this statement to apply to theoretical beliefs only when their meaning has been incompletely analyzed, and he seems, three pages later, to retract the statement when he declares: "It now begins to look strongly as if perhaps all belief might involve expectation as its essence. That is as much as can justly be said. We have as yet no assurance that this is true of every kind of belief" (5.542).

Peirce offers the following as an illustration of the way in which purely theoretical beliefs seem to involve expectation:

To say that a quadratic equation which has no real root has two different imaginary roots does not sound as if it could have any relation to experience. Yet it is strictly expectative. It states what would be expectable if we had to deal with quantities expressing the relations betwcn objects, related to one another like the points of the plane of imaginary quantity. So a belief about the incommensurability of the diagonal relates to what is expectable for a person dealing with fractions; although it means nothing at all in regard to what could be expected in physical measurements, which are, of their very nature, approximate only [5.541].

This analysis, of course, assumes Peirce's doctrine that all mathcmatical reasoning turns on the observation of diagrams or imaginary constructions. It is precisely by such means that even mathematical or necessary reasoning can be regarded as a process which begins with a percept arising from reaction with a singular and ends with a general proposition. Peirce explained in his analysis of deduction in Lecture V that "the diagram itself, in its individuality, is not what the reasoning is concerned with" (5.148). Although the mathematician begins with a perceptual judgment that in a given diagram a certain relation obtains, this judgment shades into the general proposition or expectation (usually without conscious effort on the mathematician's part) that the relation will obtain for all diagrams that are assumed to be constructed as the given one was supposed to have been. While mathematical reasoning thus turns "upon the perception

211

of generality and continuity at every step" (5.150), this does not affect its hypothetical or necessary character which is reflected in the phrase "supposed to have been" as opposed to "actually was" constructed. Otherwise, the expectations of the mathematician would be indistinguishable from those which pertain to physical measurement and would have no claim to necessity. The distinction between theoretical as opposed to practical beliefs will be considered below in B of section 3.

At the opposite extreme to abstract theoretical beliefs arising from mathematics lie the beliefs in the actual character of a given singular. In the case of a judgment like "That wafer looks red," "What element of expectation is there in the belief that the wafer *looks* red at this moment? In order to handle this question, it is necessary to draw a distinction . . . every proposition has its predicate which expresses *what* is believed, and its subjects which express *of what* it is believed" (5.542). But then the judgment, "This wafer looks red," expresses a belief that a given subject has a certain appearance.

It takes some time to write this sentence, to utter it, or even to think it. It must refer to the state of the percept at the time that it, the judgment, began to be made. But the judgment does not exist until it is completely made. It thus only refers to a memory of the past; and all memory is possibly fallible and subject to criticism and control. The judgment, then, can only mean that so far as the character of the percept can ever be ascertained, it will be ascertained that the wafer looked red [5.544].

Peirce remarks that "perhaps the matter may be stated less paradoxically" by appealing to the fact that every singular judgment involves a law. For "to say that a body is hard, or red, or heavy, or of a given weight, or has any other property, is to say that it is subject to law and therefore is a statement referring to the future" (5.545). That is, in terms of the logic of relatives, "This wafer looks red" predicates of this singular the general relation "having the same color as," which gives rise to the law, "Any red object will appear to have the same color as this wafer appeared to have."

212

One of the doctrines which Peirce defended in *The Law of Mind* (1892) and never had occasion to modify was that "we are immediately conscious through an infinitesimal interval of time" (6.110). In accordance with this doctrine, there is no difficulty in maintaining that relative to expectation and belief perceptual judgments involve memory and control, while in respect to their character as premisses of reasoning they are beyond control. Thus, the perceptual judgment, "This wafer appears to have the same color as any red object," occurs in an infinitesimal interval of consciousness and as such is an uncontrollable first premiss. However, by the principle of continuity, just as an infinitesimal interval of consciousness shades into a very small positive interval, so this judgment shades into the law or positive belief that "any red object will appear to have the same color as this wafer appeared to have." It is permissible, therefore, to assert that the beliefs arising directly from perceptual judgments provide no exception to the general principle that every belief involves expectation as its essence and at the same time to hold that perceptual judgments as immediate consciousness are uncontrollable.[3] In the process of inquiry, then, an individual's perceptual judgments may become hypotheses rather than unalterable premisses and can thus be merged with the inquiry of the community.

2. CRITICAL COMMON-SENSISM AND SELF-CONTROL

A. In addition to the more or less indubitable beliefs that arise from perceptual judgments, Peirce recognized another class of indubitables in connection with that part of his philosophy he called "critical common-sensism." Beliefs of the latter sort are "invariably vague" (5.446), and it will be well to preface a discussion of them by some consideration of Peirce's analysis of vagueness, as presented in the papers dealing with common-sensism written a few years after the lectures on pragmatism.

"Vagueness" may be characterized as

the antithetical analogue of generality. A sign is objectively *general*, in so far as, leaving its effective interpretation indeterminate, it sur-

213

renders to the interpreter the right of completing the determination for himself. . . . A sign is objectively vague, in so far as, leaving its interpretation more or less indeterminate, it reserves for some other possible sign or experience the function of completing the determination [5.505].

According to another passage, "a sign that is objectively indeterminate in any respect is objectively vague in so far as it reserves further determination to be made in some other conceivable sign, or at least does not appoint the interpreter as its deputy in this office" (5.447). In other words, a sign is objectively vague in so far as it "leaves the right of further exposition in the utterer," and it becomes objectively general only "by a well-understood convention" which transfers the right of further determination to the interpreter (5.447).

Peirce seems to use the word "objectively" here to indicate that the point at issue is the extent to which a sign determines its object. Both the vague and the general refer to a sign which is "objectively indeterminate,"[4] meaning one "whose object is undetermined by the sign itself" (5.447). Although Peirce does not specify in this passage the sense in which he is using "object," he must surely mean what he called elsewhere the *immediate* object as opposed to the *existent* object, or "that thing which causes a sign as such" (5.473). The immediate object is "the Object as the sign itself represents it, and whose Being is thus dependent upon the Representation of it in the Sign," while the existent object may be regarded as "the Dynamical Object, which is the Reality which by some means contrives to determine the Sign to its Representation" (4.536). Only the immediate object, then, can be indeterminate, either as vague or as general, since it is precisely this object and not the existent object which is itself a representation.[5] "An existing thing is simply a blind reacting thing, to which not merely all generality, but even all representation, is utterly foreign" (5.107). In so far as the immediate object is indeterminate, "the Immediate Interpretant, which is the interpretant as it is revealed in the right understanding of the Sign itself, and is ordinarily called the meaning of the sign" (4.536),[6] must of course also be indeterminate. The meaning can be made more definite only by making this object more definite, and in a fragment ca. 1902 Peirce spoke of "the complete immediate Object" as the "meaning" (2.293).[7] In the further discussion of Peirce's analysis of vagueness, "object" unless otherwise specified will always be taken in the sense of immediate object.

The indeterminateness of a sign, whether it is that of vagueness or generality, thus consists in a "latitude of interpretation" as to what is the object of the sign; and, if a sign is to be completely determinate, "there must be no such latitude either for the interpreter or for the utterer" (5.448 n.). Peirce refers to the process of rendering a sign definite and precise[8] as "an expression of determination which is made either full or free for the interpreter" (5.449). The latter case would seem to represent a passage from vagueness to generality and may be elucidated by Peirce's remark that "the general might be defined as that to which the principle of excluded middle does not apply," while "the vague might be defined as that to which the principle of contradiction does not apply" (5.505; cf. 5.448). Thus, a vague statement must be regarded as possibly inconsistent in every respect as long as the utterer does not provide further determination,[9] and the interpreter has no right to invoke the principle of contradiction and assume, for example, that triangle in a vague sense is not at the same time both scalene and equilateral. A general statement, on the other hand, leaves the interpreter free to choose any triangle he pleases as the intended object and thus to ignore the principle of excluded middle in the sense that triangle in general is neither scalene nor equilateral. In so far as the meaning is made "full" rather than "free" for the interpreter, the sign becomes definite and precise by losing its indeterminateness as well as its vagueness. In this case the sign tends to acquire an absolutely determinate and individual object—a logical atom. Peirce refers in his discussion ca. 1905 (5.506) to his paper of 1870 on the logic of relatives where he argued that a "logical atom" "like a point in space, would involve for its precise determination an endless process" (3.93). "Absolute individuality" is thus "merely ideal," and every representable object is capable of further logical division. A precise description like "the second Philip of Macedon" "is still capable of logical division—into Philip drunk and Philip sober, for example." But, then, every sign remains in some degree general because its object is always susceptible of further division.

The greatest precision is of course in mathematics, which Peirce characterized in the *Minute Logic* as reuniting "perfect exactitude and practical infallibility with unrestricted universality" (4.237). "These characters of mathematics," he continued, "are inevitable consequences of its being the study of hypothetical truth." Yet in 1906 Peirce remarked that "no concept, not even those of mathematics, is absolutely precise" (6.496), and it is clear from the context that he meant there is some degree of vagueness even in mathematics. The point seems to be simply that with respect to its subject matter mathematics can be said to achieve perfect precision because its objects, as being purely ideal, can theoretically be made absolutely determinate; however, in the actual practice of communication there may always be some respects in which the utterer has a latitude for further specification of meaning.[10] In one passage in his discussion of common-sensism, Peirce remarked that people might succeed in making their meaning determinate if "their chat is about the theory of numbers. . . . But the further their topics are from such presciss, or 'abstract,' subjects, the less possibility is there of such precision of speech" (5.447). The words "presciss" and "abstract" here refer to "dissection in hypothesis," as "in geometry, for example, we 'prescind' shape from color" (5.449). The subject matter of mathematics is thus highly presciss or abstract in the sense that by hypothesis the observable qualities of an object as distinct from its form are left out of account. But Peirce preferred to reserve "the stem 'abstract' " for signifying "hypostatic abstraction," or that operation which "is performed when something, that one has thought about any subject, is itself made a subject of thought" (5.534), as when one calls the honey sweet and then thinks of sweetness (cf. 4.235). There are thus three distinct operations to be differentiated: (1) "dissection in hypothesis," which is referred to by "prescind," "presciss," "prescission," and "prescissive"; (2) "an expression of determination which is made full or free for the interpreter," which is referred to by "precide," "precise," "precision," and "precisive"; and (3) "hypostatic abstraction" (5.449).

Peirce's analysis of vagueness may now be summarized as follows. A sign is vague in so far as the onus of further determination rests with the utterer. The utterer may try to render his meaning more precise by specifying, for instance, that in using "the second Philip of Macedon" he intends neither Philip drunk nor Philip sober but Philip in general, and the interpreter thus acquires a latitude in determining the intended object and relieves the utterer. But such latitude can never be absolutely complete if there is to be communication; the interpreter is not free to construe "Philip in general" as signifying any object he pleases, so that some onus still rests with the utterer, and hence the meaning is still to some extent vague.[11] On the other hand, the utterer may attempt precision by specifying that he means only Philip drunk, and, while this decreases the latitude of the interpreter, it does not relieve the utterer of the obligation to make further distinctions; for example, between Philip drunk alone and in a crowd. The process may go on indefinitely, and the utterer may always attempt further determination or surrender some right to the interpreter, such as specifying Philip drunk in general. The whole process is precisive, and prescission occurs whenever the utterer prescinds one aspect of the object from another aspect, as Philip drunk from Philip sober. If the utterer then declared his object to be the drunkenness of Philip, there would of course be hypostatic abstraction. But the meaning in all cases remains more or less indeterminate, in some respects as being vague and in others as

217

being general, though obviously "no sign can be at once vague and general in the same respect" (5.506).

B. Peirce's critical common-sensism may be taken in its common-sense aspect as a doctrine which attempts to account for the possibility of communication in spite of the inevitable vagueness and indeterminateness of language. "No general description can identify an object. But the common sense of the interpreter of the sign will assure him that the object must be one of a limited collection of objects" (5.448 n.). In other words, while language is never absolutely determinate, with the aid of common sense it becomes determinate enough for the purposes of communication. But then there must be certain beliefs about a common universe of discourse which everyone accepts as a matter of common sense when he becomes an interpreter of signs. He will believe, for example, that there is a universe of natural objects which always manifests a considerable degree of order, and, when he interprets the sign, "It will rain tomorrow," he does not demand of the utterer absolute precision as to the reasons for accepting weather predictions or for thinking that tomorrow will ever come. Similarly, one will assume a universe of right and wrong actions when he attempts to interpret signs expressing a normative judgment. Yet these common-sense beliefs must remain extremely vague simply because they mark a sort of boundary between what can be communicated and what must be presupposed in all communication. As interpreter, one may experience relatively little difficulty with his belief in the uniformity of nature, but, when he becomes utterer and attempts to communicate precisely in what his belief consists, he is sure to encounter difficulties before he has become very precise. For in effect he is trying to give distinct communication to what is always more or less presupposed in every communication. The indubitability of these common-sense beliefs is thus a matter of not being able to get along without them rather than of any precise reasons that can be given in support of them.

Peirce never attempted to draw up a list of indubitable beliefs, though he implied that "a fixed list, the same for all men," should be possible (5.509; cf. 5.444). There seems to be no alternative to assuming that these beliefs originate in instinct, and, while Peirce was inclined to think at first that "the indubitable propositions changed with a thinking man from year to year," he later came to the conclusion that "the changes . . . from generation to generation" are "slight" "though not imperceptible" (5.444–45). The formation of instinctive beliefs as well as that of perceptual judgments is of course initially beyond control, but if the changes in beliefs are to represent evolution "in its higher stages," which "takes place more and more largely through self-control" (5.433), there must be some respect in which these beliefs, like perceptual judgments, shade into hypotheses. In general, this respect consists simply in the fact that one is never absolutely sure a given belief is indubitable or even instinctive. In particular, instinct, Peirce holds, "can be somewhat modified in a very short time," and it is fallible, even though it "seldom errs" (5.445). Moreover, "the original beliefs only remain indubitable in their application to affairs that resemble those of a primitive mode of life" (5.445). Thus, "while they never become dubitable in so far as our mode of life remains that of somewhat primitive man, yet as we develop *degrees of self-control* unknown to that man, occasions of action arise in relation to which the original beliefs, if stretched to cover them, have no sufficient authority. In other words, we outgrow the applicability of instinct—not altogether, by any manner of means, but in our highest activities" (5.511) (Peirce's italics).

The rise of doubt seems to be an indispensable accompaniment of the development of self-control, and "there is every reason to suppose that belief came first, and the power of doubting long after. Doubt, usually, perhaps always, takes its rise from surprise, which supposes previous belief; and surprises come with novel environment" (5.512). "Genuine doubt" thus "always has an external origin, usually from surprise," and it is never possible to create a genuine doubt merely "by such an act of the will as would suffice to imagine the condition of a mathematical

219

theorem" (5.443). Yet this does not mean that the source of novelty and surprise is only in an external environment with respect to which man is entirely passive. The critical common-sensist "is not content to ask himself whether he does doubt, but he invents a plan for attaining to doubt, elaborates it in detail, and then puts it into practice, although this may involve a solid month of hard work; and it is only after having gone through such an examination that he will pronounce a belief to be indubitable. Moreover, he fully acknowledges that even then it may be that some of his indubitable beliefs may be proved false" (5.451).

The critical common-sensist's plan for attaining to doubt consists in setting himself "in serious earnest to the systematic business of endeavoring to bring all his very general first premisses to recognition, and of developing every suspicion of doubt of their truth, by the use of logical analysis, and by experimenting in imagination" (5.517). In accordance with pragmatism, this experimentation amounts to an attempt to call before the imagination all the possible kinds of circumstances under which one would expect to act on the basis of the belief in question, and, in so far as a genuine hesitation arises with respect to such "conditional resolutions as to conduct," the belief is open to doubt.[12] There is of course the danger that in this procedure one may strive to make his inevitably vague beliefs too precise and end in thinking he doubts what he really believes, or even in really doubting what he ought to believe.[13] But Peirce feels that, "on the whole," neither of these possibilities "is so unfavorable to science as for men of science to believe what they ought to doubt, nor even for them to think they believe what they really doubt" (5.498). This would certainly be the case in so far as the advance of science depends on the development of self-control, and the critical examination of beliefs which appeared indubitable in a more or less primitive mode of life is inseparable from this development.

At one point in his discussions of common-sensism, Peirce

gave a sketch of the different grades involved in the development of self-control, and the passage may well be quoted in full.

To return to self-control, which I can but slightly sketch, at this time, of course there are inhibitions and coördinations that entirely escape consciousness. There are, in the next place, modes of self-control which seem quite instinctive. Next, there is a kind of self-control which results from training. Next, a man can be his own training-master and thus control his self-control. When this point is reached much or all the training may be conducted in imagination. When a man trains himself, thus controlling control, he must have some moral rule in view, however special and irrational it may be. But next he may undertake to improve this rule; that is, to exercise a control over his control of control. To do this he must have in view something higher than an irrational rule. He must have some sort of moral principle. This, in turn, may be controlled by reference to an esthetic ideal of what is fine. There are certainly more grades than I have enumerated. Perhaps their number is indefinite. The brutes are certainly capable of more than one grade of control; but it seems to me that our superiority to them is more due to our greater number of grades of self-control than it is to our versatility [5.533].

Peirce did not illustrate these different grades of self-control with respect to an original belief, but, to judge from his sketch, the belief in the uniformity of nature, which is the one he most often cites as an example of the common-sense indubitables, would fare somewhat as follows. In everyday living and even in the practice of scientific inquiry which is restricted to the special sciences and is free from metaphysical speculation, this belief might involve besides instinctive control only that which "results from training"—from conditioning by the physical and social environment. The transition to the grade of control where a man becomes "his own training-master" marks the beginning of philosophic inquiry and requires the critical common-sensist's plan for attaining to doubt by logical analysis and experiments in the imagination. At this stage the belief is seen to be unnecessary for a logico-mathematical explanation of the validity of induction (see above, chap. v, sec. 2), and doubts arise as to whether the belief has anything to recommend it. But when the controlled thinking which occasioned these doubts is itself sub-

221

jected to control, the analysis becomes consciously moral and esthetical, and the need to hope for the indefinite continuation of induction becomes apparent. These various stages of philosophic inquiry would thus represent different levels of understanding the inevitably vague belief in the uniformity of nature, and in accordance with his synechism Peirce would have to admit that the grades of self-control involved might be indefinite in number.

It would seem that all the beliefs which appear in a primitive state as instinctive and indubitable undergo considerable transformation as inquiry develops higher grades of self-control. The vague belief, for example, that "fire burns" (cf. 5.498) must have enjoyed at one time an important place in man's knowledge of the universe, but with more advanced stages of inquiry this belief is in one sense replaced by relatively precise scientific hypotheses and in another sense is absorbed by the general philosophic belief in the uniformity of nature—fire, like any other part of nature, possesses certain habits. There is thus a twofold way in which man "outgrows the applicability of instinct" in his "highest activities" (cf. 5.511). On the one hand, inquiry in the special sciences, or what Peirce called in the *Minute Logic* "idioscopic" inquiry (cf. 1.242), supplies hypotheses which are applicable to situations where instinct had formerly been the only guide. On the other hand, critical examination by philosophic inquiry may achieve an understanding of the impossibility of getting along without certain common-sense beliefs, so that something more than the mere evidence of instinct is acquired. In his discussions of critical common-sensism Peirce was concerned to emphasize that the original beliefs could never be entirely replaced by hypotheses of the special sciences. "Any such idioscopic inquiry must proceed upon the virtual assumption of sundry logical and metaphysical beliefs; and it is rational to settle the validity of those before undertaking an operation that supposes their truth" (5.521). The critical inquiry which is to determine the validity of these beliefs would of course proceed by experimenting in the imagination, and Peirce continues that "the whole inquiry" can "be concluded before the first outward experiment is made." Moreover, precisely because idioscopic inquiry must presuppose logical and metaphysical beliefs, the wisdom of instinct with respect to these beliefs, quite apart from any philosophic examination, is more trustworthy than anything which can be discovered by the special sciences. "No 'wisdom' could ever have discovered argon; yet within its proper sphere, which embraces objects of universal concern, the instinctive result of human experience ought to have so vastly more weight than any scientific result, that to make laboratory experiments to ascertain, for example, whether there be any uniformity in nature or no, would vie with adding a teaspoonful of saccharine to the ocean in order to sweeten it" (5.522).

C. Critical common-sensism on its critical side, then, may be taken as a doctrine designed to account for the gradual refinement of more or less primitive beliefs despite the fact that inquiry, as a sign-process infected with the inevitable vagueness of language, seems always to presuppose such beliefs. The process of refinement comprises both idioscopic and philosophic inquiry, and the original beliefs rather than being shown false are usually rendered in some respects more subject to control. One may speak of a "fixed list" of instinctive beliefs "the same for all men" (5.509), inasmuch as the beliefs retain some sort of identity in the progression through the various grades of self-control. The special scientist never entirely escapes presupposing in some sense the primitive belief that fire burns, although he would never regard this vague belief as among those which constitute the principles of his science. While he may be able to explain with considerable precision the chemical reactions which take place when fire burns and to relate these reactions to a wide variety of others, he has merely subjected the primitive belief to more control rather than proving it false. He may still be said to presuppose it in the sense that in all his communications he vaguely assumes that the various parts of nature, such as fire, will continue to behave more or less as they have done before. The common-sense indubitables are thus in the nature of presuppositions required for any use of language and are in this sense quite different from perceptual indubitables. A perceptual judgment is indubitable only in the sense that it refers to the unalterable character of what is forced upon consciousness, and as it shades into an abductive inference the judgment becomes a hypothesis concerning what will be discovered in the future. The acceptance of such a hypothesis already involves the common-sense indubitables, as the belief, for example, that every red object will have the same color as this percept supposes some uniformity of nature.

However, Peirce's treatment of the perceptual judgment would seem to make common-sense indubitables in the last analysis special cases of perceptual indubitables. While every perceptual judgment as the cognitive product of a reaction uniquely determines a singular, as soon as this singular is taken as the immediate object of the sign constituting the percept it is only vaguely singular because the utterer can never succeed in making such an object absolutely determinate for the interpreter. But then there is no reason to stop short of saying that "the same ever-reacting singular" which comprises "the totality of all real objects" (cf. 5.152) is itself vaguely the immediate object of a percept.[14] In short, we do have a perception of nature, however vague it may be, and the belief in the uniformity of nature arising from such a perception is indubitable in essentially the same way as the belief arising from any other perception, namely, in referring to what is forced upon consciousness.[15] This does not affect the circumstance that common-sense indubitables are presupposed in communication regarding other perceptual indubitables and that as presuppositions in this sense they acquire a special kind of indubitability. Even though as being the results of perception the two kinds of indubitables differ only in degree, this does not prevent there being a sharp distinction between them when they are related to a universe of discourse presupposed in communication. Inasmuch as the singular determined by each perceptual judgment is itself composed of singulars, it may always be taken as comprising a perceptual universe within itself as well as forming part of a larger universe. The common-sense indubitables are then simply results of those perceptual judgments which vaguely determine the natural and moral universes more or less common to all communication, and the progress of human knowledge may be viewed as the process of subjecting these primitive beliefs to higher degrees of self-control.[16]

This interpretation of Peirce's critical common-sensism thus focuses the doctrine on the nature of communication as a process necessarily requiring self-control. Peirce held, in accordance with his pragmatism, that "the latitude of interpretation which constitutes the indeterminacy of a sign must be understood as a latitude which might affect the achievement of a purpose. For two signs whose meanings are for all possible purposes equivalent are absolutely equivalent" (5.448 n.). But then an attempt to determine the object of a sign should be followed by the specification of a purpose, and the highest grade of clearness would seem impossible without such specification. Peirce did not explicitly relate clearness and precision, but to judge from the remark just quoted clearness should be that which compensates for a lack of precision. A common-sense indubitable such as the belief in God, for example, must remain extremely vague, but in so far as the belief is understood with reference to the summum bonum—to its value in the self-controlled growth of inquiry—a purpose has been specified with reference to which the belief becomes clear. Similarly, in the case of beliefs which can be referred to a definite set of practical effects, as the belief that a certain object is hard, the element of vagueness may be compensated for by the specification of a purpose. The fact that the utterer can never make what he means by "the hardness of this object" absolutely determinate for the interpreter becomes virtually of no consequence when the meaning is clearly grasped relative to the purposes of a given experiment, and when this experiment, in turn, is understood as subserving the ultimate purpose of inquiry, the meaning would become even more clear though no more precise. The necessity for self-control, then, arises just from this need to offset vagueness by the specification of purposes. The common sense of the interpreter which enables him to cope with the indeterminateness of language thus becomes in effect a kind of natural capacity for grasping intended purposes, and the critical common-sensist's plan for attaining to doubt amounts to controlling his beliefs by imagining how he would act to achieve various purposes.

It should be remarked in conclusion that the above analysis may be sharpened by reference to Peirce's distinction between object and interpretant. "The Immediate Object of all knowledge and all thought is, in the last analysis, the Percept," and in accordance with pragmatism "the Immediate Interpretant of all thought proper is Conduct" (4.539). As already noticed, in so far as the immediate interpretant is distinguished from the immediate object, it is simply the right understanding of this object,[17] or the meaning of the sign (cf. 4.536). The percept as object in this sense is of course itself a sign determining a further object-sign, and while "the Immediate Object of a Percept is excessively vague," Peirce explains that "natural thought makes up for that lack (as it almost amounts to), as follows. A late Dynamical Interpretant of the whole complex of Percepts is the Seme of a Perceptual Universe that is represented by instinctive thought as determining the original Immediate Object of every Percept" (4.539). A "dynamical interpretant" is "the actual effect which the Sign, as a Sign, really determines" (4.536) and a "seme" is "anything which serves for any purpose as a substitute for an object of which it is, in some sense, a representative or Sign" (4.538). Thus, a late dynamical interpretant of a percept as it becomes a complex of percepts would be a representation of a perceptual universe (or situation) that would determine the immediate object of every percept sufficiently for certain conduct.

By calling the interpretant here "dynamical," Peirce seems to imply an effect resulting more from a kind of instinctive effort than from conscious control. The development of control should, presumably, amount to further specification of conduct

226

or purpose and be related to the immediate interpretant of thought proper. But the relation of the immediate to the dynamical interpretant is difficult to make out, and Peirce was perhaps too anxious to parallel his distinction between immediate and dynamical object. He speaks also of a "final interpretant," but adds: "I confess that my own conception of this third interpretant is not yet quite free from mist" (4.536). The analysis is somewhat changed in a paper written perhaps a little later (ca. 1906), where the three interpretants are the "emotional," the "energetic," and the "logical" (5.475–76).[18] The last is "closely related to," if not the same as, "the meaning of a general concept" and would seem in this sense to correspond to the immediate interpretant of all thought proper. In these terms, then, the lack of precision with respect to the immediate object may be offset, first, by an energetic (dynamical) interpretant, which is "a single act" and hence never the meaning of a general concept, and, second, by a logical interpretant which involves self-control and "habit change." The former would seem to constitute the instinctive or common-sense way of compensating for vagueness, while the latter seems to comprise the critical stages of self-control. The emotional interpretant is prior to both of these and consists in a feeling which is the "first proper significate effect of a sign." "There is almost always a feeling which we come to interpret as evidence that we comprehend the proper effect of the sign, although the foundation of truth in this is frequently very slight" (5.475). Such a feeling might not involve any degree of self-control, but the energetic interpretant could involve at least instinctive control. Inasmuch as an interpretant of any kind in some way makes up for vagueness, it would appear correct to say that precision relates to the object and clearness to the interpretant.[19]

3. INQUIRY AND THE INQUIRER

A. In 1905 Peirce referred to his critical common-sensism and scholastic realism as "two doctrines that were defended by the writer about nine years before the formulation of pragmaticism" but which "may be treated as consequences of the latter belief" (5.439; cf. 5.453). The reference to "about nine years before" is clearly to the papers of 1868–69, in which Peirce had argued against intuitive knowledge and in favor of the reality of generals. He is none too explicit in his later discussions as to how the doctrines in question actually follow from pragmatism, but the main line of argument seems obvious enough. Pragmatism makes all intellectual meaning ultimately a matter of purposive conduct, so that "being" or "reality" comes to be understood with reference to the final goal of inquiry. Inasmuch as such a goal involves the notion of inquiry prolonged indefinitely, reality as understood or represented—as the immediate rather than the dynamical object of a sign—can never be grasped by intuition or regarded as absolutely determinate. Reality in this sense is therefore general and also in some degree vague, since it must possess all the essential characteristics of representation.

The conclusion that all reality is in a sense a universe of signs is acknowledged in Peirce's comments of 1906 concerning his remarks about vagueness (indefiniteness) and generality given the year before. These remarks, he says,

made the proper distinction between the two kinds of indeterminacy, viz.: indefiniteness and generality, of which the former consists in the sign's not sufficiently expressing itself to allow of an indubitable determinate interpretation, while the [latter] turns over to the interpreter the right to complete the determination as he please. It seems a strange thing, when one comes to ponder over it, that a sign should leave its interpreter to supply a part of its meaning; but the explanation of the phenomenon lies in the fact that the entire universe—not merely the universe of existents, but all that wider universe, embracing the universe of existents as a part, the universe which we are all accustomed to refer to as "the truth"—that all this universe is perfused with signs, if it is not composed exclusively of signs. Let us note this in passing as having a bearing upon the question of pragmaticism [5.448 n.].

The universe which seems to be composed exclusively of signs constitutes all reality that can be represented by signs, whether as a mere possibility or as a real law destined to be actualized.

228

What Peirce referred to elsewhere as his second universe (see above, chap. v, sec. 3) comprises, in these terms, the existent or dynamical objects which cause or determine signs, as opposed to the immediate objects which are really signs themselves because they have no real status except as they are more or less determined by other signs.

In accordance with this conception of the universe, then, a real thing or substance has no intelligible status except as determined by a process of signification. It has been remarked in the preceding chapters of the present study that Peirce encountered some difficulties with this notion of substance when he came to account for man as the substance who conducts inquiry, who utters and interprets signs. The papers of 1868–69 had maintained that "the word or sign which the man uses is the man himself" (5.314), but by 1892 Peirce regarded his original statement as somewhat nominalistic and emphasized that "every general idea has the unified living feeling of a person" (6.270). Yet the thoroughgoing realism which Peirce claimed to have achieved in the latter case did not alleviate the necessity to distinguish between mind as architect directing the course of inquiry and mind as another object to be investigated by inquiry. The unsatisfactoriness of agapasm seemed to arise primarily from an attempt to fuse these two views of mind in a single account of evolution, and Peirce's subsequent distinction between normative and objective logic became necessary in order to remedy the situation. The problem of accounting for mind as architect in a universe perfused with signs if not composed entirely of signs would seem to require for its solution the view that a sign may be both utterer and interpreter. Yet it should be noticed that, although Peirce is able to substitute "sign" for "utterer" quite easily, the same does not hold for "interpreter." Thus, a sign "is objectively vague in so far as it reserves further determination to be made in some other conceivable sign, or at least does not appoint the interpreter as its deputy in this office" (5.447). While this statement succeeds in avoiding a reference to an utterer who is not a sign, it is clearly impossible to substitute "some other conceivable sign" for "interpreter" without completely confounding the meaning of the sentence. "Interpretant" in any of its senses would likewise confuse the meaning, at least if an interpretant is always a "significate effect" of the original sign and presupposes some activity on the part of an interpreter, such as feeling, instinctive reaction, or controlled thought. It would thus be the interpreter, as opposed to the interpretant, who could act as deputy. Moreover, "some other conceivable sign" is contrasted with "interpreter," while any interpretant would be some other conceivable sign.[20]

It would thus seem that even though every sign, or at least every general idea, has the unified living feeling of a person, there must be some essential difference between the functions of a person and those of a sign. This difference does not seem to consist so much in the office of utterer, or that of conveying information, as it does in the office of interpreter, of one who completes the meanings of signs. In so far as the interpretant of a given sign is absolutely determined by that sign, the immediate object would be completely determinate and singular, and there would be no latitude of interpretation. In this extreme case the interpreter becomes identical with or at least indistinguishable from the interpretant, but in all other cases—all the possible ones with Peirce's analysis—the interpreter remains as something not a sign which further determines the interpretants of signs.[21] It can thus hardly be said that Peirce escaped from what he appears to have regarded as the nominalistic bias of his papers of 1868. The inevitability of assuming an interpreter seems most apparent in his remark in these papers that "it follows from our own existence (which is proved by the occurrence of ignorance and error) that everything which is present to us is a phenomenal manifestation of ourselves. This does not prevent its being a phenomenon of something without us, just as a rainbow is at once a manifestation both of the sun and of the rain. When we think, then, we ourselves, as we are at that moment, appear as a sign" (5.283). In other words, every phenomenon—every representation which appears in consciousness—is

230

further determined by an active interpreter[22] and thus appears to that interpreter as a phenomenal manifestation of himself. The occurrence of ignorance and error provides the only occasion for the interpreter's becoming aware of a source of determination other than himself, and hence of becoming aware of himself in opposition to an external world.

This suggests that by analogy the external world should have the status of an active utterer, and Peirce virtually admitted the point in his lectures of 1903:

> Analogy suggests that the laws of nature are ideas or resolutions in the mind of some vast consciousness, who, whether supreme or subordinate, is a Deity relatively to us. I do not approve of mixing up Religion and Philosophy; but as a purely philosophical hypothesis, that has the advantage of being supported by analogy. Yet I cannot clearly see that beyond that support to the imagination it is of any particular scientific service . . . [5.107].

Peirce offered no further explanation in his lecture of this notion of a divine mind, but it seems quite close to his later description (1908) of God as *Ens necessarium*, as a "disembodied spirit, or pure mind," having "its being out of time" (6.490). The role of this conception of God in Peirce's metaphysics was discussed above in chapter iv, and it need only be remarked here that, while Peirce does seem forced to admit the possibility of speaking by analogy of a sort of active utterer, who is something besides a sign, the fundamental notion for his philosophy is the active interpreter, which supplies the basis for the analogy. All reference to an utterer is easily avoided by taking as ultimate the sign-phenomena themselves as they are forced into consciousness by an existent or dynamical object; but, since the signs are always more or less general and vague, such ultimacy is relative to an interpreter who must be in some degree active in determining the immediate objects of the signs.

Peirce's strictures against intuitive knowledge and a nominalistic thing in itself, in these terms, apply always to the immediate objects of signs, which can never be anything but further signs. The interpreter can never know himself except as such a sign-object, and in this sense there is no difficulty in maintaining that man is nothing but a sign. Some understanding of what the interpreter is besides a sign may be achieved by a consideration of Peirce's later descriptions of thought as "dialogic in form" (cf. 6.338). In one of the articles of 1905 on pragmatism, Peirce refers to the nature of thought in order to indicate a sense in which absolute truth may be distinguished from what an individual does not doubt.

Two things here are all-important to assure oneself of and to remember. The first is that a person is not absolutely an individual. His thoughts are what he is "saying to himself," that is, is saying to that other self that is just coming into life in the flow of time. When one reasons, it is that critical self that one is trying to persuade; and all thought whatsoever is a sign, and is mostly of the nature of language. The second thing to remember is that the man's circle of society (however widely or narrowly this phrase may be understood), is a sort of loosely compacted person, in some respects of higher rank than the person of an individual organism. It is these two things alone that render it possible for you—but only in the abstract, and in a Pickwickian sense—to distinguish between absolute truth and what you do not doubt [5.421].

The self which functions always as interpreter is thus the "critical self" which is "just coming into life in the flow of time" or, rather, is always just outside of time, since, as soon as the self enters time, it becomes a sign and is utterer rather than interpreter. The point about truth and doubt would then seem to be that if one defines absolute truth as that which his critical self will ultimately accept, he can distinguish "in the abstract" between such truth and those signs, habits, or beliefs which constitute his phenomenal self at any given time. Peirce did not explain his use here of "in the abstract," and he might have intended primarily a kind of hypostatic abstraction in which the adjectival notion of accepted-by-the-critical-self is turned into the substantival notion of absolute truth. But "prescissive" abstraction would also be involved, in that acceptance by the critical self must be a notion prescinded from reference to a phe-

232

nomenal self (or phenomenal manifestation of the self). Such "prescission" in the last analysis could hardly stop short of identifying the critical self with the unlimited community, which would represent "man's circle of society" taken in its widest sense.[23]

This "presciss" characterization of the critical self, however, can only be known as part of a phenomenal self, since it still has the nature of a sign. At the most, it would seem to be a kind of conscious projection of one's phenomenal self into the indefinitely distant future. In any case, the notion is certainly "all-important" for Peirce's philosophy, as otherwise it would be impossible to sustain the division between the objective and normative or to account for regulative principles. The objects interpreted as well as the rules of interpretation are signs, and any difference between them must be stated with reference to an interpreter, to what he interprets and his habits of interpretation.[24] Thus, if Peirce's pragmatism results in a universe perfused with signs and is led to embrace a common-sensism and scholastic realism by the vagueness and generality of the signs, it also makes the final point of reference an interpreter with instinctive common sense and a capacity for the self-controlled development of habits. In short, if reality must be determined ultimately as the outcome of purposive action, the source of such action is in effect the source of reality.

B. However obscure may be Peirce's notion of the interpreter as critical self, it is at least clear that he did not intend the notion in a sense which could be explained ultimately by psychology or any other special science. In 1905 he spoke of the position of "those who would base logic or metaphysics on psychology or any other special science" as "the least tenable of all the philosophical opinions that have any vogue" (5.452). Yet this sort of position would inevitably result if the interpreter presupposed in Peirce's normative account of meaning were a concept to be explained by the special sciences. Such explanation not only would do violence to the ordering of the sciences by reversing the relative priority of logic and the special sciences but

233

would also end by destroying Peirce's distinction between theoretical and practical.

Broadly speaking, Peirce regarded "the practical" as covering any effect that might be encountered in the course of action, and in this sense the meaning of all concepts in the sciences consists in conceivable practical effects. But this manner of specifying the meaning does not imply that the sciences themselves thereby become practical. In the *Minute Logic* Peirce declared: "I recognize two branches of science: Theoretical, whose purpose is simply and solely knowledge of God's truth; and Practical, for the uses of life" (1.239). He regards the distinction as obvious and disclaims any interest in classifying the practical sciences, which include such things as "pedagogics, gold-beating, etiquette, pigeon-fancying," and "vulgar arithmetic" (1.243). For each of these sciences practical effects, then, constitute the end of inquiry rather than the meaning of concepts. The theoretical scientist can never maintain that the actual achievement of a practical effect is all he is trying to accomplish by his inquiry, since no matter how many times he may achieve the effect he has not attained absolute confirmation of his hypothesis. In this way, the distinction between practical and theoretical becomes as sharp as that between a limited and unlimited end. But, in order to sustain such a distinction, it is necessary to admit Peirce's reinterpretation of pragmatism as a doctrine that makes the ultimate intellectual meaning of a concept consist in the manner in which it subserves the *summum bonum*. The theoretical as well as the practical scientist must endeavor to specify his meaning in the conditional form that if certain acts are carried out, certain results will follow. But the purpose of the specification in this case is to make the concept serviceable for the self-controlled growth of inquiry rather than for the actual attainment of this or that practical effect. In short, the ultimate meaning is the way the concept subserves an unlimited end.

However, when science is regarded generally as the ultimate fixation of belief, it becomes difficult to keep the distinction between theoretical and practical from becoming one of degree merely. Apparently, in order to avoid this consequence, Peirce admitted in the lectures of 1903 that, "speaking strictly, *belief* is out of place in pure theoretical science, which has nothing nearer to it than the establishment of doctrines, and only the provisional establishment of them, at that" (5.60). This conclusion is developed at some length in lectures of 1898, where Peirce asserted flatly that there is "no proposition at all in science which answers to the conception of belief" (1.635). A man believes a proposition when he is willing to act upon it under conditions that involve some personal risk, while a scientist "risks nothing" upon the propositions he accepts qua scientist, and they are therefore "but opinions at most." Now one way of making this distinction between scientific opinion and belief absolute would be to presuppose different sorts of interpreters or inquirers and to define scientific opinion as whatever is accepted by the scientific man. But one might also assume a single interpreter and distinguish different kinds of belief by the different effects produced on the interpreter.

Peirce on one occasion appears to use the second of these ways of distinguishing absolutely between scientific opinion and belief. In the fragment on belief and judgment ca. 1902, where he argued that in the last analysis all belief seems to "involve expectation as its essence" (5.542), he remarked that "there is just this difference between a practical belief and an expectation so far as it involves no purpose [or] effort; namely that the former is expectant of muscular sensation, the latter of sensation not muscular" (5.540). Thus, to use Peirce's examples, a belief like "Anthracite is a convenient fuel" is practical because the kind of expectation it arouses involves muscular sensation; and a belief like "The pole of the earth describes an oval of a few rods' diameter" is a theoretical belief (or scientific opinion) because it gives rise to a different kind of expectation. This way of drawing the distinction is clearly relative to what can be determined about an interpreter through investigation in special sciences, such as psychology and physiology. Yet, regardless of what might be established by experiments concerning the muscular sensations associated with certain beliefs, this manner of characterizing the interpreter could not be taken as the ultimate basis for differentiating the theoretical from the practical. There would be no reason for calling those beliefs which are "expectant of muscular sensation" practical rather than theoretical unless the beliefs had already been so characterized by a different type of analysis. Of course, one might say that by definition practical beliefs are beliefs of this sort, but then it would remain to be shown that this sense of "practical" had any connection with what Peirce referred to in the *Minute Logic* as "the uses of life" as opposed to "knowledge of God's truth."[25]

A reference to different kinds of interpreters rather than to different effects on a single interpreter underlies the analysis in the lectures of 1898. The "scientific man" is contrasted to one who is interested in practical matters, and Peirce declares: "The two masters, *theory* and *practice*, you cannot serve. That perfect balance of attention which is requisite for observing the system of things is utterly lost if human desires intervene, and all the more so the higher and holier those desires may be" (1.642). Peirce means by "higher" and "holier" desires those which relate to the establishment of religious and other beliefs that may afford great personal satisfaction.[26] This is not inconsistent with his assertion in the *Minute Logic* that the scientific man must have moral devotion to truth as a phase of the *summum bonum* (cf. 1.575–76). In fact, in the latter sense the scientific man would be a perfectly moral being who gave himself entirely to the service of truth. Such a being is of course an abstraction or ideal like the unlimited community, and the scientific man would seem to be simply the perfect citizen of this community. Peirce's view mentioned above that "a person is not absolutely an individual" (5.421) but involves a phenomenal self who addresses a critical or deeper self "just coming into life in the flow of time" would appear consonant with holding that there might be something of the scientific man

236

in each person, especially in so far as the critical self seems to shade into "the man's circle of society." Yet if this notion of the scientific man is to provide the basis for an absolute distinction between theoretical and practical belief it must remain a notion formed entirely from normative logic with nothing presupposed from the special sciences. The idea of an inquirer who identifies fixation of belief with the outcome of inquiry sufficiently prolonged is indigenous to Peirce's analysis of induction, and any attempt to employ induction itself to investigate the actual effects of a belief held in this capacity as opposed to one held for the uses of life must assume the logical analysis. If, on the other hand, the inquirer were conceived only as determined by inductive inquiry, the priority of logic could not be maintained, and there would be no basis for distinguishing between theoretical and practical in the sense Peirce intended.

Yet if the process of inquiry, in accordance with critical common-sensism, is to constitute an evolution in which primitive beliefs are replaced by scientific hypotheses as man outgrows the applicability of instinct, there would still seem to be a continuity between beliefs held for the uses of life and for theoretical ends. The point here is perhaps best approached by recalling Peirce's remark that we outgrow the beliefs of primitive man "as we develop degrees of self-control unknown to that man" (5.511). The higher grades of self-control, as Peirce sketched them, consisted in self-training in accordance with a "moral principle" or an "esthetic ideal" (cf. 5.533). The scientific man as a moral being who devotes himself entirely to the pursuit of truth would thus be one who has developed degrees of self-control unknown to primitive man. But then the evolution Peirce refers to in his discussions of critical common-sensism may be viewed as essentially one in which different kinds of inquirers come into being. The passage from beliefs held exclusively for the uses of life to those entertained merely as scientific opinions takes place with the emergence of an inquirer who subjects his practical beliefs to further degrees of self-control. Thus, the process of replacing the vague belief that fire burns by a relatively precise practical belief about the action of fire would involve a transition from the more or less instinctive inquiry of primitive man to that of an inquirer who controlled his practical beliefs by his scientific opinions. But the circumstance that greater precision in practical belief presupposes or is concomitant with the development of theoretical science does not mean that an absolute distinction between theory and practice is impossible. The ascertainment of truth assumes an inquirer whose self-control leads him always to regard his ultimate goal as indefinitely remote from the limited end of achieving certain practical effects, even though his inquiry by its very nature can advance only with the attainment of such a limited end.

From this point of view, the process of inquiry may be identified with that of the fixation of belief without specifying either practical or theoretical belief. For a practical belief that would suffice for every conceivable occasion, that would remain forever beyond even the possibility of theoretical doubt (i.e., genuine doubt which arises from experiments in the imagination), would have to be a belief that was in accord with the real nature of things. In other words, the ultimate fixation of practical belief through the exercise of self-control coincides with the establishment of truth. As Peirce remarked in 1905, "that ultimate state of habit to which the action of self-control ultimately tends, where no room is left for further self-control, is, in the case of thought, the state of fixed belief, or perfect knowledge" (5.420). It was in the paragraph immediately after this remark that Peirce explained that the notion of a critical self and a self which includes man's circle of society might enable one to distinguish in the abstract between absolute truth and what he did not doubt. In the last analysis, then, absolute truth is simply the object of those beliefs which will be fixed by the unlimited community, and in this case there is no distinction between practical and theoretical beliefs. It is only as the individual or limited community is opposed to the unlimited one and conceived as having ends which pertain merely to given situations that practice becomes distinct from theory. It is thus always possible for an individual not to doubt a particular belief on the basis of his limited inquiry and at the same time to distinguish in the abstract between this belief and absolute truth. Precisely such distinction is required if one is to form scientific opinions as opposed to practical beliefs. In this sense, the belief that anthracite is a convenient fuel remains practical as being held only for the purposes of action in a specific type of situation, but, if there is the additional purpose of advancing scientific inquiry by investigating the properties of various fuels through laboratory tests, the belief may be altered to the point of becoming a scientific opinion. In the latter instance the scientist may be unable at a particular stage of his inquiry to distinguish except in the abstract between his opinion and absolute truth, although at a further stage some surprise in experimental results may occasion doubts that are not thus in the abstract. Eventually the original practical belief may be entirely changed because of newly discovered fuels, and inquiry has advanced one step nearer the indefinitely remote goal of having all beliefs fixed in accordance with reality.

C. It was noticed above in chapter iii that there was a kind of discontinuity between the first three methods of fixing belief and the scientific method as they were presented in the early essay, *The Fixation of Belief*. Tenacity, authority, and taste constituted ways of settling belief relative to limited communities, while induction presupposed an unlimited community. In so far as the first three methods seemed to reflect Peirce's categories, this situation appeared analogous to those in the earlier essays where a determination of the real was the fourth step in a process that had already been divided into three stages corresponding to the categories. Scientific inquiry viewed as that of the unlimited community could be analyzed as a purely logical process proceeding by abduction, deduction, and induction independently of historical accidents. But there was then the problem of accounting for the existence of such inquiry—for its coincidence with the inquiry of limited communities. This became in effect the problem of relating human nature and inquiry, of showing that the former was such as eventually to give rise to the latter.

The resolution of this problem should be found in Peirce's doctrine of the evolution of inquiry from the instincts of primitive man to the higher grades of self-control exercised by the scientist. But there seems to be nothing in this evolution which represents a passage through the three stages of prescientific inquiry distinguished in *The Fixation of Belief*. The best indication as to how Peirce might have related these stages to such evolution seems to be the sentence he added *ca.* 1910 to his discussion in this essay of the a priori method.[27] "Indeed, as long as no better method can be applied, it ought to be followed, since it is then the expression of instinct which must be the ultimate cause of belief in all cases" (5.383). Occasions where no better method can be applied should arise for the most part only in connection with the logical and metaphysical beliefs that are "virtually assumed" by the special sciences (cf. 5.521–22), and, in so far as critical reflection on these beliefs merely confirms the expression of instinct, the latter would appear to be the ultimate cause of belief in all cases. But then the first method historically in this view would be a species of the third one according to the earlier analysis. The methods of tenacity and authority might then represent accidental obstructions which temporarily block the road of discovery, and the same would of course be true for the a priori method when it is extended beyond its proper sphere and results in rationalistic science rather than the expression of instinct. The prescientific stages of inquiry may thus be reinterpreted as unscientific varieties, as three possible ways in which human nature may react at any time to impede the advance of science. The rationale of the varieties may be taken quite legitimately from the categories without reference to history, since the question is one of determining possibilities rather than of anything which actually has or must happen in the course of events. The discontinuity between unscientific and scientific inquiry occasions no difficulty because the rise of the latter is not to be accounted for as an outgrowth from the former. The evolution from primitive man to scientific inquirer may be explained as a continuous process which consists essentially in the gradual refinement of original instinctive beliefs through the development of self-control, and the accidental interruptions of this development by unscientific modes of inquiry would represent chance deviations from the necessary laws of the process.[28]

Inquiry and the inquirer are thus related ultimately by the tendency to self-control, which starts with instinct and may perhaps advance through indefinite gradations. This tendency would appear to be the same, according to Peirce's analysis, as the tendency to take habits, and the fact that he came to use the moralistic rather than the biological term would reflect the priority which his theory of induction led him to confer upon the normative over the objective. But there would also seem to be a close connection between the degrees of self-control and the clearness of ideas. It was noticed above in section 2 that clearness appeared to be a way of offsetting the effects of vagueness, in that an interpreter might clearly grasp the meaning of a sign as entailing certain practical consequences although the sign remained objectively vague. Clearness is then a necessary prerequisite to the ascertainment of truth, since it constitutes an understanding of the meaning sufficient for the employment of induction. The important difference between clearness and truth, however, is that the former remains strictly the accomplishment of an individual inquirer while the latter can be attained finally only by the unlimited community. This distinction between clearness and truth, then, affords a much sharper break between the individual and the community than does the division of practical and theoretical. For the latter requires only the difference between the ends of a limited and unlimited community, and the "scientific man" represents a highly abstract version of the individual inquirer which inevitably shades into the notion of a community. But grades of clearness as opposed to truth mark off an individual as distinct from a social end. The tendency to self-control should thus appear, first, in the individual achievement of clear ideas and, second, in the form of inquiry which merges the individual with the community.

Yet the relation between clearness and truth in one sense suffers a rather striking alteration when pragmatism is reinterpreted so as to make the ultimate meaning of a concept consist in the manner in which it would subserve the self-controlled growth of inquiry. While in most cases this means merely that the concept would be useless for inquiry if it entailed no conceivable practical effects by which it could be tested, there are some terms, notably those of Peirce's ontology, which do not possess a meaning in this fashion and yet are not scientifically meaningless because they do serve the advancement of inquiry. But then the question arises: Are there true statements about ontology? Peirce began one of his lectures of 1903 by remarking, "I proceed to argue that *Thirdness* is operative in Nature. Suppose we attack the question experimentally" (5.93). The experiment he proposes is that of dropping a stone from his hand and predicting that it will fall to the floor. The success of the prediction is taken as showing that a general law is really operative in nature. Peirce perhaps intends here that successful prediction constitutes the practical effect comprising the meaning of the idea that thirdness is operative in nature. But such an effect is obviously of a different order from those ordinarily said to be encountered by inquiry, and the truth of an idea like the one in question is presupposed rather than established by induction. Peirce went on in his lecture to mention two conflicting "hypotheses" regarding the occurrence of successful predictions about falling stones. One is that such occurrences are "due to mere chance" and the other is that they are "due to some *active general principle*" (5.100). But there is no specific practical effect—no verifiable consequence—which will distinguish between these hypotheses with respect to their truth or falsity, nor

242

did Peirce attempt to designate any. He clearly felt that no one could genuinely doubt the falsity of the first hypothesis, and in the closing remarks of this part of the lecture he implied that such inability to doubt was tantamount to accepting the second hypothesis (cf. 5.101). This situation may obtain in so far as the alternatives are merely those between doubting and not doubting the vague common-sense belief in the uniformity of nature, but Peirce here refers to the second hypothesis as "the doctrine of scholastic realism," and in this form it certainly represents a refinement of the original instinctive belief to a point where it has frequently been doubted. How, then, can Peirce defend this refinement as true doctrine? The only possible way seems to be to maintain that, when the doctrine is clearly apprehended with reference to the way in which it subserves the advancement of inquiry, its truth is apparent. But then some ideas about reality are shown to be true simply by making them clear, and truth in this sense would seem to be attainable by an individual, or at least it does not require an unlimited community in the way a strictly inductive conclusion does.

Peirce never explicitly declared that the truth of an idea about reality might be determined only by its clearness,[29] although in his discussions of common-sensism he did speak of "sundry logical and metaphysical beliefs" which are "virtually assumed" by any idioscopic inquiry and the truth of which can "be concluded before the first outward experiment is made" (5.521). Now inasmuch as the experiments which the critical common-sensist performs in his imagination are primarily a matter of forming "conditional resolutions as to conduct" (cf. 5.517), the process would seem to be essentially one of making ideas clear. Those beliefs whose truth can be settled only by such experimentation are thus very much in the nature of ideas which can be verified only by being made clear. Presumably, such ideas for the most part should be limited to those which lay the foundations of Peirce's ontology as distinct from his scientific metaphysics. This conclusion suggests comparison with his statement that principles of ontology are not "positive truths" because they are reducible to "logical formulae" by virtue of the pragmatic maxim (cf. 5.496). Yet an ontological proposition like "Thirdness is operative in nature" is hardly analytic, at least not in the sense that propositions of formal logic and mathematics are analytic. On the other hand, while Peirce did regard this proposition as a hypothesis and even spoke of "attacking the question experimentally," it was easily seen not to be a hypothesis susceptible of inductive verification. From this point of view, the principles of ontology occupy a dubious status in Peirce's philosophy, and perhaps the best that can be said for them is that their truth is shown by their clearness and that they represent a refinement of instinctive beliefs. But then the dividing line between ontology and scientific metaphysics becomes a difficult one to draw, since certain beliefs which Peirce designated as belonging to the latter are also refinements of instinctive beliefs. While Peirce in one sense could give arguments for the reality of God, for example, and thus regard this belief as a hypothesis, he also declared that the belief as the expression of instinct was doubted only by those who misunderstood it (cf. 6.496). In this second sense, Peirce seems rather close to a form of the ontological argument for God's reality, since the truth of the belief is then to be shown only by its clearness.

However, this mingling of ontology and metaphysics does not have to result in what Peirce called "the meaningless gibberish" of "ontological metaphysics" (cf. 5.423). It was remarked above in chapter iv that an example of such gibberish might be found in Leibniz's principle of pre-established harmony as Peirce interpreted it in relation to an explanation of the interaction between mind and matter. Leibniz seemed to be saying merely that "the motions and changes of state of atoms are relative to one another, because God made them so in the beginning" (6.273). But this is hardly anything more than the assertion that the facts are so because they are so. Regardless of whether the question is taken finally as one of ontology or scientific metaphysics, this position represents a confusion between an explanation and a mere restatement which adds nothing of significance.

If the question is one of ontology, the restatement must clarify the original vague belief that mind and matter interact by adding a significance to the conception which will make it serviceable for the advancement of inquiry. While this significance may not be "positive" in the sense that verifiable consequences can be deduced from it, it is not meaningless as Peirce reinterpreted his pragmatism.

It would seem, in fact, that in the last analysis all the parts of philosophy distinguished in Peirce's ordering of the sciences, from phenomenology through at least a considerable portion of metaphysics, achieve "positive truth" only as a form of clarification. They all have in common the exclusive use in some form or other of "coenoscopic" as opposed to "idioscopic" observation (cf. 1.241–42). Their aim, in effect, is simply a clear apprehension of things which "come within the range of every man's normal experience, and for the most part in every waking hour of his life." In accordance with pragmatism, this amounts to understanding the most common elements of experience in a way that will be serviceable to the self-controlled growth of inquiry. Such an aim is individual rather than social and would seem to represent a sort of prerequisite for membership in the unlimited community of inductive inquirers. The self who is to exercise the self-control Peirce talks about so frequently is perhaps best construed as the self with a capacity for this understanding of the common elements of experience. The idioscopic inquirer can control his inquiry by a consciously formulated *logica docens* to the degree that he has clearly grasped what he must discern by coenoscopic observation. On the other hand, to the extent that he follows a *logica utens* he must be unaware, except instinctively, of matters that stare him in the face. Peirce's wide use of the term "perception" should also be remarked in connection with this distinction between coenoscopic and idioscopic observation. It was noticed above in the preceding section that even the common-sense indubitables appeared to be more or less of the nature of perceptual judgments. For inasmuch as the immediate object determined by perception is

245

never absolutely singular, there seems to be no reason to stop short of saying that even the singular which constitutes the totality of real objects is itself vaguely the object of perception. From this point of view, coenoscopic observation serves to determine the perceptual universe presupposed in communication. The common-sense indubitables in their original form would represent a clear understanding of such observation only at the level of instinctive control. The development of the various parts of philosophy would then consist in the achievement of greater degrees of clearness in this understanding.

D. Further indication of the crucial importance of clearness for Peirce's philosophy may be obtained by another comparison of the grades of clearness with the methods of fixing belief. It was suggested above in chapter iii that the three grades Peirce originally distinguished, like the first three methods, could be viewed as expressions of his categories. The fact that a fourth method but not a fourth grade was differentiated seemed to be connected with the circumstance that only in the former case were ideas referred finally to actuality rather than possibility. The continuity of the progression through the different methods was interrupted by the circumstance that the scientific method presupposed an unlimited community for the ultimate fixation of belief. But this situation, it has already been noticed, was altered in Peirce's later writings so that the three prescientific methods could be viewed as unscientific varieties which represented accidental departures from the main course of evolution. However, the fact that a determination of the real constitutes the fourth step in a process which has already been divided into three stages corresponding to the categories seems to reappear as a result of the new interpretation Peirce gave his pragmatism. He regarded the understanding of a concept with reference to the manner in which it would subserve the self-controlled growth of inquiry as "a still higher grade of clearness of thought" to be attained after the third grade mentioned in 1878 (cf. 5.3). Inasmuch as this higher grade is precisely what is necessary in order to establish the modes of being required by Peirce's ontology, a determination of the real again appears as the fourth step in a process. Yet, in this case, the continuity is not disrupted by a passage from the limited to the unlimited in so far as the concern throughout is to achieve the individual end of clearness rather than the social end of a true induction. While Peirce never indicated as much, the familiarity which constitutes the first grade of clearness would seem to represent primarily instinctive understanding. The definition which marks the achievement of the second grade should be the same as a relatively precise or definite meaning understood with reference to an object. The inevitable failure of attaining absolute precision is counteracted by an interpretation of the meaning with reference to conceivable practical effects.[30] The fourth grade then represents a grasp of the ultimate purpose of the whole process and leads to an ontology which identifies the reality of an object understood with the truth of a general idea of its conceivable practical effects. Such a reality is seen clearly at this grade to imply a mode of being distinct from that of dynamic interaction as well as from that of mere feeling.

It will be recalled that, in the original presentation (1867) of the categories, substance and being appeared as the extreme terms in a list of five and that a determination of the real was not guaranteed by the union of subject and predicate in a proposition but required a fourth step distinct from the three stages which Peirce later regarded as representing his complete list of categories. The Kantian orientation of his thought at this time was apparently sufficient to have led him to view this formation of a proposition only as an individual end. But scarcely a year later he developed his social theory of reality and defined the real as the ultimate outcome of induction. The nature of the individual inquirer, however, remained a problem which seemed to be resolved only by making the practice of induction contingent upon the moral sentiments of the inquirers. As noted above at the start of this chapter, when Peirce came to reconsider the formation of a proposition by an individual person, he marked the beginning and end of the process by perception and purposive action instead of substance and being. Statements of ontology thus come to depend finally on the clearness with which an individual can grasp the most common elements of perception in relation to purposive action—in relation ultimately to the self-controlled growth of inquiry. Peirce's philosophy, then, remains basically pragmatic in that his ontology seeks to elucidate reality by the purposes of the inquirer.

4. PRAGMATISM AND PHILOSOPHY: CONCLUSION

A. In a short fragment ca. 1905 Peirce commented on what he regarded as the main philosophic alternative to pragmatism. He declared: "I may speak of the traditional logic as the principal alternative, as presenting itself at the first and only great parting of the ways. For the old logicians, thought has no meaning except itself, any more than a fugue of Bach has" (5.500). The remainder of the fragment is somewhat obscure, but the fundamental question is clearly the conception of substance. Start with "any twig of the tree of Porphyry," Peirce says, and one comes finally to substance as the ultimate concept. While the pragmatic alternative is not presented in the fragment, the issue seems properly stated as that between the second and third grades of clearness.[31] Substance would be ultimate in the traditional sense in so far as the meaning of each concept is to be grasped by immediate reference to a certain kind of substance. In order to maintain this position, it seems necessary to fall back on some sort of intuitive apprehension of essential nature. Since Peirce considered such apprehension impossible and held that the immediate object of a thought could never be something outside the thought-process, the traditional position becomes tantamount for him to maintaining that "thought has no meaning except itself." Pragmatism is then the position which proposes a higher grade of clearness of meaning by referring a thought not merely to another thought-object but to such an object interpreted as conceivable practical effects. By thus turning finally to the process of inquiry, it becomes possible to speak of the fixation of belief as the result of an external permanence established by induction, without assuming that outside the thought-process there is a substantial thing in itself which is the real object of knowledge. The "first and only great parting of the ways," therefore, should come at the point where clearness of meaning is to be identified with the immediate apprehension of essential nature or with conceivable practical effects to be tested by inductive inquiry.

In his later writings Peirce spoke of proving the doctrine of pragmatism and went so far as to announce in a paper ca. 1906 that he could give "even two or three scientific proofs of its truth" (5.468). But, "unfortunately," he continued, "all the real proofs of pragmatism that I know—and, I hardly doubt, all there are to be known—require just as close and laborious exertion of attention as any but the very most difficult of mathematical theorems, while they add to that all those difficulties of logical analysis which force the mathematician to creep with exceeding caution, if not timorously." In order to avoid bewildering his readers with such intricate and difficult exposition, Peirce offers instead "an idea perfectly fulfilling the reader's desire, that of enabling him to place pragmatism and its concepts in the area of his own thought, and of showing roughly how its concepts are related to familiar concepts." Nothing is given in the Collected Papers which purports to be one of the "real proofs" of pragmatism, though presumably these proofs would involve the analysis which establishes the new logic of relatives and shows the incompleteness of the formal syllogistic developed by traditional logic. Peirce spoke elsewhere of his pragmatism as having "been designed and constructed, to use the expression of Kant, architectonically" (5.5), and, again, he remarked that a proof of pragmatism "would essentially involve the establishment of the truth of synechism" (5.415). It would thus appear that a "real proof" of pragmatism would amount to a kind of elucidation of most of Peirce's philosophy and formal logic. The "idea" which he offered his readers in the paper ca. 1906 begins in its first phase with a brief exposition of the categories (5.469) and involves next "the view that every thought is a sign" (5.470). The analysis proceeds with the distinctions already considered earlier in the present chapter between the existent and immediate object and the emotional, energetic, and logical interpretant. The necessity for pragmatism becomes apparent from an examination of the logical interpretant, which comprises the meaning of a general concept. But this not quite real proof of pragmatism, then, amounts to a partial elucidation of Peirce's philosophy, with particular reference to speculative grammar, or that part of his logic which properly contains the pragmatic maxim.

The fact that Peirce referred to what could hardly be anything more than a kind of exposition of his philosophy and formal logic as a "scientific proof" of pragmatism is not inconsistent with his conception of argument and demonstration. Inasmuch as every modification of consciousness is an inference and every symbol has the nature of an argument, there is no absolute distinction between interpreting a proposition and advancing an argument in favor of its truth. Every perceptual judgment shades into an abductive inference or hypothesis, and further elucidation of the meaning must involve phases corresponding to deduction and induction. Arguments with meaning only at the fourth grade of clearness, such as the hypotheses of God's reality, may exhibit aspects only loosely analogous to these two phases. Yet in so far as the analysis is to apply to all symbols and the higher degree of clearness is to be recognized, there must be something analogous, however remote. It is only with this extremely wide use of logical terms that Peirce can speak of his philosophic doctrines as hypotheses susceptible of scientific proof. An equally broad use of "perception" and "observation" is of course entailed by the view that every modification of consciousness is an inference. While this analogical use of terms may thus be required by one side of Peirce's logic, it nevertheless blurs his distinction between truth and clearness at the highest grade and leads to the position discussed in the preceding section—that some ideas about reality may have their truth shown only by their clearness.

250

Peirce's scrupulous adherence to his complete renunciation of the traditional doctrine of substance demands this broad application of logical concepts. If an idea is always taken to signify the predicate of an object or substance, logic can assume that meaning is fixed at the level of terms, or at least of propositions, and proceed to analyze arguments as complex forms of meaning. But in so far as an idea signifies nothing but conceivable practical consequences and makes no assumption of a substance which possesses these consequences as predicates, meaning is fixed only at the level of arguments. Hence, instead of analyzing arguments as complex forms of meaning, Peirce must analyze terms and propositions as partial forms to be completed by arguments. "The meaning of a proposition or term," he declared in 1903, "is all that that proposition or term could contribute to the conclusion of a demonstrative argument" (5.179).

The beginnings of this position are easily discernible in the new logic presented in Peirce's writings of 1867. The collapse of Kant's distinction between mediate and immediate inference came as the result of locating logical principles in operations of substitution rather than in forms of thought. The chief business of logic thus became the classification of arguments, and terms and propositions were to be distinguished primarily as different elements in the process of substitution which effect the construction of arguments. On this new approach to logic any attempt to fix meaning ultimately with only terms or propositions would involve an extra-logical assumption which accords the elements of arguments an independent status. The denial of intuitive faculties proclaimed in the papers of 1868 seemed to make such an assumption impossible and led to the position that every modification of consciousness is an inference. A definition of reality as the ultimate outcome of inductive inquiry appeared to be the only other possibility. The manner in which terms acquire meaning ultimately in a demonstrative argument is clearly illustrated by Peirce's later analysis of perception and the perceptual judgment. A red percept, for example, acquires meaning as a term in the context of a demonstrative argument in which "Any red percept will have the same color as this percept" is deduced from "This percept is red." The alternative to this analysis, as Peirce saw it, is to assume that the percept is ultimately a predicate attached to a possible object, specified perhaps only as a certain space-time region. But then, in so far as an immediate intuition of such an object is impossible so that the percept can mean (as opposed to indicate) nothing outside of consciousness, this alternative position amounts to the view that "thought has no meaning except itself." The only way of referring meaning to reality, then, is to understand or interpret the percept as ultimately the conclusion of an argument predicting the nature of future percepts.[32]

B. The reality determined by this procedure is of course always in the form of a general law stating that, if certain actions are performed, certain results will follow. The existent object or singular which reacts to produce the percept is precisely what is never represented. It may be pointed to or indicated by dynamically directing the attention of an interpreter to it, but, as soon as one attempts to represent it, he ends by talking about certain practical consequences that would be encountered under certain conditions. Individual existence thus remains unintelligible and falls under the category of struggle rather than that of representation. When Peirce in his lectures of 1903 referred to his second category as consisting in the element of struggle, he admitted that the notion was anthropomorphic (cf. 5.47). He explained ca. 1905: "I heartily embrace most of the clauses of that doctrine [anthropomorphism], if some right of private interpretation be allowed me. I hold, for instance, that man is so completely hemmed in by the bounds of his possible practical experience, his mind is so restricted to being the instrument of his needs, that he cannot, in the least, mean anything that transcends those limits" (5.536). This passage emphasizes again that man, the individual interpreter or inquirer, becomes the ultimate point of reference for Peirce's pragmatic philosophy. The passage also suggests what is perhaps the fundamental difference between Peirce and Kant. By regarding all possible experience as possible practical experience, Peirce collapses Kant's distinction between theoretical and practical reason and defines the limits of intellectual meaning by the purposes of action rather than the conditions of experience.[33]

The difficulties which Peirce encountered with his notion of the inquirer may be seen in a new light by this contrast with Kant. Peirce's polemic against substance is made in terms of the first critique and is basically a flat denial of "the proposition that a thing-in-itself can, however indirectly, be conceived" (5.452).[34] Yet this did not prevent Peirce from asserting that "we have *direct experience of things in themselves*," and hence that "all experience and all knowledge is knowledge of that which is, independently of being represented" (6.95) (Peirce's italics). But he hastened to add after these remarks, "At the same time, no proposition can relate, or even thoroughly pretend to relate, to any object otherwise than as that object is represented." These statements, he continued, become intelligible "as soon as you take into account that Secondness that jabs you perpetually in the ribs." The existent or dynamical object which reacts to cause the percept, in other words, is the thing in itself, but the immediate object referred to by the perceptual judgment can only be an object as represented by the percept. The thing in itself, thus, is always experienced in the element of struggle, although it can never be conceived or represented. When this analysis is accepted, any attempt to refer meaning to reality by a doctrine of independent substance can yield at the most a verbal explanation of truth. "That truth is the correspondence of a representation with its object," Peirce declared, "is, as Kant says, merely the nominal definition of it" (5.553). Kant's endeavor to go beyond a verbal explanation involves, of course, the logic of truth given by his transcendental analytic taken as a canon for judging the empirical use of the understanding. After the above statement, Peirce explained his alternative to Kant's solution as follows:

Now thought is of the nature of a sign. In that case, then, if we can find out the right method of thinking and can follow it out—the

253

right method of transforming signs—then truth can be nothing more nor less than the last result to which the following out of this method would ultimately carry us. In that case, that to which the representation should conform, is itself something in the nature of a representation, or sign—something noumenal, intelligible, conceivable, and utterly unlike a thing-in-itself.

It should be noted here first that Peirce does not use the word "noumenal" in Kant's sense as opposed to the phenomenal. Every representation, every phenomenon, possesses an element of thirdness and is thus intelligible and noumenal.[35] The truth of a representation, then, consists in its conformity to that representation which would result from sufficient employment of the right method of transforming signs. A second fundamental difference from Kant is that Peirce's explanation of that to which a true representation must conform depends on a method rather than an analytic. The final statement of Peirce's explanation thus assumes the form of a hypothetical imperative giving a prescription for the right conduct of inquiry rather than an analysis of the necessary conditions for the empirical use of the understanding. In this way, Kant's distinction between theoretical and practical reason is collapsed, and the limits of intellectual meaning which Peirce finds in the explanation of truth must be specified with reference to possible practical experience. Problems which are posed and professedly resolved in the first critique are thus referred by Peirce to considerations that Kant reserved for the second critique. Yet the character of these considerations is radically altered by Peirce's identification of the noumenal with the intelligibility to be found in every phenomenon. Kant's *praktisch* as distinct from his *pragmatisch* becomes unnecessary with this conception of the noumenal, and Peirce declared that these two terms in Kant "were as far apart as the two poles, the former belonging in a region of thought where no mind of the experimentalist type can ever make sure of solid ground under his feet, the latter expressing relation to some definite human purpose" (5.412). Peirce thus chose to call his doctrine "pragmatism" rather than "practicalism" and always intended "practical" as a synonym for "prag·matic."

Kant's distinction between noumena and phenomena was precisely what enabled him to account as he did for an individual person as a moral being, or free agent. Any such account is clearly impossible for Peirce in so far as he restricts his analysis to the three elements of phenomena expressed by his categories. A noumenal self or person in this case would be simply any general idea or symbol and would constitute the self as thirdness. A self not a sign but an individual in some way determining signs would always be one term in the dyadic affair constituting the element of struggle. The first category is strictly prior to any distinction between sign and individual and hence can contribute nothing to an account of the self without the aid of the other two categories. The reactions which constitute secondness are usually characterized by Peirce as dynamic and energetic, although, when he turned to the normative sciences, he described them as treating of "Phenomena in their Secondness" (5.123). Moral and physical compulsion are thus essentially of the same character, and with this much of Peirce's philosophy there is certainly no way of distinguishing action by self-control from physical reaction. Nor is there any way left to achieve such distinction by means of the laws or habits constituting the third category, since in this case the identity of the moral and the physical is if anything more pronounced. The laws or habits by virtue of which men are destined eventually to attain goodness and truth are essentially of the same sort as those by which dice are destined to turn up pairs of sixes.[36]

The one remaining factor in Peirce's philosophy which makes intelligible a distinction between moral and physical action is his fourth grade of clearness. At this level, distinctions which would otherwise be meaningless acquire significance as they subserve the development of concrete reasonableness—the self-controlled growth of inquiry. The individual self that is neither sign nor physical reaction but an inquirer capable of moral self-control may thus be understood as that which makes such development of inquiry possible. Inasmuch as the modes of being which comprise Peirce's ontology are to be explained finally as elements of co-operation toward this self-controlled growth—toward the *summum bonum* (2.118)—the possibility, existence, and reality of the self presupposed by the process cannot be accounted for in turn by these modes of being. Peirce's characterization of the normative sciences as treating of phenomena in their secondness was given in the context of his ordering of the sciences where it served to differentiate the parts of philosophy, but the notion of moral as distinct from physical action was then assumed and not explained. A sort of remnant of Kant's noumenal as opposed to phenomenal is thus to be found in Peirce's fourth grade of clearness, and the self understood at this level is presupposed but not explained by Peirce's ontology just as the noumenal self is presupposed but not explained by Kant's ethics. Again, as Kant's categories could never apply to noumena, so Peirce's categories should never apply to those ideas which can only be conceived with the highest grade of clearness.[37] Peirce's "anthropomorphic" declaration that man cannot in the least mean anything that transcends the limits of possible practical experience appears as an analogue of Kant's statement that man's understanding is limited by possible experience. But Kant's statement would itself be meaningless if the understanding were unable to reflect on the source of its own cognition and determine its limitations. The attainment of Peirce's fourth grade of clearness is then the analogue of this reflection, and far from constituting a violation of the pragmatic criterion of meaning it represents an understanding of the criterion itself.

C. What appears to be a conflict in Peirce between a scientific empiricism or naturalism and an anti-empirical metaphysics or transcendentalism may be centered around the issue of the third and fourth grades of clearness in their relation to truth. In his dictionary article of 1902 where he explicitly distinguished the fourth grade, Peirce referred to his original pragmatic maxim as appearing to assume a "stoical" doctrine that "the end of man is action" (5.3). Such a doctrine, Peirce says, becomes inadequate if one admits that action itself "wants an end." He did not elaborate the stoical view, but what he intended by it seems clear enough. Man has no end but action if all action is physical, or, in other words, if man's nature, as the stoics maintained, can only be conceived as part of physical nature. With this naturalistic position, as Peirce saw it, it is impossible to distinguish between the end of inquiry as the ascertainment of general ideas expressing scientific truth and the particular acts—the practical effects—which are necessary for the achievement of this end. Such distinction assumes the reality of general laws apart from existential facts, and this reality in turn assumes a conception of man as a being able to discern an ultimate goal beyond the particular acts which comprise his physical nature. Peirce was careful to point out in his dictionary article that his paper of 1878 departed from naturalism so far as to embrace a doctrine of scholastic realism. "Indeed," he says with reference to his own paper, "the writer practised better than he preached; for he applied the stoical maxim most unstoically, in such a sense as to insist upon the reality of the objects of general ideas in their generality" (5.3).

It was in connection with this doctrine of realism that Peirce had already been led to assert in his paper of 1869 that "logic rigidly requires, before all else, that no determinate fact, nothing which can happen to a man's self, should be of more consequence to him than everything else. He who would not sacrifice his own soul to save the whole world, is illogical in all his inferences, collectively" (5.354). While this clearly entails the notion of an end beyond the particular acts which comprise a man's physical nature, Peirce hesitated to describe the end except as something which man is biologically and socially compelled to follow. The tendency to waver between a naturalistic and ethical account of the end appears in The Doctrine of Chances (1878). After describing his three logical sentiments, Peirce declared: "It may seem strange that I should put forward three sentiments . . . as indispensable requirements of logic. Yet, when we consider that logic depends on a mere struggle to escape doubt, which, as it terminates in action, must begin in emotion, and that, furthermore, the only cause of our planting ourselves on reason is that other methods of escaping doubt fail on account of the social impulse, why should we wonder to find social sentiment presupposed in reasoning?" (2.655). The suggestion of an ethical determination of the end appears in Peirce's further comment, "It interests me to notice that these three sentiments seem to be pretty much the same as that famous trio of Charity, Faith, and Hope, which, in the estimation of St. Paul, are the finest and greatest of spiritual gifts."

Now, there is nothing in Peirce's doctrine of scholastic realism that would be contrary to the view that man's pursuit of an end beyond his individual acts may be explained as a biological and social phenomenon. Yet such explanation can characterize the end only as a type of action or behavior which results from certain biological and social compulsions. Hypotheses like that of "emotion," "the social impulse," and "social sentiment" might easily find a place in this sort of explanation, which would presuppose that logic is manifested in a struggle that "terminates in action." But the notion of "the greatest of spiritual gifts," at least with anything like the sense intended by St. Paul, obviously could have no place as a hypothesis in the account. However, in so far as the problem is that of the ultimate assumption required for the practice of induction, any explanation which used induction could of course not provide a justification for such an assumption. It has been argued in the preceding chapters of the present study that Peirce was forced to take an ethical account of man as ultimate in order to avoid a paradox in connection with this assumption, although the question as to whether such an account might be in conflict with the pragmatic maxim was not considered.

Peirce decided four years later that his dictionary article of 1902 was "quite mistaken" in its suspicion that his pragmatic maxim as originally formulated "expressed a stoic, that is, a nominalistic, materialistic, and utterly philistine state of thought" (5.402, n. 3). He continued:

No doubt, Pragmaticism makes thought ultimately apply to action exclusively—to conceived action. But between admitting that and either saying that it makes thought, in the sense of the purport of symbols, to consist in acts, or saying that the true ultimate purpose of thinking is action, there is much the same difference as there is between saying that the artist-painter's living art is applied to dabbing paint upon canvas, and saying that that art-life consists in dabbing paint, or that its ultimate aim is dabbing paint. Pragmaticism makes thinking to consist in the living inferential metaboly of symbols whose purport lies in conditional general resolutions to act. As for the ultimate purpose of thought, which must be the purpose of everything, it is beyond human comprehension; but according to the stage of approach which my thought has made to it . . . it is by the indefinite replication of self-control upon self-control that the vir is begotten, and by action, through thought, he grows an esthetic ideal, not for the behoof of his own poor noddle merely, but as the share which God permits him to have in the work of creation.

Throughout this passage Peirce is of course speaking at the fourth grade of clearness. His statements have no meaning when interpreted at the third grade, as hypotheses to be verified by specific practical consequences. But they have the same meaning as the expression of the pragmatic maxim, which is itself not a hypothesis to be tested in this manner. In fact, the statements here constitute simply a somewhat elaborate expression of the maxim and provide the beginnings of a "proof" of pragmatism. The vir begotten by "the indefinite replication of self-control upon self-control" is quite different from the man determined to action through biological and social compulsion. Yet this does not mean that the two accounts of man are necessarily incompatible, since both may be correct in their appropriate spheres of meaning, just as a painter may be both a man biologically and socially compelled to dab paint on canvas and an artist expressing an esthetic ideal.

The appearance of a conflict between the two accounts in Peirce's thought may be referred to the peculiar status of truth

259

in relation to the fourth grade of clearness. As noted above in section 3, Peirce's coenoscopic observation seemed for the most part to yield "positive truth" only in the sense of clarifying beliefs which could not be doubted once they were properly understood. Peirce liked to call himself an experimentalist and to insist that all truth should be determined experimentally. While he occasionally restricted the phrase "positive truth" to something like its ordinary usage and implied that ontological propositions were "reducible to logical formulae" (5.496), he usually spoke of all the parts of philosophy as determining positive truth and was hence obliged to use "experimentation" in a very wide and analogical sense. The clarifications achieved in coenoscopy constitute in this sense the results of internal experiments performed in the imagination and are not to be taken as exceptions to the principle that all truth is determined experimentally. But the great difficulty with this analogical use of terms is that experimentation always supposes a distinction between clearness and truth; one first obtains a clear understanding as to the meaning of a hypothesis and then tests its truth by experiments. It is only after some degree of verification has been achieved that one becomes unable to doubt the hypothesis. Yet in coenoscopic observation where the concepts have no meaning except at the highest grade of clearness both the meaning and the verification lie in "the conditional resolutions as to conduct." One grasps the meaning of the proposition that thirdness is operative in nature by imagining what difference there would be in his conduct if he accepted or rejected the proposition. Experimentation should then consist in testing the proposition by actually trying the different forms of conduct. But if, as Peirce holds, the proposition in this case is virtually assumed by all idioscopic inquiry and a person is unable genuinely to adopt a conditional resolution to act in accordance with its denial, there is hardly a distinction between clearness and truth. The inability to doubt comes immediately with a clear apprehension of the meaning and does not require a separate process of verification. In this respect, then, the analogy between philosophy and scientific experiment breaks down completely.

When Peirce's constant injunctions to test truth experimentally are taken in a literal sense, they of course preclude any attempt to give a true account of man's ultimate end except as that course of action which human nature is biologically and socially compelled to follow. Peirce himself wavered as to how literally he should take his own injunctions, and the so-called naturalistic strain in his thought seems to result partly from this wavering and partly from the ease with which many of his statements, stripped of their analogical meaning, fit into naturalistic theses. The pragmatic maxim itself is an excellent case in point. Literally, this maxim appears to render any proposition scientifically meaningless that implies no specific practical effects which would constitute its experimental verification. Peirce's suspicion that his maxim was stoic and nominalistic is in this respect justified, but he was also correct in pointing out that the realism he had advocated at the same time was inconsistent with this interpretation of the maxim. The recognition of a fourth grade of clearness, however, is necessitated not only by his realism and his coenoscopic inquiry generally but in particular by any attempt to explicate and prove his pragmatism.

If Peirce had met the challenge to defend his maxim by arguing exclusively from man's biological and social nature, he would have been open to the objection that his arguments were not a proof of the maxim but merely an application of it to the investigation of human nature. The objection might be answered by the reply that, if one wished to obtain scientific truth, he would have to conform to the maxim and that a scientific account of man and his struggle to attain fixation of belief was perhaps the best way of making the situation clear. But this reply already supposes the fourth grade of clearness, since it refers to the general end of truth and the advancement of inquiry without designating specific practical effects. The reply thus becomes intelligible only to an individual who is capable of grasping an end beyond that of action itself, and further clarification of the reply would involve an explication of what the end is apart from the forms of action required for its attainment. In this context the pragmatic maxim may be construed as an injunction to seek the ultimate meaning of a concept in relation to such an end. After his dictionary article of 1902, Peirce did not continue to distinguish between a third and fourth grade of clearness but simply refrained from taking his maxim in a literal sense. The idioscopic inquirer may refer scientific meaning to the end of specific practical effects, and the philosopher by analogy may refer all such meaning to the *summum bonum*. While the pragmatic maxim may be taken to cover both cases by virtue of the analogy, in this sense it is clearly inconsistent with a philosophic naturalism.

D. When Peirce turned in 1891 to plan the construction of a philosophy, he may perhaps have preached better than he practiced. He cautioned at the outset against those "one-idea'd philosophies" that result when "an idea which has been found interesting and fruitful has been adopted, developed, and forced to yield explanations of all sorts of phenomena" (6.7). But in a fragment ca. 1897 he described himself as "saturated, through and through, with the spirit of the physical sciences" and emphasized his primary concern with methods of inquiry, particularly those "of the most exact sciences" (1.3). If Peirce fell into a "one-idea'd" philosophy despite his own warnings against it, the one dominant idea is certainly the precept that whatever is taken as true must have experimental verification. A survey of Peirce's philosophy as an attempt to force this idea to yield explanations of all sorts of philosophic problems may begin conveniently with his logic.

As remarked in B above, Peirce differed from Kant in making his final explanation of that to which a true representation must conform depend on a method rather than an analytic. Although this may suggest that the precept just mentioned should turn Peirce's logic into a doctrine of methods of experimental verification, methodology comprises only the third branch of his logic. Critic, or the second branch, is properly an analytic of arguments and precedes methodology, while speculative grammar or stoicheiology comes first in the order and provides the foundations for the analysis. However, the influence of the precept of experimental verification is evidenced in the fact that the stoicheiology of logic culminates in the pragmatic maxim, which prescribes that discourse can be related to reality only by identifying meaning with conceivable practical effects. Terms and propositions can thus acquire meaning only in the context of arguments predicting future consequences, and pragmatism begins the logic of abduction at the same time that it ends speculative grammar. Even though this procedure is variously suggested in the new approach to logic inaugurated by Peirce's early papers on the classification of arguments and especially in his views on the faculties of knowledge, the precept that truth can never be grasped immediately but only as the outcome of a process of experimental verification seems well taken as the dominant idea of the analysis. The second branch of logic affords an account of the validity of induction in a fashion which requires no assumption about the actual constitution of the universe but which does require a certain hope or sentiment on the part of individual inquirers. Speculative rhetoric or methodeutic, "the highest and most living branch of logic" (2.333), is then to provide a reflective study of "methods of attaining purposes, in general" (2.108), and should, if Peirce had ever completed the study as he proposed, make clear the sense in which the practice of logical methods depends on moral sentiment.

The fact that Peirce did not profess to take up the question of modes of being without supposing his speculative rhetoric implies that his logic is, after all, dominated by a methodology. If his speculative grammar had proclaimed an ultimate determination of meaning at the level of terms or propositions, discourse could have been related to reality without reference to the results of inquiry. Categories of being would then have been determined at this level and would have preceded the analysis of arguments and the exposition of methods. But, in accordance with the pragmatic maxim, parts of discourse can come to express parts of reality only as the final result of following a proper method of inquiry. By analogy, then, the ultimate parts or modes of reality should be expressed by the fundamental stages in the process of following the right method. Since modes of being have no meaning as specific practical effects to be verified by inquiry, they must be taken analogically with reference to the ultimate goal—the *summum bonum*. As normative logic culminates in methodology, it thus appeals to ethics and esthetics at the same time that it prescribes the principles for objective logic and ontology.

Peirce's categories as generated by the simplest mathematics appear as the three fundamental forms of relation, the monad, the dyad, and the polyad. They constitute a formal representation of the principal moments in a process rather than three modes of a fixed and permanent being. When they are taken as categories of phenomenology, they thus determine three fundamental stages of what appears in consciousness rather than three modes under which a single phenomenon may be apprehended. There is no fixed thing, the appearance, which retains a substantial identity while it is successively apprehended under the modes of feeling, struggle, and representation. On the contrary, the phenomenon itself is the process of apprehension, and any notion of a fixed appearance susceptible of further apprehension must be replaced by that of a continuum of phenomena in which every phenomenon is the representation of another. A priority of process and becoming over permanence and being is of course in accord with the precept that all truth is the outcome of inquiry, and Peirce's categories determine his ontology as three moments in the becoming toward an end rather than, strictly speaking, three modes of being. The central theme of his metaphysics is thus easily taken as that of cosmic evolution, and regulative principles like synechism and the hope for further explanation are easy corollaries of the idea that truth must be determined experimentally and is hence never absolute.

Not even mathematical subject matter and method are exempt from process and experimentation. While the objects of mathematics are regarded metaphysically as Platonic ideas in the first universe, they surrender their traditional immutability in submission to the principle that all things evolved from an original nothingness. Characterized by its method, mathematics is the science which draws necessary conclusions, but it still provides no exception to the rule that all truth must be obtained by experimentation. The necessity of its conclusions arises from the hypothetical character of its objects rather than from a nonexperimental method, and the analogy with physical experiment here does not blur the distinction between clearness and truth as it does in the case of ontological propositions. Since the mathematician proceeds by observing the consequences of performing certain transformations in his diagrams, he must first have a clear idea of the operations which constitute a given transformation before he can test its effects within his system. Even the basic premisses, the axioms and definitions, are shown to be true ultimately by the noncontradictory character of their consequences rather than by the clearness with which the mathematician grasps them.

The most difficult phase in Peirce's analogical extension of the idea of experimental truth appears in his forced appeal to the *summum bonum* in order to give sense to his ontology. In so far as the virtual identification of clearness and truth in this context is unavoidable, the analogy between philosophizing and scientific experiment fails. Moreover, Peirce's claim that he escaped from anything like the traditional doctrine of substance (which appeared in A above to be the main alternative to pragmatism) hardly seems justified at this point. If clearness is to be taken as evidence of truth, what is apprehended should be more in the nature of a fixed and permanent being to be cognized by an individual than a real probability to be evaluated by an unlimited community. This does not mean that the

265

propositions of Peirce's ontology have to be taken as results of immediate intuition in no sense inferred from previous experience. Quite to the contrary, they may remain as inferences from coenoscopic observation, although the truth which they profess to determine has for its analogue in scientific practice the clearness of a hypothesis rather than the truth of an induction. This achievement of truth through clearness even remains in a sense a social enterprise, since the critical self which becomes unable to form genuine doubt of ontological truths merges with a man's circle of society. But inasmuch as the procedure is not literally inductive, the goal is not social in the sense of presupposing an unlimited community. An appeal to the *summum bonum* is necessary only to conform by analogy to the maxim that all meaning must consist in conceivable practical effects. While the abandonment of this analogy might have led Peirce away from his pragmatism and back to something like the traditional doctrine of substance, it also could have saved him from resting his ontology on ethics and esthetics. And even in this final appeal to the self-controlled growth of inquiry, some remnant of the doctrine of substance persists in the notion of a self which exercises the control and renders the development possible.

If Peirce's philosophy, as this survey of it would indicate, is open to the charge of being "one-idea'd," the wide analogical use given that idea saves the philosophy from more serious limitations. In fact, when the precept of experimental verification is taken in its most literal sense, the result, in Peirce's terms, is not philosophy at all but idioscopic inquiry. The wide variety of problems treated in the *Collected Papers* as well as the subtle and penetrating character of many of the analyses would have been impossible if Peirce had remained more literal in his use of terms. The fact that his analogies break down at crucial moments does not prevent them from throwing new light on the problems even at the very points where they fail.[38] While the old doctrine of substance may seem unnecessary and untenable at certain stages in the exposition of pragmatism, the thoroughness with which Peirce carried out his analogies serves in the end to suggest a new argument for the inevitability of something like the notion of substance. In contrast to Kant, Peirce might be characterized as a philosopher who sought the significance of the experimental method in the relation of scientist to truth viewed as that of forecaster to successful prediction rather than in the relation of reason to nature viewed as that of judge to witness. The foundations of science for Peirce are thus to be found in the rules of action which lead to successful predictions rather than in the forms of reason which lead to a proper interrogation of nature. Yet in so far as Peirce's analogy no less than Kant's requires in the last analysis something like the permanence of substance as opposed to the flux of phenomena, both men might be said to have approached the same philosophic truth from different directions. Philosophy may be impossible without extensive use of analogy, as it certainly is with Peirce, and perhaps any philosophy may be construed in some fashion as "one-idea'd." But then the value of the philosophy will in a sense depend more on the careful development and ramification of the analogies than on the extent to which the one idea originally selected is applicable to the problems of philosophy. For the limitations of the applicability may always become evident through the failure of the analogies in certain contexts, unless the analogical development is arrested by a literal interpretation which would make these contexts meaningless. While the precept of experimental truth construed in some form as the dominant idea of philosophy is at least as old as Francis Bacon, it was virtually ignored by many of Peirce's contemporaries and taken so literally by others as to reduce philosophy to little more than the dogmatic assertion that truth is natural science. Peirce avoided both of these extremes in his pragmatism, and, if in doing so he attempted to force his one idea to yield more than it can for philosophy, he also was not content with literal meanings which would have concealed the limitations of his idea at the expense of his philosophy.

NOTES

NOTES TO INTRODUCTION

1. The Charles S. Peirce Society was formed on February 22, 1946, at the annual meeting of the Eastern Division of the American Philosophical Association.

2. See, e.g., the disagreement between Professors Buchler and Weiss: J. Buchler, "The Accidents of Peirce's System," *Journal of Philosophy*, XXXVII (1940), 264–69; P. Weiss, "The Essence of Peirce's System," *Journal of Philosophy*, XXXVII (1940), 253–64. Professor T. A. Goudge (*The Thought of C. S. Peirce* [Toronto: University of Toronto Press, 1950], p. 345) concludes that "Peirce's subtle, original, and wide-ranging intellect was struggling to break loose from the patterns of thought typical of his own century, and to point the way to the next. His naturalism I take to be the measure of his success in this struggle. It is directly 'in the general line of growth' of the ideas which dominate the philosophical arena today." But Professor R. B. Perry ("Is There a North American Philosophy?" *Philosophy and Phenomenological Research*, IX [1949], 356–69) has been unable to read Peirce as "a forerunner of American Naturalism" and prefers to describe him as an American philosopher "who stands like a lonely peak," "belonging to no school."

3. This reference is to Volume I, paragraph 3, of the *Collected Papers of Charles Sanders Peirce*, ed. Charles Hartshorne and Paul Weiss (6 vols.; Cambridge, Mass.: Harvard University Press, 1931–35). All references to these papers will be given in this manner, following the custom of the editors. When a quotation from Peirce is cited only as appearing in an independent publication, it has not been reprinted in the *Collected Papers*.

NOTES TO CHAPTER I

1. This reference is to the appendix of Volume II of the *Collected Papers*. When a single work is referred to in its entirety, the reference will always be given by volume number, book, and chapter, or paper, rather than by volume and paragraph number.

2. Peirce remarked ca. 1905 concerning the second of these two

271

papers: "But although I received some complimentary letters about that paper at the time, it is now utterly unintelligible to me, and is, I trust, by far the worst I ever published" (4.333).

3. *Die falsche Spitzfindigkeit der vier syllogistischen Figuren erweisen* (1762).

4. Peirce's spelling, "premiss" instead of "premise," is used throughout the present work. Peirce insisted that "it is entirely contrary to good English usage to spell premiss, 'premise,'" and explained that "premiss" is derived from the medieval logicians' *praemissa*, while "premise" is properly a legal term and is correctly used to refer to "items in an inventory, etc., and hence buildings enumerated in a deed or lease" (2.253). Cf. 2.582.

5. The examples in this illustration are taken from 3.166, from a paper, *On the Algebra of Logic*, 1880. The illustration given in this paper is somewhat more elaborate, though in complete accord with that given in the paper of 1867.

6. This position, it will be noted, provides no way for distinguishing particular from universal propositions with respect to existential import. It was not until Peirce had worked in the logic of relatives that he made this distinction. In a paper of 1869 he remarked that "there are two kinds of universals, those which do not assert the subject to exist . . . and those which do assert that the subject exists," and, in the latter case, "an inference from a universal to the particular under it is always valid" (5.338). See below, p. 55. In his paper of 1880 he adopted the unqualified view that "universal propositions do not, while particular propositions do, imply the existence of their subjects" (3.178).

7. Peirce could derive affirmative conclusions in the third figure by holding that the denial of a first-figure premiss and conclusion involved a change of "*quality* alone" when the second figure was generated and a change of "*quantity* alone" when the third figure was generated. Thus, the major premiss in Barbara changed in quantity (to "Some M is P") follows from the minor premiss and the conclusion changed in quantity (to "Some S is P"), and this is the third-figure Disamis. Cf. 2.498.

8. This same second-figure syllogism is given by Leibniz (*New Essays*, Bk. II, chap. 2) as a demonstration of the conversion of the traditional E proposition. Leibniz mentions Peter Ramus as having already remarked the demonstrability of conversions by second- and third-figure syllogisms. But Peirce makes no reference in the *Collected Papers* or in any other of his published writings to Leibniz

or Ramus on this point. To judge from 4.2 (quoted above at the beginning of this chapter), Peirce discovered this method of demonstrating conversions entirely on his own.

9. *Kant's Introduction to Logic, and His Essay on the Mistaken Subtility of the Four Figures,* trans. T. K. Abbott (London, 1885), p. 83.

10. In the *On a New List of Categories,* published (May, 1867) a month after the classification of arguments, Peirce gives further indication of the nature of this attempt to reduce mathematical reasoning to syllogistic form. In respect to a proposition:

"The objects indicated by the subject (which are always potentially a plurality—at least, of phases or appearances) are . . . stated by the proposition to be related to one another on the ground of the character indicated by the predicate. Now this relation may be either a concurrence or an opposition. Propositions of concurrence are those which are usually considered in logic; but I have shown in a paper upon the classification of arguments that it is also necessary to consider separately propositions of opposition, if we are to take account of such arguments as the following:

"Whatever is the half of anything is less than that of which it is the half:

"A is the half of B;
A is less than B.

"The subject of such a proposition is separated into two terms, a 'subject nominative' and an 'object accusative'" (1.559).

According to this, "A" is the subject nominative, "B," the object accusative, and "is half of," the predicate. The objects indicated by the subject are thus of two distinct sorts and must be considered as in some way other than or opposed to each other, rather than as being all concurrently the same sort, as in the ordinary "S is P." But this does not enable the above argument to be interpreted as involving nothing but the substitutions occurring in an ordinary three-termed syllogism.

In a paper entitled *Grounds of Validity of the Laws of Logic: Further Consequences of Four Incapacities* (1869), Peirce makes his final attempt, in view of De Morgan's memoir on "the logic of relatives" (to which he refers in a footnote), to reduce all inference to syllogistic form. Cf. 5.322. Less than two years later (1870), Peirce published his first paper on the logic of relatives and analyzed the syllogism as one form of logical relation rather than as the fundamental formula of all arguments. Cf. 3.66.

11. Peirce went on to explain that traditional logic is thus tied down to the single relation of similarity because it considers only genera and species, i.e., classes, and "a *class* is a set of objects comprising all that stand to one another in a special relation of similarity" (4.5). The logic of relatives, on the other hand, "talks of *systems,*" and "a *system* is a set of objects comprising all that stand to one another in a group of connected relations" (4.5). When Peirce remarks elsewhere that "analytical reasoning depends upon associations of similarity, synthetical reasoning upon associations of contiguity" (6.595; cf. 1.383, 2.451 n.), he has reference to what he considered the iconic or diagrammatic character of reasoning. The similarity here holds between iconic signs which constitute various stages in the reasoning process and not between objects signified which belong to the same class. Peirce's iconic theory of reasoning is considered below in chap. v, sec. 1.

12. Peirce later differentiated three distinct processes in what he refers to here as a single process, called "abstraction" or "precision." See below, pp. 216–17.

13. "*Embodying blackness is the equivalent of black*" (1.551).

14. Cf. a comment ca. 1899: "I observed in 1867 that dual relations are of two kinds according as they are or are not constituted by the relate and correlate possessing non-relative characters. This is correct. ... We see, then, that the first category of relations embraces only similarities; while the second, embracing all other relations, may be termed dynamical relations" (1.566–67).

15. In 1902 Peirce analyzed relations as "either *Genuine* or *Degenerate.*" Similarity is a "more" and difference a "less" degenerate relation, while dynamical relations are genuine (2.91 ff.).

16. This particular correlation between the genera of arguments and the kinds of signs did not prove very satisfactory, and after he developed his theory of probability Peirce came to connect hypothesis with an icon, deduction with an index, and induction with a symbol. Cf. 2.96 (1902).

17. Peirce always maintained that plural relations or "polyads" "do not introduce any radically different elements from those that are found in triads" (1.293). His endeavors to substantiate this contention are in some respects open to question. Cf. R. B. Braithwaite, review of the *Collected Papers,* Vols. I–IV, *Mind,* XLIII (new ser., 1934), 491–92. This point will be discussed below, pp. 160, 285.

18. Cf. R. B. Perry, *The Thought and Character of William James* (Boston: Little, Brown & Co., 1935), II, 223.

19. In the footnote of 1893 "the breadth of an argument is the aggregate of possible cases to which it applies," while its depth "is the importance of the conclusions which it draws." Peirce did not explain how the "importance" was to be determined. His final remarks on the problem (ca. 1906) make the distinction between the breadth and depth of an argument that "between the state of things in which its premisses are true and the state of things which is defined by the truth of its conclusion" (5.471). The latter seems to be what is demanded by his basic analogy between subject and predicate and premiss and conclusion. The definition of the information of a symbol as "the sum of synthetical propositions in which the symbol is subject or predicate" must of course be modified by adding "antecedent or consequent." Cf. 2.364 (1902).

NOTES TO CHAPTER II

1. See above, p. 14.
2. See below, pp. 55–56, for Peirce's solution to Zeno's paradoxes.
3. These three general references involved in any sign also serve to determine aspects of the thought-sign itself and not merely the nature of its references. There is, first, that aspect of the sign which pertains to it as something "not identical with the thing signified," and which may be termed its "material qualities" (5.287). Second, there is the "real, physical connection of a sign with its object, either immediately or by its connection with another sign," which may be called "the pure demonstrative application of the sign." Both of these aspects are distinct from "the representative function of a sign," since this function "is something which the sign is, not in itself or in a real relation to its object, but which it is to a thought, while both of the characters just defined belong to the sign independently of its addressing any thought."
In regard to its material quality, "no present actual thought (which is mere feeling) has any meaning, any intellectual value; for this lies not in what is actually thought, but in what the thought may be connected with in representation by subsequent thoughts; so that the meaning of a thought is altogether something virtual" (5.289). This statement shows clearly that a pragmatic criterion of meaning is a direct consequence of the analysis in Peirce's earliest papers. In a paper explaining his pragmatism, ca. 1905, Peirce quoted this statement and remarked that the paper in which it was originally made "in fact expresses a kind of pragmatism not unlike that of Professor James" (5.504 n.).

4. A possible objection is that inference deals only with general terms and that an image, or absolutely singular representation, cannot therefore be inferred. But an examination of the nature of an image shows that "we have no images even in actual perception" (5.303). For if images are "absolutely determinate representations in perception," then there are "materials in each such representation for an infinite amount of conscious cognition, which we yet never become aware of" (5.305). In other words, by the continuity of the thought-process each event or individual thought has an infinite number of events, each of them partially determining it, between it and any given previous event, so that it cannot in itself possibly constitute a consciousness of an absolutely determinate or singular representation.

Moreover, there are no "general conceptions" except "in judgments" (5.307). Although "a mere general concept of a thing is in no case a cognition of it as existing," it still seems impossible "to call up a concept" without making some judgment. For example, "in order to conceive the number 7, I suppose, that is, I arbitrarily make the hypothesis or judgment, that there are certain points before my eyes, and I judge that these are seven." But if this is always the case, "what goes by the name of the association of images is in reality an association of judgments." The association of ideas has been assumed to proceed according to the principles of resemblance, contiguity, and causality, but "it would be equally true to say that signs denote what they do" according to these same principles. The association of ideas, then, "consists in this, that a judgment occasions another judgment, of which it is the sign." All association is therefore an inference, and, to the objection that such association could never produce novelty, it can be said that, while this is true of inferences expressed in the form of a complete argument, such inferences "hardly occur outside of a logic book" (5.308).

5. The "pure demonstrative application" of a thought-sign consists in "attention," or the "power by which thought at one time is connected with and made to relate to thought at another time" (5.295). While a single act of attention is an induction in the form of a simple enumeration, and hence "does not increase our knowledge," in virtue of the representative function of the thought-sign acts of attention may produce "habits, or nervous associations," which constitute genuine inductions (5.296–97). Presumably the latter is properly "understanding," although Peirce actually uses the term only in the quotation given above from 5.298.

276

A differentiation of "sensations proper," "emotions," and the "feeling of a thought" results from further characterization of thought-signs by their material qualities. Since "there is some reason to think that, corresponding to every feeling within us, some motion takes place in our bodies," this animal motion, having no "rational dependence upon the meaning of the sign," may be compared to the material quality of the sign (5.293). However, such motion is different from the material quality as above defined in that "it is not essentially necessary that it [the motion] should be felt in order that there should be any thought-sign." In these terms, a sensation differs from an emotion in that the former "produces no great commotion in the bodily organism" and does not exercise "a very strong influence upon the current of thought except by virtue of the information it may serve to afford," while the latter "produces large movements in the body, and independently of its representative value, strongly affects the current of thought." Sensations proper and emotions may be differentiated from the "feeling of a thought" by the fact that "in the case of the two former the material quality is made prominent, because the thought has no relation of reason to the thoughts which determine it, which exists in the last case and detracts from the attention given to the mere feeling" (5.294). Where there is such a relation of reason, the thought is always "complex," whereas a strictly "incomplex thought" can be "nothing but a sensation or emotion, having no rational character.

6. In later writings Peirce spoke of his first declaration of realism as appearing (1871) three years after the above statement in his extended review of Frazer's *The Works of Berkeley, North American Review*, CXIII (1871), 449-72. Cf. 1.20, 5.453, 5.527. The looseness of this statement of 1868 is indicated by the use of "existence" to characterize the reality of generals, a procedure which is directly contrary to Peirce's later formulations of realism.

7. This point is actually made in the examination of the third proposition, where the thought-sign is characterized by its "material quality": "Every thought, however artificial and complex, is, so far as it is immediately present, a mere sensation without parts, and therefore, in itself, without similarity to any other, but incomparable with any other and absolutely *sui generis*. Whatever is wholly incomparable with anything else is wholly inexplicable, because explanation consists in bringing things under general laws or under natural classes" (5.289).

8. See above, chap. i, n. 10.

9. For Peirce's later treatment of Zeno's paradoxes, cf. 6.177 ff. and 2.666. For the liar, cf. 2.352, 2.618, and 3.446.

NOTES TO CHAPTER III

1. In the essay *How To Make Our Ideas Clear*, immediately following *The Fixation of Belief*, Peirce indicates what he thought this progression was in actual history. The method of tenacity is exemplified in "the literature of the dark ages." In the later medieval period the method of authority prevailed and "the truth meant little more than the Catholic faith." Since "the time of Descartes," the a priori method has been prominent (cf. 5.406).

2. According to notes in the *Collected Papers* (5, Bk. II, Paper V, p. 248), this paper was to have been Essay IX. However, in view of the fact that it was immediately preceded in the original series, "Illustrations of the Logic of Science," by the *Fixation of Belief*, Essay VII, and seems clearly a direct continuation of the latter, it is extremely difficult to imagine what could have been the subject of the missing essay interposed between these two. The numbering of the essays is in all probability incorrect.

3. Cf. J. Buchler, *Charles Peirce's Empiricism* (New York: Harcourt, Brace & Co., 1939), p. 238. Buchler feels that in these notes Peirce is "unjust to himself" in the way he criticized his definition of 1878, since he confuses "in spite of himself" "a ratio of the specific occurrences to all *possible* occurrences with a ratio of the specific occurrences to the generic occurrences *examined*." T. A. Goudge (*The Thought of C. S. Peirce* [Toronto: University of Toronto Press, 1950], pp. 169–70) seems more plausible in arguing that Peirce's later criticism comes from recognizing what appears to be a fundamental difficulty inherent in the frequency theory of probability, viz., that "the series of values involved is both *empirical* and *infinite*." However, Peirce insists elsewhere in his writings that there is no need for assuming that the series is infinite but only that a sufficiently large finite number of cases has been examined (cf. 2.784, 5.170). This is perhaps why Buchler finds the criticism of 1910 so puzzling. Yet the puzzle disappears in so far as the issue is that of the reality which a probability has independently of the occurrences examined. The latter can yield only an *estimate* of the real probability, not a *definition* of it. If, as the paper of 1878 asserts, we could get a definition in this way then the number of cases examined would have to be infinite. But if the real probability is defined as that which *would be* realized in an infinitely long run, then we can get an esti-

mate as close to this as we please by examining a sufficiently large finite number of cases.

Further consideration of this point is given below, chap. v, sec. 2.

4. The notes in the *Collected Papers* do not specify this essay as belonging to the *Search for a Method*, but since it originally appeared as the fifth paper in the series "Illustrations of the Logic of Science," between the papers later intended for Essays XI and XIII, it is almost certainly the missing Essay XII.

5. "But to say that a body is hard, or red, or heavy, or of a given weight, or has any other property, is to say that it is subject to law" (5.545, ca. 1902). The law in this case is a cause "really operative in nature." Cf., e.g., the discussion of 1903, 5.93–101. While in 1878 Peirce was far from having worked out his position to the point where he found it necessary to regard laws as operative causes, his conception here of cause as law or defining property of a class is an important step toward the later development, which requires that laws operate through final, and facts through efficient, causation.

6. While Peirce worked out fairly definite answers for these questions, he seems never to have reached a conclusion as to which of the ways of relating the genera of arguments to the categories was most fundamental. In 1903 he frankly admitted, "concerning the relations of these three modes of inference to the categories and concerning certain other details, my opinions, I confess, have wavered" (5.146). As noted above (chap. i, n. 16), Peirce in 1902 related the three modes of inference to the three kinds of signs so as to make hypothesis a first, deduction a second, and induction a third—the same result with respect to the categories as that obtained from the classification based on "a difference in the mode of apprehending facts."

NOTES TO CHAPTER IV

1. Cf. Peirce's elaboration of this passage in his reply to the criticisms of Paul Carus in 1893 (6.612).

2. Law is definitely specified as a secondness in the triad, chance, law, and the tendency to take habits, given later in *The Architecture of Theories* (6.32). The same triad appears (1.409) in *A Guess at the Riddle*, ca. 1890. The quotation given above about brute force (1.427) is from a paper ca. 1896, where law is definitely specified as thirdness (1.420). However, in a fragment which the editors of the *Collected Papers* have dated as late as ca. 1897 with some hesitation (see their note to 1.155), Peirce still refers to laws as "forces

of nature" which cannot be left "absolutely blind and inexplicable" (1.175). The main issue here seems to be the relation of continuity to law and generality, and in Peirce's final view all these notions constitute thirdness. For the role of continuity in this fragment ca. 1897 see below, n. 6. The complete dissociation of law from the reactions of secondness is explicitly stated in a paper ca. 1906, where Peirce speaks of " 'secondness,' or brute actions of one subject or substance on another, regardless of law or of any third subject" (5.469). Peirce's discussion of cause in *The Order of Nature* seems to come rather close to his later conception of law as thirdness (see above, p. 94, and chap. iii, n. 5). In his later view, laws have the force of final but not efficient causation—the force of thirdness but not secondness.

3. This apparently refers to Paul Carus' "two-aspect monism." Cf. H. W. Schneider, *A History of American Philosophy* (New York: Columbia University Press, 1947), p. 333.

4. Cf. A. O. Lovejoy, "A Note on Peirce's Evolutionism," *Journal of the History of Ideas*, VII (1946), 351–54. Professor Lovejoy points out that Peirce is here faced with the apparent dilemma of having to assume either an infinite time or that the habit-taking tendency is a favored possibility which will turn up in a finite time. In so far as Peirce's cosmic evolution is interpreted in strict analogy with the Darwinian principle, either assumption seems unjustified. But, as will appear below, Peirce seems never to have regarded this analogy as very strict. In his final view the situation is complicated by the fact that time itself is something that evolved, though this is hardly analogous to anything in Darwin.

5. Peirce remarks in a marginal note dated 1903, written in his personal copy of the *Century Dictionary* (1889) opposite his entry on the continuum, that he had misunderstood Kant's definition of continuity (6.165–68). Kant, Peirce says, defined a continuum "as that all of whose parts have parts of the same kind," but then failed to understand the full import of his own definition and took it to mean merely that a continuum is that which is infinitely divisible. Peirce implies that in his *Law of Mind* he shared with Kant this misunderstanding of Kant's words but later came to see that, properly understood, the definition means that "a continuum, where it is continuous and unbroken, contains no definite parts; that its parts are created in the act of defining them and the precise definition of them breaks the continuity" (6.168).

According to the present interpretation, the factor which enabled

Peirce to gain this new understanding of Kant was a recognition of continuity as a distinct and ultimate category—as thirdness. The possession of definite parts marked off by discrete acts is characteristic of secondness, and endless divisibility into such parts is therefore not the proper mark of continuity itself. The issue, then, concerns the role of continuity in a system of philosophy, i.e., its role as a category and its relation to other categories, such as act and possibility.

6. When he did not regard synechism as a regulative principle, Peirce needed a separate doctrine which he termed "fallibilism." This was related to synechism as follows: "The principle of continuity is the idea of fallibilism objectified. For fallibilism is the doctrine that our knowledge is never absolute but always swims, as it were, in a continuum of uncertainty and of indeterminacy. Now the doctrine of continuity is that all things so swim in continua" (1.171) (Peirce's italics).

The actual word "fallibilism" occurs as the expression of a doctrine in the *Collected Papers* only in the fragment from which this quotation was taken and in another fragment (1.8-14) of the same date, ca. 1897. The manner in which synechism as a regulative principle takes over the function of fallibilism is clearly indicated in the article in Baldwin's dictionary. One of the things prescribed by this principle is that "it is not a hypothesis fit to be entertained that any given law is absolutely accurate" (6.173). The circumstance that synechism becomes a regulative principle does not, however, mean that continuity is no longer regarded as real, although Peirce's later doctrine of modes of being is required in order to explain the situation.

7. When Peirce came to analyze mathematical or necessary reasoning as the observation of diagrams, he was forced to admit that such reasoning "turns upon the perception of generality and continuity at every step" (5.150 [1903]). But this admission is the result of a logical and epistemological analysis made in accordance with synechism as a regulative principle and is prior to anything in psychology. See below, chap. vi, sec. 1.

8. *The Monist*, II (1891-92), 574.

9. *Ibid.*, p. 572.

10. According to this scheme, the Darwinian theory is first, Lamarck's is second, and cataclysmal evolution is third. The first effort of this sort occurs in *A Guess at the Riddle*, ca. 1890, where three principles of Darwinian evolution alone are found to reflect

the categories. Sporting is first, heredity is second, and "the elimination of unfavorable characters" is third (1.399). Peirce's main concern here seems to be to show that this triad in evolution reproduces the one he had distinguished in his molecular theory of protoplasm, which he had just presented for the first time in the preceding section, but he admits the triad is "a somewhat imperfect reproduction." The same triad, except that the third member is specified in a positive form as "the process whereby the accidental characters become fixed," is given as one of the illustrations of the categories at the close of *The Architecture of Theories* (6.32). In an earlier section of the latter work, a scheme is given similar to the one ca. 1896, except that the theory of Clarence King (*Catastrophism and the Evolution of Environment* [1877]) is specified as the third (6.17). Peirce seems also to have had in mind the theories of Cuvier and Agassiz as illustrations of this third type of evolution. Cf. Philip P. Wiener, "The Evolutionism and Pragmaticism of Peirce," *Journal of the History of Ideas*, VII (1946), 329 ff. The Lamarckian theory appears as a third only in the presentation of agapasm.

11. Peirce did not always employ the expression "objective logic" in the sense taken here, which represents his later views. In 1893 he remarked that "second intentional, or, as I also call it, Objective Logic, is much the larger part of formal logic" (4.80). In 1896 he spoke of objective logic as being the same as speculative rhetoric (cf. 1.444, 3.430, 3.454). But by 1898 he was using the expression more or less in the general manner assumed for the present discussion (cf. 6, Bk. I, chaps. 7–8). Further consideration of objective logic and its relation to speculative rhetoric and normative logic generally will be given below, chap. v, sec. 3.

12. The account here is oversimplified by dovetailing Peirce's distinction of three modes of being quoted above from the paper of 1906 with his lectures of 1898 on objective logic, where he recognized only two modes of being, possibility and actuality. But the categories as determining three elements of experience are no less necessary in an explanation of evolution with the two universes of possibility and actuality (cf. 6.192) than they are when the three universes in the paper of 1906 are assumed (cf. 4.545 ff. and 6.455, 1908). The essential point for the present account is simply the general character of objective logic as a way of conceiving evolution. The question of modes of being is considered below, chap. v, sec. 3.

13. But there is still the difficulty that inductive inquiry always moves toward the goal of establishing complete uniformities; and,

while Peirce often speaks of his cosmic evolution as proceeding toward concrete reasonableness with the eventual elimination of chance variations, he emphasizes almost as frequently the continual emergence of greater variety and spontaneity in the course of evolution. Lovejoy (op. cit., p. 354) has noted this apparent inconsistency. See also Wiener's remarks (op. cit., p. 340).

Two points might be urged in defense of Peirce. (1) As he developed his position to include three modes of being corresponding to his categories, rationality or thirdness could have no reality without the brute facts of secondness, which in turn always involved an element of spontaneity or firstness. Thus, any movement toward further concrete reasonableness would at the same time entail a greater variety of facts, each with its own element of spontaneity. (2) A somewhat analogous point may be made in terms of the essays of 1891–93, where modes of being are not distinguished, if evolution is viewed in terms of the process of inquiry. Let the evolution of inquiry through infinite time be represented by any infinite series of rational numbers, say, the series of rational fractions from 0 to 1. The goal of the unlimited community is to write down every number in this series. But each time a new number has been written down, two new infinite series will appear which have to be filled in, one between this number and its predecessor and another between it and its successor. Let the appearance of each new term represent an increase in rationality and the appearance of each new series to be filled in, an increase in variety and spontaneity. Then, while it may be said that the ultimate goal is complete rationality—the final crystallization of mind in the infinitely distant future—at every stage except the last, where the infinity is actual, spontaneity as well as rationality is increasing.

14. Peirce regarded all internal relations as instances of similarity, which would accord with his conception of generalization in these essays as the spreading of ideas. All other dyadic relations were "dynamical relations" and would cover all cases of interaction between organism and external environment. Cf. 1.566–67 and above, pp. 26–27.

15. Peirce did remark in 1903 that "the laws of gravitation, elasticity, electricity, and chemistry" could hardly be taken as escaping "the great law of evolution" (1.348). But the context of this remark makes it clear that he means "the great law" as referring to an objective logic which presupposes a moralistic account. He declares a few sentences later: "That truth and justice are great powers in the

world is no figure of speech, but a plain fact to which theories must accommodate themselves." The manner in which an objective logic which assumes final causation presupposes a normative logic is discussed below, chap. v, sec. 3.

16. Cf. W. B. Gallie, "The Metaphysics of C. S. Peirce," *Proceedings of the Aristotelian Society*, XLVII (new ser., 1946-47), 27-62. Professor Gallie notes (p. 56) that agapasm has no place in a scientific theory of evolution, but he does not connect it with Peirce's position on the priority of normative science. The emphasis here given to that position is perhaps the principal difference between the present account of Peirce's metaphysics and that developed by Gallie.

17. The "second subclass" is called "theorics" and embraces two "families," "chronotheory" and "topotheory" (1.278).

18. It is open to question whether Peirce meant this phrase to be limited to scientific metaphysics in the sense just explained. While it seems probable that he meant "positive" here (5.423) as he used it in 5.496, it is possible he meant it in the broader sense. This second interpretation becomes possible in so far as Peirce regarded propositions of ontology as in a sense scientific hypotheses rather than statements "reducible to logical formulae." This difficulty with regard to the propositions of his ontology is considered below, chap. vi, sec. 3, C and D.

19. Further consideration of this point involves Peirce's reinterpretation of his pragmatic criterion of meaning as referring ultimately to the *summum bonum*. This reinterpretation is discussed below, chap. v, sec. 3.

20. It might seem that, from this way of looking at the matter, Peirce could have tested his hypothesis of God's reality by deducing from it the conceivably verifiable consequence that those who have advanced the progress of science are believers in God. But the difficulty with this would be in determining who are believers, since Peirce seems to construe the hypothesis in such a way that what a man explicitly says about it is not evidence of his belief or disbelief. Thus, in the paper ca. 1906 Peirce remarks: "I further opine that pretty nearly everybody more or less believes this [God's reality], including many of the scientific men of my generation who are accustomed to think the belief is entirely unfounded. The reason they fall into this extraordinary error about their own belief is that they precide (or render precise) the conception, and, in doing so, inevitably change it; and such precise conception is easily shown not to be

warranted, even if it cannot be quite refuted" (6.496). This is in accord with Peirce's "critical common-sensism," which holds that man's fundamental beliefs are the result of instinct and are inevitably vague. But, then, the consequence suggested above becomes virtually a tautology, since "doing what one can to advance inquiry" seems to be part of what is meant by "believing in God."

21. For a discussion of this difficulty in Peirce's conception of God cf. C. Hartshorne, "A Critique of Peirce's Idea of God," *Philosophical Review*, L (1941), 516–23.

22. He claimed in his paper ca. 1906 that the mutation-theory was in accord with the way he had "*always* insisted . . . species have arisen" (6.498) and that this insistence would form part of his logic of events.

23. In a fragment ca. 1897, Peirce explained his "semiotic" or doctrine of signs as an attempt to discover "the character of all signs used by a 'scientific intelligence,' that is to say, by an intelligence capable of learning by experience" (2.227). He then added: "The modes of thought of a God, who should possess an intuitive omniscience superseding reason, are put out of the question."

NOTES TO CHAPTER V

1. Cf. J. Buchler, *Charles Peirce's Empiricism* (New York: Harcourt, Brace & Co., 1939), pp. 224–27. The difficulties which Buchler finds with Peirce's doctrine of mathematical reasoning arise from regarding the *logica utens* here as though it should have the same justification as the *logica utens* of the natural scientist. Buchler thus assumes at the start that Peirce's conception of mathematical subject matter is wrong.

2. This last quotation is from the paragraph where Peirce gives his attempt, criticized by R. B. Braithwaite (review of *Collected Papers*, Vols. I–IV, *Mind*, XLIII [new ser., 1934], 491–92), to reduce a tetradic relation to a set of two triadic ones. It seems possible to admit Mr. Braithwaite's point that the meaning of "transaction" is irreducibly tetradic and still grant Peirce's main contention that such a relation can be diagramed with only three elements. Peirce does, as Braithwaite points out, object to a similar attempt by A. B. Kempe to reduce a triad to a set of dyads (cf. 3.424), yet the attempts are not entirely similar, in so far as Peirce intends only to diagram a tetrad by lines with nothing but three-way forkings, while Kempe wants to diagram a triad by using only dif-

ferent sets of straight lines. However, it is true that, in the example of "transaction" which Braithwaite picks, Peirce certainly does not make it clear that this is all he intends.

3. Cf. the statement, 1906, concerning the way in which a mathematical form represents its objects: "A *mathematical form* of a state of things is such a representation of that state of things as represents only the samenesses and diversities involved in that state of things, without definitely qualifying the subjects of the samenesses and diversities. It represents not necessarily all of these; but if it does represent all, it is the *complete* mathematical form. Every mathematical form of a state of things is the complete mathematical form of *some* state of things. The complete mathematical form of any state of things, real or fictitious, represents every ingredient of that state of things except the qualities of feeling connected with it. It represents whatever importance or significance those qualities may have; but the qualities themselves it does not represent" (5.550). In another paper of the same year, Peirce remarked: "No pure Icons represent anything but Forms; no pure Forms are represented by anything but Icons" (4.544).

4. The term *stoicheiology* means "doctrine of elements" and is taken from Sir William Hamilton. Cf. his *Lectures on Metaphysics and Logic* (1864), p. 46.

5. In the lectures of 1903, Peirce identifies pragmatism with "the logic of abduction" but argues that it in no sense directly affects deduction and induction (5.196). While this might seem to make pragmatism belong to the first branch of "critic," it must be remembered that on Peirce's analysis a perceptual judgment "shades into" an abductive inference "without any sharp line of demarcation between them" (5.181) and that, consequently, an analysis of assertion would inevitably pass into one of abductive inference or hypothesis. This is, of course, but an application of Peirce's general principle that every modification of consciousness is an inference. Pragmatism, then, is to be identified with the logic of abduction precisely because it completes the analysis of significant assertion given by speculative grammar. The function of pragmatism in the logic of abduction is examined below in chap. vi, sec. 1.

6. Cf. 1.501 ff. Peirce came later to regard the sciences of measurement, comprising the laws of space and time, as bridging the gap between metaphysics and the special sciences. According to the classification of sciences in the *Minute Logic*, "they are thus of a nature intermediate between coenoscopy and idioscopy; but in the

main their character is philosophical." "They form, therefore, a second subclass of philosophy, to which we may give the name of theorics. As inquiry now stands, this subclass has but two divisions which can hardly rank as orders, but rather as families, chronotheory and topotheory" (1.278). This position is anticipated in the paper ca. 1896. Cf. 1.514.

7. Peirce's later views concerning a determination of reality in relation to the grades of clearness and the methods of fixing belief are considered below, chap. vi, sec. 3, C and D.

8. The aim of the present discussion is simply to determine the general character of Peirce's final views on the validity of induction. When all his writings are taken into account, a number of complications arise concerning the different types of probable inference which are not essential for the purpose here. For a discussion of these complications see Buchler, op. cit., pp. 229-54 and Appendix I; T. A. Goudge, The Thought of C. S. Peirce (Toronto: University of Toronto Press, 1950), pp. 172-80.

9. In his lectures of 1903 Peirce characterized abduction as "an act of insight, although of extremely fallible insight" (5.181). He thus seems open to the objection of giving an undue extension to the word "reasoning" when he applies it to abduction. Professor Arthur W. Burks ("Peirce's Theory of Abduction," Philosophy of Science, XIII [1946], 301-6) has shown that this view of abduction as reasoning must be understood in the light of Peirce's conception of logic as a normative science. Considerations relevant to this point occur throughout the remainder of the present work. See esp. chap. vi, sec. 1.

10. The manner in which this relation constitutes a support of pragmatism is considered below in section 1 of the next chapter.

11. Yet in comments on Kant in 1885 with reference to the first critique, Peirce remarked that the proposition that "no general description of existence is possible" is "perhaps the most valuable proposition that the Critic contains" (1.35). This certainly calls for Peirce's later distinction between existence and reality when the latter is defined as the general laws ultimately discovered by induction.

12. Peirce does say in a paper ca. 1897: "According to my view, there are three categories of being; ideas of feelings, acts of reaction, and habits. Habits are either habits about ideas of feelings or habits about acts of reaction" (4.157). But as the second sentence here

suggests, Peirce goes on in this paragraph to say that there are two worlds, the "Inner" and the "Outer," with habits or laws appropriate to each. There is no indication of a third world or universe comprising those possibilities that are "destined" to be actualized. The phrase "categories of being" in the above quotation should thus be taken as "categories of phenomena" and not as referring to the three modes of being which Peirce later distinguished. The meaning of "destined to be actualized" and "third universe" is discussed below.

13. Peirce declared earlier in the *Minute Logic*: "This list of categories may be distinguished from other lists as the *Ceno-Pythagorean Categories*, on account of their connection with numbers" (2.87).

14. This is clearly indicated in Peirce's remark that "reality, like every other quality, consists in the peculiar sensible effects which things partaking of it produce" (5.406).

15. Quoted in R. B. Perry, *The Thought and Character of William James* (Boston: Little, Brown & Co., 1935), II, 223.

16. The issue of real possibility is also discussed in another paper of 1897, *The Logic of Relatives*. Cf. 3.526 ff. Also cf. 4, Bk. I, Paper V, ca. 1897.

17. While the account is in the traditional terms of the inherence of qualities in subjects when the issue of real possibility is being argued, Peirce refers to individual existence in terms similar to those he used in his original pragmatic definition of reality. "Not only is this opposition essential to an individual thing or subject, but also to an individual fact. Its truth, or existence, is the sum of its effects" (1.457). The distinction implied here between "thing" and "fact" reflects the traditional terminology and is not sustained by Peirce's later analysis. The pragmatic phrase "the sum of its effects" points clearly to the third mode of being which he had distinguished by 1902.

18. Cf. Perry, *op. cit.*, p. 224.

19. The editorial footnote here that modes of being are "usually called categories by Peirce" is incorrect in the light of the present discussion, especially with reference to the explicit distinction between categories and modes of being quoted above from 2.116. However, Peirce does at times in a phenomenological discussion of the categories use "being" when, strictly, he should mean "appearing." Cf. the discussion earlier in the *Minute Logic* of "being in

the present instant" and "being *in futuro*" (2.85–86). See above, n. 12.

20. In his lectures of 1903 Peirce spoke of this third mode as that "mode of being which *consists* in the fact that future facts of Secondness will take on a determinate general character" (1.26).

21. The example here is taken from the paper *Multitude and Number* (1897), already referred to, where Peirce offers a tentative proof of the possibility of always having such a one-to-one relation. This amounts, of course, to attempting a proof for an equivalent of what is usually called the multiplicative axiom, or axiom of selection. Peirce's proof depends on supposing the relation to remain forever in the realm of possible construction, but in such a way that there is no need for a special axiom to guarantee its reality. The proof is expressly in answer to a philosophic question rather than a mathematical one (cf. 4.177) and is inseparably bound up with Peirce's theory of real possibility. Cf. *The Logic of Relatives* (1897), esp. 3.526 and 3.549 n.

22. In *The Logic of Relatives* (1897) Peirce remarked: "I formerly defined the possible as that which in a given state of information (real or feigned) we do not know not to be true" (3.527). This definition was the only one given even in *The Regenerated Logic* (1896). Cf. 3.442. In a paper of 1905 such a definition is specified as pertaining to "subjective" as opposed to "objective modality" (5.454–55). The latter represents the doctrine of modality interpreted in accordance with modes of being. Time is "a particular variety of objective modality," and the past is "the Existential Mode of Time" (5.459). The future is either destined or undecided, i.e., necessary or possible. The necessary and the possible are "of the same mode since . . . Negation being outside the category of modality cannot produce a variation in Modality." The present is "that Nascent State between the Determinate and the Indeterminate."

23. Peirce's article on pragmatism for Baldwin's *Dictionary* (1902) clearly states the point as a reinterpretation of this doctrine. After describing the maxim as stated in *How To Make Our Ideas Clear* (1878), Peirce remarks that he "would venture to suggest that it should always be put into practice with conscientious thoroughness, but that, when that has been done, and not before, a still higher grade of clearness of thought can be attained by remembering that the only ultimate good which the practical facts to which it directs attention can subserve is to further the development of

concrete reasonableness; so that the meaning of the concept does not lie in any individual reactions at all, but in the manner in which those reactions contribute to that development" (5.3). Cf. 5.433 (1905), where such development is specified as constituting the *summum bonum*. In a paper of 1906 Peirce decided that this reinterpretation was in accord with the spirit of his early paper. Cf. 5.402, n. 3.

24. This does not mean that the objective logic of 1898 is made incorrect by the later analysis but only that a full development of objective logic requires contrast with normative rather than subjective logic. See below, chap. vi, sec. 1.

25. In 1908 Peirce added the following marginal note to a passage about the ideal and real worlds in his *The Logic of Relatives* (1897): ". . . the real world is a part of the ideal world. namely, [sic] that part which sufficient experience would tend ultimately (and therefore definitively), to compel Reason to acknowledge as having a being independent of what he may arbitrarily, or willfully, create" (3.527, n. 1). In this sense the problem is not that of connecting the two worlds but rather that of distinguishing one as part of the other by means of inquiry. While this way of viewing the matter emphasizes the final dependence on the hope for sufficient inquiry, it does not bring out the need for a third universe, which requires further analysis of what is meant by "the real world."

26. Probably 1855, when Peirce in his sixteenth year read Schiller's *Aesthetische Briefe*. Cf. 2.197.

27. This is suggested in Peirce's remark: "Reasoning essentially involves *self-control*; so that the *logica utens* is a particular species of morality" (5.108).

NOTES TO CHAPTER VI

1. Cf. 6.189 and above, p. 193. Peirce does not use the phrase "objective logic" in this discussion of "premisses of nature," but then his remarks on this subject in the *Minute Logic* had already made the fundamental contrast that between objective and normative rather than subjective logic.

2. While Peirce spoke in these lectures of "a perception of generality and continuity" and admitted that this might provide a difficulty for "the theory of vision" (cf. 5.148–50), his analysis throughout is logical and epistemological and hence prior to anything in psychology. The perceived generality he refers to here would thus be

a result of synechism as a regulative principle in the analysis, and the theory of vision would have to presuppose such perception and attempt to explain how it takes place.

3. It is precisely in this manner that metaphysics and the other sciences of reality, although they start with facts of immediate perception, can be said to treat of phenomena in their thirdness—of phenomena as ends or general predictions in some sense already achieved—while the normative sciences treat of phenomena in their secondness (see above, pp. 170–71). The latter provide norms for the control to be exercised by the former, and in doing so they oppose phenomena to ends which ought to be pursued.

4. In another paper of 1905 Peirce gave as an example of a thing which is objectively general "a statue of a soldier on some village monument," which "is for each of a hundred families the image of its uncle, its sacrifice to the Union." Though the statue "is itself single," it "represents any one man of whom a certain predicate may be true" (5.429). In other words, it is a sign whose object is general. On the other hand, Peirce goes on to explain, a symbol, such as an ordinary word, has "subjective generality" in the sense that it is a "type" or "form" to which the individual marks or sounds which occur each time the word is written or spoken must conform. Peirce means of course that the symbol has real generality as its mode of being and is not an "existent thing" as the statue is. This use of "objective" and "subjective" corresponds to the medieval esse objectivum and esse subjectivum, being as an object thought or represented and being as a real subject, or substantial being. Cf. R. P. McKeon, Selections from Medieval Philosophers (New York, 1930), II, 474, 499. The statue is thus general by virtue of the object it is thought or represented to be, while a word is general by virtue of the kind of subject it really is, qua word.

5. Throughout this discussion of vagueness, Peirce speaks of signs without specifying icon, index, or symbol. The reason for this would be that "the division into Icons, Indices, and Symbols depends upon the different possible relations of a Sign to its Dynamical Object" (4.536), while the concern here is only with the immediate object.

6. The complications that arise when the different kinds of interpretants which Peirce distinguished are taken into account will be considered below, pp. 226–27. The concern here is simply to point out that the immediate object is closely connected with the meaning, if it is not in a sense identical with the meaning.

7. Here Peirce does say the immediate object of a symbol rather

than a sign, but there would seem to be no objection to saying that the complete immediate object of a sign is also its meaning. Cf. 5.473, where the immediate object of an index is referred to as "a mental representation of the index," i.e., of the pointing. In a footnote to 2.293 Peirce specifies that "the immediate object of a symbol can only be a symbol." By analogy, then, the immediate object of an icon should be a mental representation of the likeness. The statue of the soldier (from the example in 5.429) would be an icon whose immediate object or meaning is a mental representation of any soldier the statue is like.

8. "In those respects in which a sign is not vague, it is said to be *definite*, and also with a slightly different mode of application, to be *precise*" (5.449). But Peirce did not go on here to specify any difference between "definite" and "precise." In another paper (1906), after remarking that "no Sign is absolutely precise," he continued: "Indefiniteness is of two kinds, indefiniteness as to what is the Object of the Sign, and indefiniteness as to its Interpretant, or indefiniteness in Breadth and in Depth" (4.543). It might seem from this that "objectively" vague and general should refer to indefiniteness in breadth, but Peirce's further remarks in 4.543 show that such is clearly not the case. In speaking of breadth, Peirce has reference to existent or dynamical objects as they constitute the subjects of propositions, as "Somebody gives something to some person" is analyzed in the logic of relatives as involving three subjects (or objects), the giver, the gift, and the receiver. Words like "donation" and "gives" are indefinite in breadth as long as these objects which react dynamically to determine the sign are not indicated. All mere predicates are indefinite in breadth in this way, and their "informative depth (*i.e.*, all the depth except an essential superficies) is indefinite" (4.543). Cf. Peirce's remarks (1906) in the footnote to 5.448, where he says that his discussion of the objectively vague and general "with a view to brevity, omitted to mention that both indefiniteness and generality might primarily affect either the logical breadth or the logical depth of the sign to which it belongs." He goes on here to explain that in speaking of logical depth one turns a predicate into an object by "hypostatic abstraction," as the depth of *sweet* is said to be *sweetness*. Now in this case, sweetness is the immediate object of "sweet" and is called the depth only when "sweet" is regarded as a predicate as well as simply a sign.

The introduction of the notions of breadth and depth thus gives rise to an analysis of indefiniteness or lack of precision which is centered around signs as predicates of propositions and presupposes the analysis which considers all signs indifferently with reference to their immediate objects. The latter alone is sufficient for "objectively" vague and general as they are crucial for Peirce's critical commonsensism. For the present consideration there is no need to attempt a distinction between "definite" and "precise" or to examine Peirce's analysis of indefiniteness in breadth and depth. Justus Buchler (*Charles Peirce's Empiricism* [New York: Harcourt, Brace & Co., 1939], pp. 24 ff.) discusses Peirce's doctrine of vagueness in relation to breadth and depth but does not connect it with Peirce's distinction between existent and immediate objects.

9. "Every concept that is vague is liable to be self-contradictory in those respects in which it is vague" (6.496).

10. Buchler (*op. cit.*, p. 30 n.) feels that there is an incompatibility between the statements quoted above from 4.237 and 6.496, but he does not draw the distinction made here between subject matter and communication with respect to mathematics. The point is perhaps stated better by referring to the *practice* of mathematics, which is correctly called the drawing of necessary conclusions (cf., e.g., 4.238–39) but which is also subject to error. The vagueness of mathematical signs could then be described as consisting in the latitude which the utterer claims for further checking of his reasoning.

11. While further generalization thus achieves less vagueness, it can never entirely overcome the vagueness because absolute generality, or complete surrender of the right of determination to the interpreter, would be no communication at all and would be the same as absolute vagueness, or the complete failure of the utterer to give any determination. Thus, "notwithstanding their contrariety, generality and vagueness are, from a formal point of view, seen to be on a par" (5.506). In accordance with his synechism, Peirce had to admit that there should be some sort of "intermediacy between generality and vagueness," and even "an endless series of such intermediacies" (5.450). While he seems to have found no use for these intermediacies and never specified what any of them would be, in his doctrine of objective modality he relied on the analogous notion of "an intermediate, or nascent state, between determination and indetermination" to define the present (5.450 and 5.459). See above, chap. v, n. 22.

12. Peirce remarked in 1878 in his *How To Make Our Ideas Clear*: "Feigned hesitancy, whether feigned for mere amusement or with a lofty purpose, plays a great part in the production of scien-

tific inquiry. However the doubt may originate, it stimulates the mind to an activity which may be slight or energetic, calm or turbulent" (5.394). But in *The Fixation of Belief* Peirce had declared: "When doubt ceases, mental action on the subject comes to an end; and, if it did go on, it would be without a purpose" (5.376). His footnote of 1903 ("Except that of self-criticism. Insert here a section upon self-control and the analogy between Moral and Rational self-control") indicates that Peirce did not attach as much importance to feigned doubt in his earlier papers.

13. Belief in God is one of the common-sense indubitables, and Peirce's remarks in 6.496 imply that this is one of the beliefs which scientists may think they doubt (because they have tried to make it too precise) while they really believe it. Presumably, they might even come really to doubt it. See above, chap. iv, n. 20, for an indication of the sense in which "doing what one can to advance inquiry" seems to be part of what is meant by "believing in God." It would seem that a scientist vaguely presupposes a belief in God in about the same way that he does a belief in the uniformity of nature.

14. Peirce comes virtually to this conclusion in 4.539 (1905) and remarks, "Of course, I must be understood as talking not psychology, but the logic of mental operations." In his statement of the conclusion here he speaks of a "complex of percepts" as giving rise to a perceptual universe and of "adjunctions to the Perceptual Universe" as eventually producing a representation of "that highest of all Universes which is regarded as the Object of every true Proposition." But since in the logic of mental operations no percept is absolutely simple and determinate in its character as a sign, there would be no absolute distinction from this point of view between a percept and a complex of percepts.

15. The belief in God would of course be difficult to explain in this fashion, in so far as Peirce held that, although God is directly perceived, He has no existence as a reacting singular. Cf. 6.495 and above, pp. 147–48.

16. This interpretation of the common-sense indubitables is contrary to the one given by Buchler (*op. cit.*, pp. 59–61), who holds that Peirce distinguishes in effect between social and perceptual indubitables. But such a view does not take account of Peirce's wide use of "perception." A further point in favor of the interpretation given here is the way in which it accords with Peirce's notion of "coenoscopic observation." See below, sec. 3, D.

17. Peirce actually says "the right understanding of the Sign itself" (4.536), but this would certainly amount to an understanding of that object which is nothing except "as the sign itself represents it, and whose Being is thus dependent upon the Representation of it in the Sign."

18. That Peirce meant his immediate, dynamical, and final interpretants in 4.536 to be essentially the same as the emotional, energetic, and logical in 5.475–76 is certainly suggested by his opening remarks in 4.536: the interpretant is "that which the Sign produces in the Quasi-mind that is the Interpreter by determining the latter to a feeling, to an exertion, or to a Sign." The extracts from Peirce's letters (1908–9) to Lady Welby published in C. K. Ogden and I. A. Richards, *The Meaning of Meaning* (London and New York, 1923; 8th ed. rev., 1946), Appendix D, sec. 6, afford some clarification as to the nature of the three interpretants. The final interpretant is characterized as "the effect the Sign would produce upon any mind upon which circumstances should permit it to work out its full effect" (p. 287). This is considerably simpler than the characterization of the final interpretant given in 4.536, as that interpretant "which refers to the manner in which the Sign tends to represent itself to be related to its Object." Peirce seems to have written the latter primarily with the intention of using the final interpretant as a means for distinguishing arguments from terms and propositions (cf. 4.572), while his remarks to Lady Welby were intended only to clarify the general notion of a final interpretant and seem in accord with the more technical discussion of the logical interpretant given in 5.476. The phrase "the Immediate Interpretant of all thought proper" (4.539) remains difficult and is surely a very special case of the immediate interpretant.

19. Peirce's statement that "indefiniteness is of two kinds, indefiniteness as to what is the Object of the Sign, and indefiniteness as to its Interpretant, or indefiniteness in Breadth and in Depth" (4.543) would suggest a kind of precision relating to the interpretant. However, upon closer analysis indefiniteness in depth turns out to involve the interpretant as object rather than as properly an interpretant. Peirce explained about a year later: "When we speak of the depth, or signification, of a sign we are resorting to hypostatic abstraction, that process whereby we regard a thought as a thing, make an interpretant sign the object of a sign" (5.448 n.).

20. Peirce does at times use the word "interpreter" as though it referred to something which is itself a sign. Cf., e.g., 5.3, where he

speaks of "general ideas" as the "true interpreters of our thought"; and 1.553, where he introduced the word "interpretant" (1867) with the remark, "Such a mediating representation may be termed an *interpretant*, because it fulfils the office of an interpreter, who says that a foreigner says the same thing which he himself says." John Dewey ("Peirce's Theory of Linguistic Signs, Thought, and Meaning," *Journal of Philosophy*, XLIII [1946], 87) remarks: "To Peirce, 'interpreter,' if he used the word, would mean *that which interprets*, thereby giving meaning to a linguistic sign." According to Dewey, this is the same as the interpretant and is hence always another sign.

The case for holding that Peirce did not succeed in avoiding the notion of an interpreter who is in some sense active in determining signs and is not himself a sign will be argued variously throughout the remainder of the present chapter. Of course, a definition of "interpretant" as a significate effect on the interpreter decides the issue at the start, but the main argument here will turn on the general character of Peirce's pragmatic approach to philosophy and not on this definition. Dewey says at the end of his article (p. 95) that Peirce would deny that "the names *Self, Mind, Knowing Subject, Person* as user of signs, apply to anything except a particular sort of natural existence, or 'thing,' which can be known only through and by means of the best knowledge we have of other 'things,' physical, biological, and socio-cultural." But this conclusion holds only in so far as Peirce did succeed in avoiding the notion of an interpreter who is not an interpretant.

21. Another point may be urged in favor of the view that Peirce succeeded in identifying "interpreter" and "interpretant." The further determination which must always be supplied by the interpreter may be regarded as entailing no more than an infinity of interpretants in a continuum of signs. But this account of the interpreter will not sustain Peirce's distinction between normative and objective, or his reliance on the notion of self-control. And even aside from these factors, Peirce remarked with reference to this infinity of interpretants: "No doubt, intelligent consciousness must enter into the series" (2.303). He did not make clear what he meant by such consciousness, but it is at least that which possesses "memory or other significant effect of the sign" and thus seems rather close to an interpreter distinct from the interpretant.

22. Peirce's use of "phenomenal manifestation" here suggests, in analogy with Kant, a noumenal self, but Peirce never explicitly held such a doctrine, and he even used the word "noumenal" in a

sense that would preclude it. A comparison of Peirce and Kant on this point is given below in B of section 4. While Peirce himself never spoke of an "active interpreter," the phrase is used here merely to indicate the contrast between the self as the sign-phenomena presented and as that which further determines the phenomena by interpretants.

23. Peirce's comments in "Questions on William James' *Principles of Psychology*" imply that any notion of an individual self is largely an illusion. "It is not quite purely illusory, but it is mainly so. It is true, for instance, that men are *selfish*, that is, that they are really deluded into supposing themselves to have some isolated existence; and in so far, they *have* it" (quoted in R. B. Perry, *The Thought and Character of William James* [Boston: Little, Brown & Co., 1935], II, 107, and in Buchler, *op. cit.*, p. 19). In terms of the present discussion, these remarks suggest that "the critical self" may be the real self, although any attempt to identify it as a phenomenon will result in a kind of illusion.

24. Peirce's view that the immediate object of every symbol is itself a symbol would of course make it impossible for him to locate regulative principles finally in a semantic metalanguage which is about the use of symbols as opposed to an object-language which is about objects that are not symbols. Cf. Dewey's remarks, *op. cit.*, pp. 88–92, concerning the manner in which Peirce would relate signs to things. While Dewey's interpretation is in accord with the view expressed here that Peirce could not locate regulative principles in a semantic metalanguage, Dewey does not admit the necessity for reference to an interpreter. But, then, Dewey does not comment on such points as, for instance, the fact that Peirce characterized his logic as "normative semeotic" (2.111).

25. Buchler (*op. cit.*, p. 63) finds Peirce's distinction between theoretical and practical belief in terms of muscular sensation the result of a nominal definition and concludes that Peirce does not seem to realize that any of the usual distinctions between theoretical and practical are ones of degree rather than of kind. But Buchler does not consider the manner in which the *summum bonum* may figure in Peirce's attempt to draw the distinction and, on the contrary (p. 71), represents Peirce as dreading "the introduction into scientific inquiry of moral or quasi-moral considerations."

26. In terms of these lectures, such desires are matters of "vital importance," but it is difficult to make out exactly what Peirce meant

by this phrase. His reason for using it in the first place seems to have been simply the fact that it occurred in the description he was given of what his lectures should cover (cf. 1.622). He remarked near the beginning of his first lecture, "I do not hold forth the slightest promise that I have any philosophical wares to offer you which will make you either better men or more successful men" (1.621). In this sense, Buchler's view that Peirce wished to keep scientific inquiry free from moral or quasi-moral considerations (see the previous note) is justified, but it is clear from the context of these lectures that "better" and "more successful" here refer to individual satisfaction rather than to anything "moral," as that term is used in the *Minute Logic*. Peirce appears to have intended "vital importance" to characterize religious and moral beliefs as matters which affect the life and well-being of the individual as opposed to the social end of goodness and truth. Later in the lectures he emphasized that ethics as a science is quite useless and not a matter of vital importance (cf. 1.666 ff.).

27. In a fragment ca. 1906 Peirce gave a hasty summary of the four methods of fixing beliefs which he had distinguished in 1877, but he provided no indication as to how they might be fitted into the evolution he had referred to in his discussions of critical common-sensism. The inaccuracy and the cursory nature of the summary are well illustrated by the looseness of his characterization of the scientific method, which he refers to merely as "the idea of truth as overwhelmingly forced upon the mind in experience as the effect of an independent reality" (5.564). According to the paper of 1878, this is an explanation of truth and reality only at the second grade of clearness (cf. 5.405), and without further elaboration it could easily be construed as inconsistent with the pragmatic conception of reality. The description of the a priori method given in the summary as "the idea of a settlement of opinion as the result of a fermentation of ideas" (5.564) may be taken as similarly loose and inaccurate.

28. This point seems clearly implied in a paper of 1905, in which Peirce remarks that "thought, controlled by a rational experimental logic, tends to the fixation of certain opinions, . . . the nature of which will be the same in the end, however the perversity of thought of whole generations may cause the postponement of the ultimate fixation" (5.430).

29. Yet he seems virtually to admit the point in his discussion of modes of being in the *Minute Logic*, where he remarked concerning

the being of a symbol: "This mode of being seems to claim immediate recognition as evident in the mere idea of it. One asks whether
there is not a fallacy in using the ordinary processes of logic either
to support it or to refute it" (2.115). Something like this appeal to
clearness as evidence of truth may be found in Peirce's paper of 1869,
where he attempts to "deduce" the validity of the laws of logic.
After stating the principle of the syllogism, he comments that it is
"not doubted by anybody who distinctly apprehends the meaning
of these words" (5.320). But his definition of reality then figures
in his further explication of the syllogism in a manner which implies
that the truth of this definition is likewise to be shown by its clearness. See above, pp. 54-55. Peirce's ultimate requirement of logic—
his hope that inquiry will continue indefinitely—is then a further
complication which arises from his definition of reality and indicates that a clear understanding of the definition requires a reference
to the *summum bonum*.

30. In accordance with this rendering of Peirce, the three grades
of clearness represent three different determinations of the logical
interpretant. For the issue throughout is that of fixing the meanings of general concepts. While only the dynamical interpretant may
properly involve instinctive control, there seems no reason why this
same control would not produce at least the beginnings of a logical
interpretant. The circumstance that many beliefs seem to be instinctive when they are not may then be explained by the fact that
whatever is perfectly familiar is likely to be taken as instinctive, since
instinct by itself would produce familiarity rather than knowledge.
The second and third grades of clearness, as will be argued below
(sec. 4, A), represent the difference between traditional logic and
pragmatism, as Peirce saw the issue.

31. Thus, in *How To Make Our Ideas Clear* Peirce referred to
the second grade as the highest recognized by traditional books on
logic. Cf. 5.390, 5.392. In a paper of 1897 (3, Paper XVI) he discusses the term "relation" as it appears in the three grades of clearness. At the first grade a relation is no more than the familiar notion
of a connection between two things (cf. 3.458-64), while at the
second grade the traditional notion of the copula "is" remains central to the explanation. "A *relative*, then, may be defined as the
equivalent of a word or phrase which, either as it is . . . or else when
the verb 'is' is attached to it, . . . becomes a sentence with some
number of proper names left blank" (3.466). The third grade in-

volves the graphic representation of relatives and a considerably expanded notion of the copula (cf. 3.473).

32. Cf. 5.142, where Peirce "corrects" the traditional distinction between *logical truth*, or truth of arguments, and *material truth*, "which belongs to propositions, being that which veracity aims to be." He concludes: "Consequently, the only difference between material truth and the logical correctness of argumentation is that the *latter* refers to a single line of argument and the *former* to all the arguments which could have a given proposition or its denial as their conclusion."

33. "Pragmatism is the principle that every theoretical judgment expressible in a sentence in the indicative mood is a confused form of thought whose only meaning, if it has any, lies in its tendency to enforce a corresponding practical maxim expressible as a conditional sentence having its apodosis in the imperative mood" (5.18). Peirce's own distinction between theoretical and practical is thus closer to Kant's pure and applied, which is a distinction applicable to both the first and second critiques.

34. Cf. the discussion of the thing in itself (5.525). Peirce begins here with the remark: "Kant (who I more than admire) is nothing but a somewhat confused pragmatist." This remark and all those quoted in the present paragraph are from writings of 1903 or later.

35. Cf. 5.49, where Peirce refers to his third category as that of "Nous, or intelligibility."

36. Cf. 5.430 and 4.547 n. Cf. 2.664, where Peirce refers to the real probability that a die will turn up a certain number as a habit "quite analogous to any *habit* that a man might have."

37. Again, the status of God in Peirce's philosophy remains problematic. The denial that God exists would be in accord with making Him beyond the categories (and this is perhaps the influence of Kant on Peirce), but, in so far as there are arguments for the reality of God, He should fall under all three categories. At least, Peirce did not attempt to give reasons for the reality of the *summum bonum*, the unlimited community, or the critical self.

38. Peirce remarked in a paper of 1897, after admitting that his analogy between chemical compounds and logical relatives "quite breaks down," "yet I cannot resist the temptation to pursue it. After all, any analogy, however fanciful, which serves to focus attention upon matters which might otherwise escape observation is valuable" (3.470).

SELECTED BIBLIOGRAPHY

Selected Bibliography

PEIRCE'S WRITINGS

Collected Papers of Charles Sanders Peirce. Edited by CHARLES HARTSHORNE and PAUL WEISS. 6 vols. Cambridge, Mass.: Harvard University Press, 1931–35.

Chance, Love and Logic. Edited with an Introduction by M. R. COHEN. New York: Harcourt, Brace & Co., 1923. (This book contains a lengthy bibliography of Peirce's publications, including his book reviews.)

The Philosophy of Peirce: Selected Writings. Edited by JUSTUS BUCHLER. New York: Harcourt, Brace & Co., 1940.

The Thought and Character of William James. Edited by R. B. PERRY. 2 vols. Boston: Little, Brown & Co., 1936. (Selections from Peirce's letters to James appear in both volumes.)

Classic American Philosophers. General editor, MAX H. FISCH. New York: Appleton-Century-Crofts, Inc., 1951. (Selections from Peirce with an Introduction by ARTHUR W. BURKS comprise chapter i.)

WRITINGS ON PEIRCE

BRAITHWAITE, R. B. Review of Collected Papers of Charles Sanders Peirce, Vols. I–IV, Mind, XLIII (new ser., 1934), 487–511.

BRITTON, KARL. "Introduction to the Metaphysics and Theology of C. S. Peirce," Ethics, XLIX (1938–39), 435–65.

BUCHLER, JUSTUS. Charles Peirce's Empiricism. New York: Harcourt, Brace & Co., 1939. (This book gives a bibliography of biographical material on Peirce and a list of his published writings not appearing in the Collected Papers and not mentioned in the bibliography given in Cohen's Chance, Love and Logic.)

———. "Peirce's Theory of Logic," Journal of Philosophy, XXXVI (1939), 197–215.

———. "The Accidents of Peirce's System," ibid., XXXVII (1940), 264–69.

BURKS, ARTHUR W. "Peirce's Conception of Logic as a Normative Science," Philosophical Review, LII (1943), 187–93.

303

BURKS, ARTHUR W. "Peirce's Theory of Abduction," *Philosophy of Science*, XIII (1946), 301–6.

———. "Icon, Index, and Symbol," *Philosophy and Phenomenological Research*, IX (1949), 673–89.

BURKS, ARTHUR W., and WEISS, PAUL. "Peirce's Sixty-six Signs," *Journal of Philosophy*, XLII (1945), 383–88.

DEWEY, JOHN. "The Pragmatism of Peirce," *Journal of Philosophy*, XIII (1916), 709–15. (Reprinted in Cohen's *Chance, Love and Logic*.)

———. "Peirce's Theory of Linguistic Signs, Thought, and Meaning," *Journal of Philosophy*, XLIII (1946), 85–95.

FEIBLEMAN, JAMES K. *An Introduction to Peirce's Philosophy*. New York: Harper & Bros., 1946. (Professor Feibleman's various articles have been incorporated in this book.)

FREEMAN, EUGENE. *The Categories of Charles Peirce*. Chicago: Open Court Publishing Co., 1934.

GALLIE, W. B. "The Metaphysics of C. S. Peirce," *Proceedings of the Aristotelian Society*, XLVII (new ser., 1946–47), 27–62.

———. *Peirce and Pragmatism*. ("Pelican Philosophy Series.") Harmondsworth, Middlesex, England: Penguin Books, 1952.

GENTRY, GEORGE. "Peirce's Early and Later Theory of Cognition and Meaning: Some Critical Comments," *Philosophical Review*, LV (1946), 634–50.

GOUDGE, THOMAS A. *The Thought of C. S. Peirce*. Toronto: University of Toronto Press, 1950.

———. "The Views of Charles Peirce on the Given in Experience," *Journal of Philosophy*, XXXII (1935), 533–45.

———. "Further Reflection on Peirce's Doctrine of the Given," *ibid.*, XXXIII (1936), 289–95.

———. "Peirce's Treatment of Induction," *Philosophy of Science*, VII (1940), 56–68.

———. "The Conflict of Naturalism and Transcendentalism in Peirce," *Journal of Philosophy*, XLIV (1949), 365–75.

HARTSHORNE, CHARLES. "A Critique of Peirce's Idea of God," *Philosophical Review*, L (1941), 516–23.

———. "Charles Sanders Peirce's Metaphysics of Evolution," *New England Quarterly*, XIV (1941), 49–63.

HILL, W. H. "Peirce's 'Pragmatic Method,' " *Philosophy of Science*, VII (1940), 168–81.

LEONARD, HENRY S. "The Pragmatism and Scientific Metaphysics of C. S. Peirce," *Philosophy of Science*, IV (1937), 109–21.

LOVEJOY, A. O. "A Note on Peirce's Evolutionism," *Journal of the*

History of Ideas, VII (1946), 351–54. (Reprinted as Appendix E in Wiener's Evolution and the Founders of Pragmatism. Cambridge, Mass.: Harvard University Press, 1949.)

MOORE, EDWARD C. "The Scholastic Realism of C. S. Peirce," Philosophy and Phenomenological Research, XII (1952), 406–17.

MUIRHEAD, J. H. "Peirce's Place in American Philosophy," Philosophical Review, XXXVII (1928), 460–81.

———. The Platonic Tradition in Anglo-Saxon Philosophy. New York: Macmillan Co., 1931. (Chapter iii of Part III is a discussion of Peirce.)

NAGEL, E. "Charles S. Peirce, Pioneer of Modern Empiricism," Philosophy of Science, VII (1940), 69–80.

QUINE, W. V. Review of Vol. II of Collected Papers of Charles Sanders Peirce, Isis, XIX (1933), 220–29.

WEISS, PAUL. "The Essence of Peirce's System," Journal of Philosophy, XXXVII (1940), 253–64.

WEISS, PAUL, and BURKS, ARTHUR W. "Peirce's Sixty-six Signs," Journal of Philosophy, XLII (1946), 383–88.

WIENER, PHILIP P. "Peirce's Metaphysical Club and the Genesis of Pragmatism," Journal of the History of Ideas, VII (1946), 219–34.

———. "The Evolutionism and Pragmatism of Peirce," ibid., pp. 321–50. (These articles, with some revision, also appear in Wiener's Evolution and the Founders of Pragmatism. Cambridge, Mass.: Harvard University Press, 1949.)

WIENER, PHILIP P., and YOUNG, FREDERIC H. (eds.). Studies in the Philosophy of Charles Sanders Peirce. Cambridge, Mass.: Harvard University Press, 1952. (A collection of twenty-four essays on Peirce by various authors. The appendixes contain hitherto unpublished biographical and bibliographical material on Peirce.)

Index

A priori method of fixing belief, 72–79, 239–41, 278

Abduction: as act of insight, 287; first stage of inquiry, 142; and perceptual judgments, 171, 209–10, 224, 250; and pragmatism, 165, 210, 263, 286; as probable inference, 174, 176–77

Abstraction: degrees of, in the order of the sciences, 166–67, 170; hypostatic, 216–17, 232, 292, 295; as precision, 21–23; prescissive, 216–17, 232–33

Action, moral and physical, 255, 257–62

Actuality as a mode of being, 182, 187–89, 193–94; see also Existence

Aesthetics; see Esthetics as normative science

Agapasm, 128, 131, 136, 137, 229, 282, 284

Agapism; see Agapasm

Agassiz, L., 282

Agnosticism, 153–54

Analogical use of terms in Peirce, 250–51, 260–62, 264–67, 300

Anancasm, 136

Anthropomorphism, 252

Architectonic: in construction of philosophic systems, 108–9, 114; as a way of approaching Peirce's philosophy, xiv–xv; see also Sciences, ordering and classification of

Arguments: classification of, 4 ff., 97–99, 251, 263; complete and incomplete, 7–9; as kinds of signs, 28–29, 97–99, 274, 279; logi-

cal breadth and depth of, 35–36, 275; and Peirce's categories, 29, 98, 274, 279; probable (see Hypothesis; Induction); in relation to terms and propositions, 17–19, 28–29, 36, 66, 251; three kinds of, 13–14, 28–29, 97–99, 123, 274, 279; see also Inference

Aristotle, 155

Assertion; see Propositions

Association always an inference, 276

Authority as method of fixing belief, 71–79, 239–41, 278

Bacon, Francis, 267

Becoming or process prior to being, 264–67

Beginning of universe, 114–17, 124, 128, 151–53, 265

Being: as a category, 20–36; meaning of, 42, 183–84, 190, 246–47; and substance, 20–26, 69, 82, 169, 202–3, 206, 247–48; see also Modes of being

Belief: and doubt, 44–45, 68–71, 78; and expectation, 210–13, 235; as habit, 80–81; indubitable, 213, 218–27; methods of fixing, 71–79, 81–84, 169, 239–41, 246, 278, 298; out of place in pure theoretical science, 235; production of, 53; theoretical and practical, 210–13, 235–39, 297; vague, 213, 218–27

Berkeleian mind of God, 58

Boole, G., 3

Braithwaite, R. B., 274, 285–86

307

Buchler, J., 271, 278, 285, 287, 293, 294, 297, 298
Burks, A. W., 287

Cartesian philosophy, 44–45, 278
Carus, P., 115, 121, 127, 128, 129, 131, 137, 146, 151, 279, 280
Categories: in analysis of logical breadth and depth, 33–36; application of, in interpreting Peirce, 45–52, 76–79, 81–84, 108–9, 239; central role of, in development of Peirce's philosophy, 97–99; and genera of arguments, 29, 98, 274, 279; as generalized by logic of relatives, 31–33, 46–47; and logic, 19–36, 46–47, 113; and modes of being, 133, 147, 155, 182–83, 192–93; as ordering events in thought-process, 50; original list of five, 25–26, 202, 247; Peirce's first statement of, 19 ff.; and phenomenology, 32–33, 36, 161, 182–83, 198; in proofs of pragmatism, 249; reasons for not including substance and being, 29–32; in theories of evolution, 128, 132, 133–37, 281, 282; see also Firstness; Secondness; Thirdness
Causality, principle of 93–95
Cause: efficient, 132, 135, 279, 280; final, 132, 133, 135, 151, 193–94, 279, 280; as law, 94, 279, 280
Chance: absolute, 111, 114–18, 127, 134, 283; laws of, 115–16; and necessity, 64, 103, 115–18, 134–37; as outward aspect of feeling, 125–26; see also Tychism
Chance-world as self-contradictory, 56–57, 91, 94–95, 97, 99–100, 115–16
Chaos; see Beginning of universe
Charles S. Peirce Society, 271
Class defined by a property, 94–95
Clearness, 79–84, 165, 169, 246–47, 248; and degrees of self-control, 241–42; fourth grade of, 82–84, 246–47, 250, 255–56,

259–62, 289–90; and precision, 225, 227, 241, 247; three grades of, 79–84, 103, 108–9, 169, 246–47, 248, 298–99; and truth, 84, 241–43, 247–48, 250, 265, 299; and vagueness, 225–27, 241–42
Cognition, 38–43, 45–52, 203–4, 206; see also Thought-process as process of signification
Comparison, act of, in determining categories, 24
Comte, Auguste, 145, 156, 166
Conceptualism, 186
Concrete reasonableness, 255, 283; see also Self-controlled growth of inquiry
Consciousness, 32, 118–20, 125, 200, 224, 252, 264; as cognitive process, 38–43, 49, 122–24; continuity of, 122–23, 127, 148; every modification of, as an inference, 50, 147–48, 171, 250, 251; questioning of, as method in ethics, 195–96, 200
Continuity: as basic conception in philosophy, 113, 121–23; definition of, 280; and generality, 113, 280, 281; as regulative principle, 123, 206; as thirdness, 113, 118, 121, 279–81; of time and consciousness, 122–23, 127, 148; see also Synechism
Continuous quantity, 85, 116–17
Copula, logical, 17
Cosmic evolution, 33, 114, 264, 280; and the hypothesis of God, 145, 150–54; of laws, 111, 124, 128–37; as objective logic, 133–37, 150–54, 180–81, 192, 229; as producing both uniformity and variety, 283
Cosmology; see Metaphysics; Philosophy, cosmogonic
Critic: as critical logic, 28, 164, 165, 179, 191, 192, 263; order of procedure in, 174; and possibility of induction, 169, 171–72
Critical common-sensism, 148–49, 206; common-sense aspect of, 218–23; critical side of, 223–27,

308

309

modification of consciousness an, 50, 147–48, 171, 250, 251; immediate, 12–14, 251; knowledge always by, 53; probable, 14, 16, 56–67, 134, 172–79, 287 (see also Probability); retroductive or abductive (see Abduction); statistical, 58, 99; validity of, 54–67

Inquirer: difficulty in defining, 66–67, 253–56; final aim of, 143; and inquiry, related ultimately by self-control, 241; as mind, 130, 133–37; moral nature of, 89, 142–44, 194, 236–37, 247; and pragmatic philosophy, 248, 252; as a sign, 65–67, 229, 236–39; theoretical and practical beliefs of, 237; see also Man

Inquiry: begins in doubt and ends in belief, 68–71; blocking the way of, 143, 145, 154, 240; existence of, as metaphysical postulate, 100; and human nature, 79; idioscopic, 222–23, 243, 245; philosophic, 222–23; process involving organism and environment, 65, 92–93, 137; seemingly requires two faculties, 64–66

Instinct, 78–79, 149, 219, 221–23, 240

Intelligence, 92–93

Intentions, first and second, 28

Interpretant, 24–29, 33–34, 49, 123–24, 152; dynamical, 226–27, 295, 299; emotional and energetic, 227, 250, 295; final, 227, 295; and hypostatic abstraction, 295; immediate, 214–15, 226–27, 295; and interpreter, 24, 230, 296; logical, 227, 250, 295, 299; and object, 226–27

Interpreter: active, 231, 297; as correlative of utterer, 214–18, 224–26, 229–32; as fundamental notion in Peirce's philosophy, 231–33, 252; and kinds of belief, 235–36; not a sign, 229–30, 295; office of, fulfilled by interpretant, 24, 296; as quasi-mind, 295; in universe of signs, 228; see also Inquirer

Introspection: not used in determining categories, 22–23; power of, 38, 46

Intuition: as defined in Peirce's early papers as premiss not itself a conclusion, 38–43, 45, 228, 251; none of God, 148; and Peirce's propositions of ontology, 266; required in traditional logic, 248, 252

James, William, 35, 122, 186, 187, 275, 297

Judgment; see Perceptual judgment; Propositions

Kant, I, and Peirce, xvii; on architectonic, 108, 249; on categories, 30–31, 54, 247; on cognition, 37–39; on continuity, 280–81; on existence, 287; fundamental differences between, 252–56, 267; on logic, 3–5, 14, 16–17, 19, 54, 251, 254, 262; on noumena and phenomena, 254–56, 296–97; on possible experience, 252–53; on pragmatic, 254–55, 300; on preconditions of knowledge, 78, 252–53; on theoretical and practical, 62–63, 252–56, 300; on thing in itself, 58, 253; on truth, 253–54

Kempe, A. B., 285

King, C., 282

Knowledge: always by inference, 53; perfect, 238; and philosophy, 110; of scientific law, 110–11; see also Belief

Kölliker, A., 128, 136

Lamarck, J. B., 128, 131, 136, 137, 281

Law: as cause, 94, 279–80; and destiny, 133–34, 188–89, 228; distinct from possibility and existence, 116; evolution of, 111, 114, 116, 283; as fact, needing explanation, 110–11; as force, and hence secondness, 110, 279–80; as mode of being, 188–89, 193, 228; necessary and contingent, 167–68; as a real probability, 175–78, 185, 189; reality of, 88, 130, 134, 136–37; as related to singulars, 212–13; as thirdness, 110, 134, 188–89, 279–80

Leibniz, G. W., 145–46, 244, 272

Liar paradox, 55–56, 278

Likelihood, 177

Likeness; see Icon

Logic: cannot be based on psychology, 233–34; as classification of arguments, 4, 97–99, 251; depends on ethics, 89, 103, 160, 163, 178, 179–80, 194–201, 203; formal, as simplest mathematics, 32–33, 97, 101, 159–62, 168, 203; fundamental character of Peirce's approach to, 18–19; importance of, in a commentary on Peirce, xvi–xvii; and mathematics, 156–63, 166, 168–70; Peirce's dominated by methodology, 262–64; and phenomenology, 156–63, 166, 168–70; prior to metaphysics, 144–45, 166–72; prior to ontology, 55, 63, 100, 103, 166–72; prior to the special sciences, 233–34, 237; proper, 160, 162, 163, 178, 193, 194; as second intentions applied to first, 27–28; traditional as principal alternative to pragmatism, xvi, 248–49; ultimate assumption or requirement of, 60–63, 75, 88, 91, 129–31, 135, 144, 194–95, 257; validity of laws of, 53–67, 128; see also Normative logic; Objective logic

Logic of relatives: affords new analysis of subject and predicate, 204–5, 212; as determining Peirce's categories, 31–33, 46, 161; different from ordinary logic, 16, 274; essentially triadic, 160–62; in proofs of pragmatism, 249; as simplest mathematics, 101, 160–61

Logica docens, 157, 158, 162, 163, 245

Logica utens, 157, 158, 200, 245, 285, 290

Logical breadth and depth: of arguments, 35–36, 275; essential and substantial, 34–36; informed, 33–36; of propositions, 35–36; of terms, 9–10, 15, 33–36; and vagueness, 292–93, 295

Logical operations, 18–19, 203; see also Substitution

Logical sentiment, 89, 103, 135, 137, 144, 178, 257, 263

Love, evolutionary; see Agapasm

Lovejoy, A. O., 280, 283

McKeon, R. P., 291

Man: as identical with a sign, 52, 65–67, 229; moral nature of, 71, 75, 236–37; see also Inquirer; Person as general idea or symbol

Materialism, 112, 118

Mathematics: as diagrammatical or iconic, 157–63, 211–12, 281, 285; dichotomic and trichotomic, 160–61; draws necessary conclusions, 265, 292; generalization in, 113; and habits of inquiry, 102–3; as hypothetical science, 138–40, 170, 211; involves only *logica utens*, 157–58, 285; and logic, 156–63, 166, 168–70; as observational science, 102, 139, 157–63, 211–12, 265, 281; and phenomenology, 156–63, 166, 168–70, 196, 200; precision and vagueness in, 216, 293; as prior to and independent of all other sciences, 170, 179, 196, 200; of probabilities, 85–88, 97; in relation to the empirical, 94–95, 97, 100–103; simplest, as formal logic, 32–33, 97, 101, 159–62, 168, 203, 264

Matter, 109, 120, 124–26

Meaning: criterion of, as reference to *summum bonum*, 183–84, 190–92, 225, 234, 262, 264–66; as immediate interpretant, 226–27; as immediate object, 291; limits of, 254; necessary for truth or falsity, 79, 241, 250; of ontological terms, 103, 183–84, 242, 246–47, 265; of pragmatic max-

312

im, 258–59, 263; as reference to substance, 248, 251–54; *see also* Clearness
Mechanical explanation, 96, 115, 124–26, 127
Mental action; *see* Thought-process as process of signification
Metaphysics, 92, 96–97, 100, 103, 114, 155; anti-empirical, 256; depends on logic, 135, 144–45, 166–72; ontological, 138–39, 146, 154, 244–45; prior to idioscopic inquiry, 222–23, 233; scientific, xvii, 107, 137–53, 181, 191, 243–45; and *summum bonum*, 197; treats phenomena in their thirdness, 170, 291
Methodeutic; *see* Speculative rhetoric
Methodology, Peirce's logic dominated by, 262–64
Mill, J. S., 57, 92–93
Mind: continuous with matter, 120, 124–26; continuous with other minds or personalities, 120, 126, 149–50; fundamental law of, 111–12, 118; of God, 152–53, 231; as inquirer, 130, 133–37, 229; and intelligence, 92–93; and nature, 92–93, 96–97, 111; and reality, 63, 92–93, 100, 103; reality of, 52
Modes of being: and fourth grade of clearness, 246–47, 256; not in Peirce's early philosophy, 33, 35, 88, 133, 181–87, 287–88; and objective logic, 133, 181, 282–83; as ontological question, 137–38; and Peirce's categories, 133, 147, 155, 182–83, 192–93; Peirce's final development of, 187–94, 263–64; and pragmatism, 190; and *summum bonum*, 183–84, 191–92, 197–98, 256, 264
Monads, 160, 167
Monism, 112, 280
Multiplicative axiom, 289
Musement, 141–42
Mutation-theory, 285
Mystical theory, 96

Nägeli, K. W., 128, 136
Naturalism and transcendentalism, conflict of, in Peirce, xii, 256–62, 271
Necessity: and chance, 64, 103, 115–18, 134–37; and destiny, 133–34; mathematical, 158–63; and possibility, 159–63, 168; principle of universal, 115–18
Nominalism, 51–52, 96, 129, 145–46, 186, 231; and the nature of man, 66, 118–21, 229–30; and synechism, 126; tendency to, in Peirce's early writings, 66, 118, 121, 229; and theory of induction, 57–60, 90
Normative logic: and criterion of meaning, 183, 192, 233; depends on prior normative sciences, 194–201; distinct from formal logic, 32–33, 97; indication of need for, in Peirce's early views, 75, 103; and objective logic, 33, 130, 135, 137, 154, 180–81, 192–93, 197, 204, 229, 241; place of, among the sciences, 139–40, 162–63, 170–71; prior to objective inquiry, 151, 237, 241; regulative principle of, 153; to avoid paradox in Peirce's theory of inquiry, 178
Nota notae, principle of, 7–8
Noumenal, 254–56

Object: existent or dynamical, 214, 227–29, 231, 250, 252, 253, 291–93; immediate, 206, 214, 224, 226–29, 231, 245–46, 250, 253, 291–92; and interpretant, 226–27; and subject, 204
Objective logic: as logic of events in cosmic evolution, 133–37, 150–54, 180–81, 192–93, 204, 229; and modes of being, 133, 181, 282–83; Peirce's early conception of, 282; posterior to normative logic, 33, 180–81, 197, 204, 229, 241; and subjective logic, 193, 204
Objective modality, 289, 293

313

Observation, coenoscopic and idioscopic, 245–46, 260, 266
Ockham's razor, 112, 127; see also Principle, of economy
Ogden, C. K., 295
One-idea'd philosophies, 108, 262, 266–67
Ontological argument, 244
Ontological line in the order of the sciences, 168–72, 178, 193
Ontological principles: determined by speculative grammar, 137–39, 164; in ontological line of sciences, 168–69; truth and clearness of, 242–45, 247–48, 265; validity of, 191, 242–45, 247–48, 284
Ontology, 36, 46–47, 52; and being and substance, 202–3; distinct from ontological metaphysics, 137–39, 146, 154, 244–45; and fourth grade of clearness, 82–83, 247, 256; logic prior to, 55, 63, 100, 103, 156, 166, 171–72; and modes of being, 137–40; and pragmatic philosophy, 248; socialistic or agapastic, 129–30
Order in the universe, 56–57, 92–93, 96–97, 99–100, 102–3; see also Uniformity of nature, principle of

Paradox in Peirce's assumption of the indefinite continuation of inquiry, 61–63, 67, 89–91, 103, 128, 178, 198–200, 258
Perception, 202–3, 208, 245–46, 250, 251–52
Perceptual judgment, 171, 202–13, 224–25, 250, 251–52, 253; shades into abductive inference, 209–13, 224, 250
Perry, R. B., 271, 274, 288, 297
Person as general idea or symbol, 66, 119–20, 229–30; see also Man
Personality, 119–20, 149–50
Phaneroscopy, 159, 161; see also Phenomenology
Phenomenology, 139, 140, 154, 179, 203, 245, 264; and categories, 32–33, 36, 161, 182–83, 198; and logic, 156–63, 166, 168–70; and mathematics, 156–63, 166, 168–70, 196, 200
Philosophy: and architectonic, 108–9; basic conceptions in, 110–14, 155; cosmogonic, 109, 114; and evolution, 132–33; pragmatic, xiii, 156, 202, 248, 262–67; see also Metaphysics
Plato, 197–98
Platonic ideas, 193, 265
Plausibility, 142, 151, 177
Polyads, 160, 167, 274
Porphyry, 248
Positivism, 145–46
Possibility: definition of, 289; distinct from existence and law, 116; essential, 35; as a mode of being, 35, 186–89, 193–94, 228, 288–89; and necessity, 159–63, 168; substantive, 35
Potentiality as a mode of being, 182, 186–88
Practical: distinguished from theoretical, 234–39, 241, 297; in relation to pragmatic, 255
Pragmaticism, 202, 227, 228
Pragmatism: and abduction, 165, 210, 263, 287; applications of, 83–84, 125–27, 140; as criterion of meaning, 81–84, 103, 138–39, 164–65, 183–84, 191, 192; and critical common-sensism, 220, 227–28; and interpretant, 226; as maxim of logic, 138–39, 164–65, 202–3, 210, 263; Peirce's first formulation of, 79–84; and Peirce's philosophy, xiii, 96, 135, 202, 248, 262–67; Peirce's reinterpretation of, 143–44, 190, 234, 242, 245, 246, 289; principal alternative to traditional logic, xvi, 248–49; proofs of, 249–50, 259, 261; and realism, 227–28, 256–58, 261; stated as a principle, 300; support of, in necessary relation between the general and the singular, 175, 207
Precision: as abstraction, 21–23,

314

38–39; and clearness, 225, 227; and vagueness, 215–17, 292–93

Predicate: of perceptual judgments, 204–13; related to subject as consequent to antecedent, 17, 30–31, 123–24, 275; and subject in syllogistic premisses, 9–14

Prediction, 143–44, 146, 148, 242

Premiss: of nature, 204; and premise, 272; in relation to conclusion, 17, 30–31, 123–24; syllogistic, 5–14, 17, 30–31

Prescission, 216–17

Presumption, 174; see also Abduction

Principle: of causality, 93–95; of economy, 43, 48 (see also Ockham's razor); leading, 5–8; of nota notae, 7–8; regulative (see Regulative principle); of uniformity of nature (see Uniformity of nature, principle of)

Probability, xvii, 85–95, 129, 172–78, 194–95, 278; definition of, 86–89, 175; real or objective, 88, 173, 175–78, 185, 189, 265, 278, 300

Property as defining a class, 94–95

Propositions: categorical and conditional, 16–17; existential import of, 55, 272; as kind of symbol, 28; logical breadth and depth of, 35–36; nature of, as significant assertion, 165, 203, 210; Peirce's restriction to, in his first analysis of categories, 31, 36; in relation to terms and arguments, 17, 28, 36, 66, 251; universal and particular, 208, 272; see also Perceptual judgment; Premiss

Psychology: in determination of categories, 22–24; as distinguishing theoretical and practical belief, 235; and ethics, 195; not used in Peirce's analysis of perceptual judgment, 207, 290, 294; and physiological analogues, 112, 114, 125–26; posterior to logic, 166; and pragmatism, 210; as providing concepts for philosophy, 111–12; and the self, 233

Purpose, specification of, as a determination of meaning, 225–27, 247–48

Purposive action, 202–3, 206, 233, 247–48, 257–62

Qualities: of feeling, 198–99; as mere potentialities, 186; perceived, 147–48; in phenomenology, 162, 170; reference to, as a category, 23–27, 33, 49; relative, 26; as sensible effects, 83–84

Ramus, Peter, 272

Reaction: as category, 33; cognitive product of, 206–7; sensation of, 147–48, 185

Realism: and conceptualism, 186; and critical common-sensism, 227–28, 233; and paradox in Peirce, 89–90; Peirce's first statement of, 51–52, 277; and pragmatism, 227–28, 256–58, 261; and synechism, 120; and theory of mind, 120, 229; and tychism, 129; and validity of induction, 58–59; as verifiable hypothesis, 243

Reality: cannot be doubted, 73–74; definition of (see Definition of reality); determination of, as fourth step beyond categories, 36, 82–83, 169, 171, 239, 246–47; independent of thought, 83; and mind, 63, 100; in relation to existence, 84, 147–48, 182–85, 187, 228, 287; social theory of, 129–30, 247 (see also Unlimited community); source of, 233; as thirdness, 170

Reasoning, iconic nature of, 157–63, 211–12, 274, 281

Regulative principle: in normative logic, 153, 233; in ontological line of sciences, 167–68; in Peirce's architecture of theories, 114, 124, 127, 156; in semantic

metalanguage, 296; synechism as, 123, 134, 206, 264, 281, 290
Relations: of contiguity, 118, 274; dual, 31–33, 160–61, 274; dyadic, 27, 46–47, 136, 160–61, 283; dynamical, 27, 274, 283; genuine and degenerate, 274; internal, 283; plural, 31–33, 160–61, 274; polyadic, 46, 160–61; of similarity, 27, 118, 273–74, 283; tetradic, 285; transitive, 101; triadic, 160–61, 274, 285; see also Logic of relatives
Religion, 121
Retroductive inference; see Abduction
Revolutions in history of philosophy, 108–9
Richards, I. A., 295

Schneider, H. W., 280
Schröder, E., 164
Science: of discovery, 155; philosophy of, 156; practical, 155, 234–39; of review, 155–56; theoretical, 155–56, 234–39
Sciences, ordering and classification of, 107, 139, 155, 202; in a commentary on Peirce, xiii–xv; in ontological line, 166–72, 178; and paradox in Peirce, 199–200; and Peirce's categories, 169–70
Scientific method of fixing belief; see Induction
Secondness, 33, 35, 46–47; as brute reaction, 148, 283; as discrete, 280; as dynamical object, 253; and genera of arguments, 98; and law, 110, 134, 279–80; and moral consciousness, 198–99; and normative science, 171, 256, 291; in the ordering of the sciences, 169–71; in relation to firstness and thirdness, 198; as struggle, 252, 255
Self: critical, 232–33, 236–37, 238, 245, 297; noumenal, 255–56, 296–97; as phenomenal manifestation of subject, 49, 230–33, 236–37; as sign, 49, 52, 229–33, 255; and substance, 266

Self-consciousness, 38–39, 41, 47–48, 119, 200, 230–31
Self-control, 71, 135, 201, 202–4, 207, 219–27, 259; and doubt, 219–21, 226, 238, 294; grades of, 221–22, 225, 227, 237–38, 240–41; and physical reaction, 255
Self-controlled growth of inquiry: and clearness of meaning, 225, 234, 242, 246, 248; and coenoscopic observation, 245; as concrete reasonableness, 255–56; requires a substantial self, 266; and test of hypotheses, 143–44, 146, 154, 183–84
Self-questioning as method in ethics, 195–96, 200
Seme, 226
Semiotic (semeotic), xvii, 163, 180, 285, 297
Sensation; see Feeling; Perception; Reaction
Sign, central notion in Peirce's philosophy, 162–63; see also Interpretant; Symbol
Sign-process; see Thought-process as process of signification
Signs: all reality a universe of, 228–29, 233; all thought occurs in, 42, 152, 190, 249–50; and modes of being, 191, 193
Singular, 205–7, 211–13, 252; necessarily related to the general, 175, 206–8; as totality of all real objects, 207, 224, 294
Social impulse, 71, 74, 78, 258
Sophisms, 55–56
Space: an elementary conception, 22; laws of, 286; perception of, 40
Speculative grammar, 28, 163–66; defines reality, 164, 171; determines ontological principles, 138–39, 164; formulates pragmatism, 138–39, 164, 179, 191–92, 203, 250, 263; in ontological line of sciences, 168, 178
Speculative rhetoric, 28, 171, 179–80, 191–93, 194, 263